2.69

WINES AND PEOPLE
OF ALSACE

Other books by T. A. Layton include:
CHOOSE YOUR WINE   Duckworth
CHOOSE YOUR VEGETABLES   Duckworth
WINECRAFT: AN ENCYCLOPEDIA   Harper
WINES AND CASTLES OF SPAIN   Michael Joseph
A YEAR AT THE PEACOCK   Cassell
WINES AND CHATEAUX OF THE LOIRE   Cassell

WINES AND PEOPLE OF ALSACE

T. A. Layton

CASSELL · LONDON

CASSELL & COMPANY LTD
35 Red Lion Square, London, WC1
Melbourne, Sydney, Toronto
Johannesburg, Auckland

© T. A. Layton 1970

All rights reserved. No part of this publication
may be reproduced, stored in a retrieval system,
or transmitted, in any form or by any means,
electronic, mechanical, photocopying, recording
or otherwise, without the prior permission of
Cassell and Company Ltd.

First published 1970

S.B.N. 304 93448 8

Printed in Great Britain by
The Camelot Press Ltd., London and Southampton
F. 1269

To my son
Thomas George Layton

CONTENTS

1. Preparations 1
2. The Cellars of Reims 11
3. Épinal 20
4. The Growers 26
5. The Road to Mulhouse 39
6. About Alsatian Wines 46
7. The Wine Regions and the Confrérie St-Étienne 58
8. Route du Vin 76
9. Colmar 83
10. Cabbages and Kuehn 94
11. Riquewihr 105
12. Snails and Storks 113
13. Beer 124
14. *Foie gras* and Feyel 131
15. More about *foie gras* 142
16. Rouget de Lisle 151
17. The Presence of Strasbourg 163
18. Saverne 172
19. Wissembourg, and a new Route du Vin 184

APPENDIX A 193
APPENDIX B 197
BIBLIOGRAPHY 199
INDEX 203

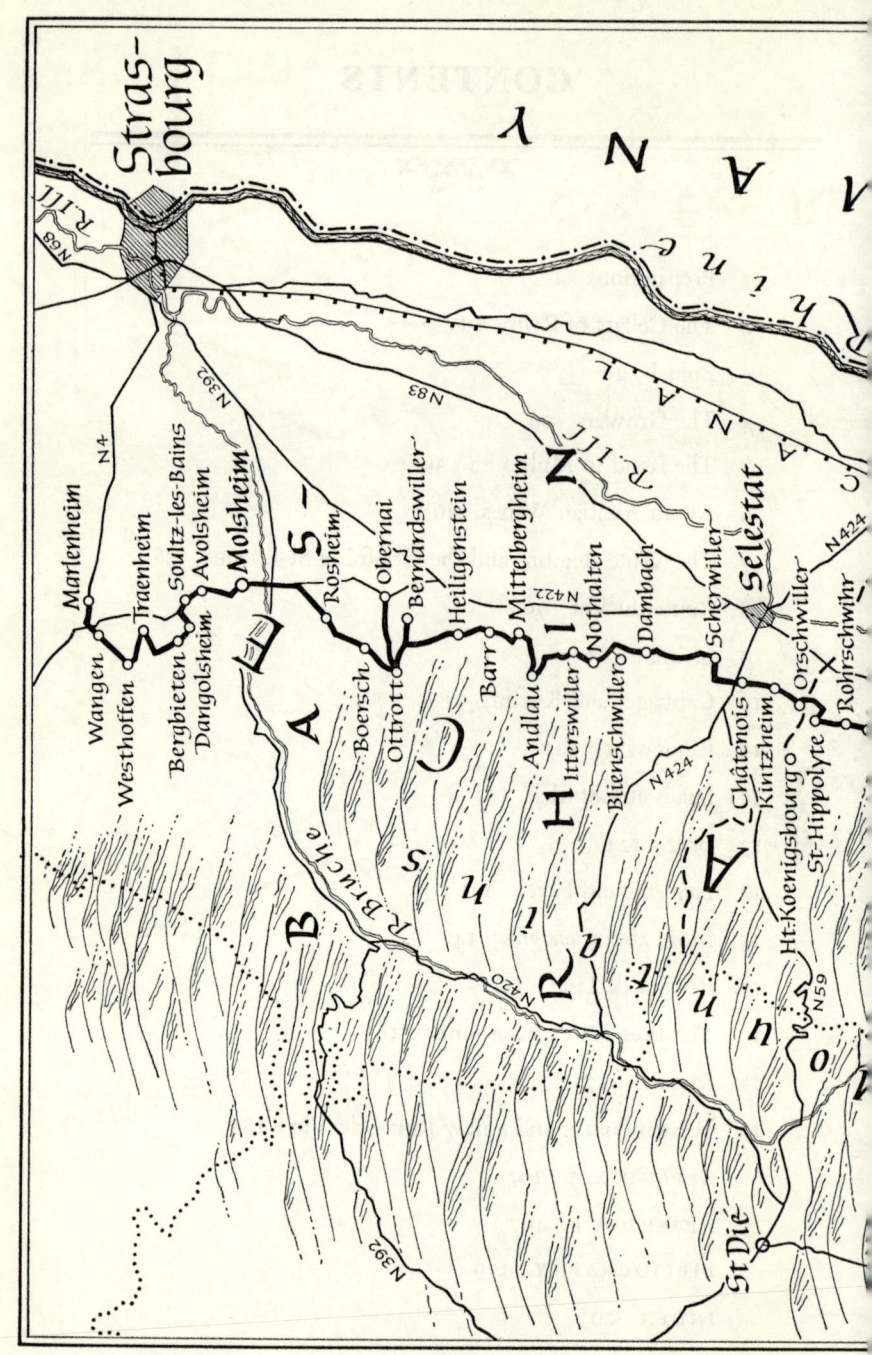

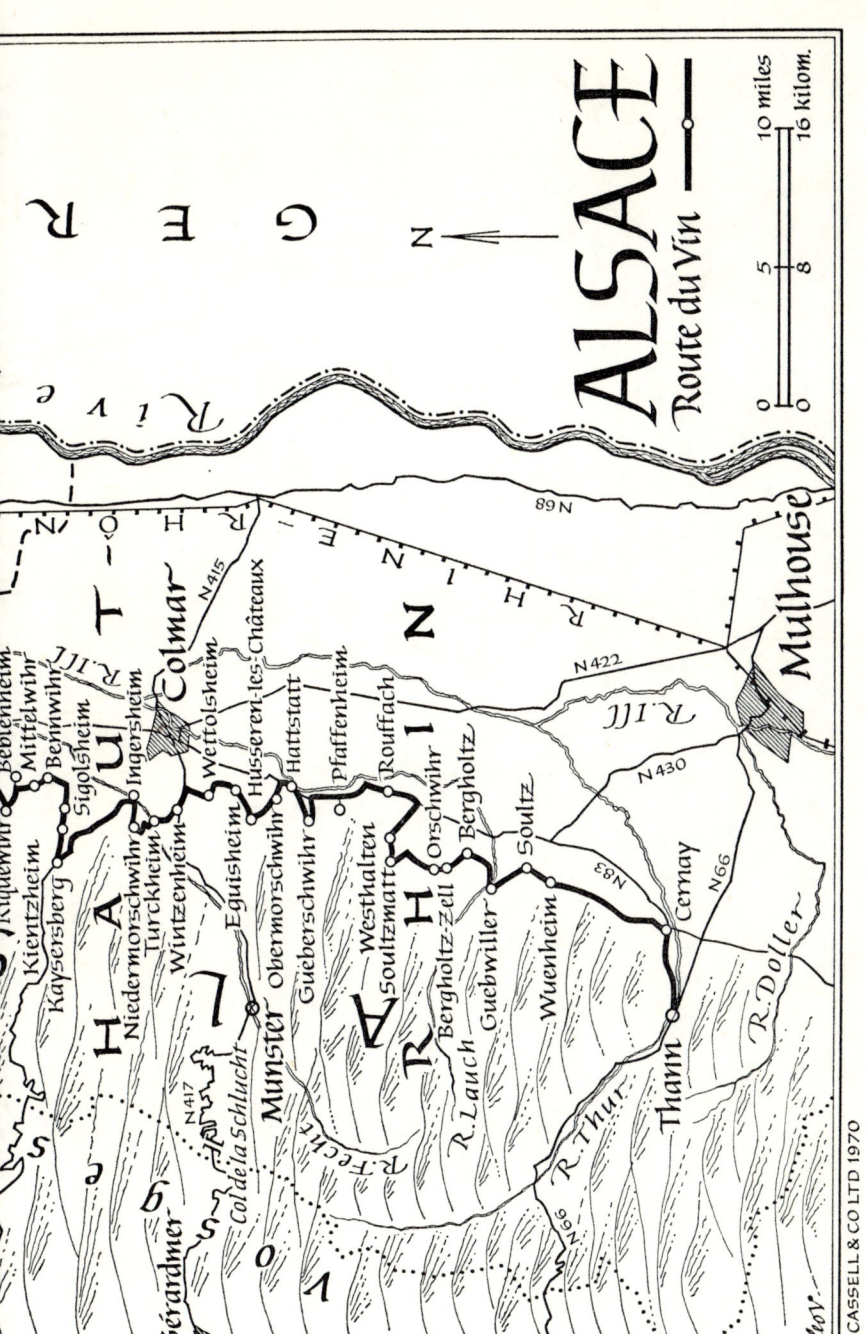

1

PREPARATIONS

WHICH came first? A sudden urge to drink only a Sylvaner or a Riesling as an apéritif? Or a growing feeling that my next book must be about Alsace?

At the moment of writing I am of the opinion that the wines of Alsace are the cleanest, most honestly made, most 'moreish' and best value of all the white wines of Europe. But did I come to that opinion objectively and fairly, or was it that knowing the Vosges mountains and forests, the beauty of the vineyards between Colmar and Strasbourg, and the history of the extraordinary Franco-German tussle for Alsace and Lorraine* made me feel that here were the germs of a book; and that I started cultivating a palate for the wines *before* I suggested such a work?

When I got the go-ahead I laid my plans carefully.

My visit to Alsace was to take place under the recent currency-export restrictions. And when one is alone in a car which has to travel thousands of miles, the petrol bill soon mounts up. The curious thing is that it was not until after I had taken various elaborate steps that I realized I could, for a bona-fide book, easily get a business travel allowance, which at the last minute I did. But before then I was in a high old flap, and so, months before I was due to leave, I went through my *Guide Michelin* and selected no less than eighty hotels the length and width of the Vosges and Alsace and Lorraine, and wrote them not a duplicated but an individual letter in which I explained my anticipated chronic shortage of cash and asked if I could have a bedroom at a very special price. Not only this, but as I always buy a good

---

* Note that I have not used the hyphen. André Maurois once said: 'There isn't an Alsace-Lorraine. This is a German creation by Bismarck; there is Alsace and there is Lorraine.' But none the less the French adopted the hyphen to denote the territory which the Germans annexed in 1872 until 1918, and again from 1940 to 1944, because it was much better for propaganda purposes than saying 'Alsace and the northern half of Lorraine' or, even worse, 'the *départements* of Moselle, Bas-Rhin and Haut-Rhin'.

collection of French and Spanish stamps to send out to people in those countries, every hotel had a stamped addressed envelope enclosed. Finally, instead of just putting on a dull ninepenny stamp, I made up the sum with a series of lower amounts, all of attractive recent issues, and put as a P.S.: *I hope you like the nice stamps I have put on the envelope.*

I was so enthusiastic that I did the same with some thirty restaurants. Off they went, and I waited. And waited. And waited.

At the end of ten days not a single person had replied, and I wondered if they had gone astray. Then a solitary letter trickled in. It said yes; my hopes soared like mad. They would all say yes, I thought. What would I do then? Then more silence, and more trickled in. Most said they were not interested; some said they would think it over; others pretended (the letter was professionally translated) rather sarcastically that they did not understand and offered to reserve me rooms at the full price. The whole operation was not such a success as I had anticipated.

Another brainwave was more productive. If, I thought, you think these Alsace wines are so good, and if you have got to go out there to study them again, why not take up an agency? What with amalgamations and other changes in the wine trade on both sides of the Channel, agencies are becoming fewer and fewer, but to have one for firms like Roederer, Mumm, Adolph Husgen or Louis Latour still has a considerable snob appeal. Its one disadvantage is that there is no contract: everything is founded on trust. I well remember being amazed when Guy Gordon Clark, whose family have had the Martell Cognac agency for generations, told me that there was no written agreement between the two firms.

'But surely, Guy,' I said, 'you must lie awake at nights, worrying.'

'It's a tradition of the trade,' he replied, and that was that.

I would now trust, I thought; anyway, there was not much to lose, and so I put an advertisement in the *Journée Vinicole* of Paris, under their 'Let Us Do Business Together' column.

COMMERCIAL PROPOSITIONS

Alsatian Wines in England. Retail firm of wine merchants, well established in one of the best parts of London, wants to represent a firm of Alsatian wine-growers.—Reply to T. A. Layton, 2a, Duke Street (Manchester Square), London, W.1.

PREPARATIONS

The advertisement cost the price of a good lunch for two at the Savoy. When they sent me a voucher copy I saw that I was in a rare old gallery.

Maître de chais, under 40, required, with perfect knowledge of laboratory work and tasting.

Salesman in Val de Loire will be offered a good job if he can make a go of pushing Appellation Contrôlée wines, but must have car.

Cognac for sale, exceptionally low price; agency would be accepted.

20,000 Burgundy bottles for sale.

I am in the market to buy port.

For Sale: Quarter-bottles of wine, supplied in cartons of 30.

We Want to buy: 200–300 small oak casks of the very best quality for the purpose of ageing the wines of Cahors.*

To Let: 50,000 gallons of glass containers.

We Will Buy: Several thousand wooden wine cases to take 12 bottles (2 × 6)† and in excellent condition.

Casks: Tonneaux (4 hogsheads), casks, half-casks, firkins—every size. We do yours up ready for filling with wine, or will sell or hire new or second hand.

The number of replies I got greatly surprised me, and I was particularly astonished at the numerous small Cognac firms who wrote in wanting to get established in England. Another district interested was Châteauneuf-du-Pape.

* We live and learn! The wines of Cahors are the roughest, purplest wines of all the rough purple wines of south-western France; I never thought anyone would want to age them.
† As distinct from 3 × 4, which makes a much squarer pack and is far more popular these days.

The most bizarre letter from Alsace itself came from a wine-broker in Mulhouse, Théo Gustave Drouet, who said that he had read somewhere that you could get peasant cottages in Southern Ireland for a song, he was going to Bantry Bay to prospect, and would I go and meet him there to discuss the question of agencies. He added that he realized this was an unusual suggestion but that as he did not speak any English he would be happy to let me have five cases of fine Alsace wines if I would act as a sort of interpreter. I was about to tear the letter up when I remembered that my sister, Peggy, had just come back from Cork and was wild with enthusiasm for the bargain she had got and the beauty of the scenery. So I decided to buy a cottage too. I looked at the letter again and realized what a lot of trouble M. Drouet had taken, for he had not only given the time of the boat-train to Fishguard, but had enclosed an A.A. route from Gloucester across Wales to the port if I decided to take my car. He had given a choice of venue: Actons' Hotel (rooms 55s. plus ten per cent) or Sea View (rooms 25s. inclusive) at Kinsale, or the Anchor Hotel at Bantry. I sent him a wire: SUGGEST EIGHT CASES FAIRER OWING COST OF TAKING CAR. We settled for six; and we both got our cottages.

Nearly a score of people answered from the Haut- and Bas-Rhin, but a little paragraph in the famous 'Faber' weekly gossip column of *Harpers Wine and Spirit Gazette* brought an introduction from every worth-while grower in town who had an agency in Alsace.

It also brought me a splendid send-off lunch with the chef of the Dorchester, Eugene Kaufeler, the doyen of West End chefs, in his private dining room.

When I was writing my book *Cheese and Cheese Cookery* for the Wine and Food Society's library I thought that a chapter entitled 'Twentieth-Century Chefs and their Cheese Recipes' would fill the bill well. That was at the time when the Gas Board had just produced a remarkable advertisement—a photograph of the twelve leading London chefs (all looking horribly serious) all stating, of course, that they cooked only by gas. I wrote to all of these, and, casting my net wider, contacted at the same time a number of other people whose gastronomic reputations were high. In this way I made a number of pleasant new friends, and was, at the same time, given some remarkably good meals.

There was that brilliant caterer Geoffrey Sharp, who entertained me at Le Carrosse Restaurant, Elystan Street, and gave me, among other things, his braised endives with cheese and tarragon sauce; there was a fabulous haddock and cheese soufflé at the Café Royal with my good friend Louis Cipolla; followed the next week by braised chicory and veal at the Waldorf Astoria, in the same excellent company.

The next week I had a curious session with René Giordano, which was sheer joy. When I went to dine with him and his wife at the May Fair, of which he has been manager for some years now, we happily decided not to have a main course before the cheese soufflé (the *raison d'être* for the luncheon) but settled for a dozen oysters and a bottle of Corton Charlemagne 1960, of the mighty Louis Latour.

The soufflé should have finished the meal, but for a chance remark of mine. We were talking about food, naturally, and I said something about loving hot pimentos, which caused René Giordano's wife to extol her hot Camembert and pimento savoury, and, before we could say 'Jack Robinson', chef Rusconi, who had come up to chat to us, disappeared back into his kitchen and the savoury (quite scrumptious!) was on our table.

In the case of the Dorchester my contact was Marjorie Lee, whom I have come to know well and who, for twenty years now, has been that hotel's most loyal and efficient Public Relations Officer. She went to work with a will and saw chef Kaufeler, with the result that a few days later I was sitting down in the grill-room to a luncheon of rare refinement, which started with an Evesham Flan.*

'What did you think of it?' said Marjorie Lee, over coffee and liqueurs.

'Think!' I said. 'It was so marvellous I want to go down and see the chef this minute.'

Chef Kaufeler was waiting for us when we descended into the huge, noisy, bustling kitchen (the best of London's hotel kitchens, I think) and into the complete calm of his neat little office, which is, incidentally, next door to his own private dining-room. After I had duly praised the Evesham Flan the conversation could well have got stilted, but we found we had several friends in common in the world of *haute cuisine*, from the days when I had taken my summer holiday working in the kitchens of the Café Royal and then, later, at the Ritz.

'You'd better come and have another lunch down here with me next week,' said Kaufeler. . . .

That lunch was superb! The excuse was for me to try the Dorchester's

---

* Take ½-pint chopped asparagus, 4 eggs, ½-pint milk, and 5 oz. grated cheese. Line a flan-ring with a short paste and bake. Put the cheese and asparagus in the flan case. Beat eggs and pour, with milk, on top. Bake in a moderate oven.

cheese soufflé, but we started with a creation of the chef's which was pure joy. In the first place, you hardly ever get real, home-made fish *quenelles* these days; and, in the second, even when you do they can be somewhat insipid. We had *Quenelles de brochet*, which, instead of being poached, were lightly fried and then served with a rich, deep brown sauce—a marvel. Then we had the juiciest, tenderest bits of saddle of hare, thinly sliced and covered with a light cream sauce, and accompanied by home-made ravioli filled with a stuffing of hazelnuts and ham. And throughout the meal, Bollinger.

'Chef,' I said, 'this is Lucullan! I will bring you the first signed copy of my book.' A year later I was as good as my word, and again descended the stairs to the kitchen and duly presented my cheese book to chef Kaufeler. There was no doubt: he was very impressed. While he was thumbing through the pages in walked George Ronus, the manager of the hotel, and my old friend Allan Arnold, who has the Mumm Champagne agency and also the coveted one for Hugel's wines in Alsace.

'Gracious, Tommy!' said Arnold. 'I thought you were in Alsace. Didn't I send you an invitation to call on the Hugels?'

'Yes, but you put me as going out three weeks too early.'

Arnold was unperturbed. 'Fine! I'll let them know out there; I'm taking George Ronus out tomorrow. How are you going?'

'By car,' I said. 'First night Reims.'

'Then why don't you let Mumm put you up for the night, and you could have lunch with them the next morning?'

'Why not?' I said, thinking too of my ever-growing passion for Champagne.

Then chef Kaufeler came up to the others and said, 'Look at my present.' They all looked at my book.

Then one of those things that spontaneously happen just happened.

'The chef makes some very good Alsatian dishes,' said Ronus.

'I shall be bringing back some magnificent Rieslings and Traminers from Riquewihr,' said Arnold.

'How interesting,' I said, naïvely. 'You know, a book like this has to have a beginning, a sort of jumping-off meal.'

'And it needn't necessarily start in France,' said Marjorie Lee....

The pause was not long.

'Will you come and have lunch with me the day before you go off to Alsace?' said Kaufeler.

'May I come too?' said George Ronus.

PREPARATIONS

And that was how, fourteen days later, we were sitting down to:

ALSATIAN LUNCHEON

Muscat 1964,	Les Paillettes de Fromage
Réserve Exceptionnelle,	Les Ramequins
Sélection Personnelle Jean Hugel	
Hugel Riesling,	La Truite au Bleu
Grand Cru 1963	
Traminer 1961,	Le Coq au Vin d'Alsace
Réserve Exceptionnelle,	Les Nouilles Fraîches
Sélection Personnelle Jean Hugel	
Tokay 1964,	Le Coeur d'Artichaut
Réserve Exceptionnelle,	au Foie Gras de Strasbourg
Selection Personnelle Jean Hugel	
	Les Fruits en Saison
	Les Fromages
Eau-de-Vie d'Alsace	
Mirabelle, Framboise	Le Café

I think this memorable repast would have gone on till suppertime if George Ronus's secretary had not called him. George has got himself one of those little walkie-talkie instruments so popular among the house surgeons of the big hospitals, so that he and his secretary can keep in touch as he sallies forth over the vast Dorchesterial domains.

Suddenly the little bleeps were heard and, to a man, we all looked at the chef's great clock in his private luncheon room: twenty past four!

Quickly ash was knocked off long cigars, liqueurs were drained, hands were pumped, and as I struggled into my hat Allan Arnold handed me a minute piece of paper, saying, 'That's the address of the place they put you up; and there is Jean Couvreur's phone number. He is the director who will be looking after you.'

A well planned beginning, I thought.

★

When I told my vintner friends that I was going on a wine fact-finding trip at the end of November, they, thinking I had missed a trick, were condemning.

'But you'll have missed the vintage!' they would exclaim.

'Naturally,' I would retort, a little sarcastically. 'I want to *talk* to the *vignerons*, not watch them sweat.'

It is heartbreaking to deglamorize anything, especially when it is connected with one's life's work, but the mystique surrounding the gathering-in of the grape harvest is horribly exaggerated. In the 1920s, when motor transport in the vineyards and electric presses in the cellars were unheard of, when wages were ridiculously low and time was not an enemy, and when the owner could stand his pickers a jolly good feast at the end, then the vintage was a wonderful event with a certain olde-worlde charm, and of course I was thrilled to be honoured by being asked to cut the first branch of grapes with a silver pair of scissors on an estate near Bordeaux. But those pictures of lovely girls dressed in spotless starched linen, and wearing the traditional headgear of whatever region it was, were a little exaggerated even in those far-off days, and I fear that the near rags which, in fact, are now worn are far from sightly. And anyway, the last job a really pretty girl would do is grape-picking, for fear of the blazing sun ruining her complexion.

Then there is the music. We laugh in a rather superior way when we hear of pop-tunes being piped out to factory workers, and yet we will trek up a mountainside in the blazing sun along the Douro to see the barefoot men trampling the red bunches to the sound of a guitar. The point in both cases being that the sound dished out is an antidote to the deadly monotony of the job. In Portugal it has been scientifically established that music makes the feet tread faster.

Time-and-motion studies are regarded as both ultra-modern and necessary, and yet at the same time as a rather inhuman way of getting more work out of employees. But our forebears have been carrying out the same sort of exploitation for centuries, only more subtly.

Take such things as: tossing a truss of hay at the local fair; world speedy sheep-shearing competitions; ploughing matches; log-felling competitions; and hop-stringing matches. What all these 'games', and scores more of a similar nature, have in common is that, once the knack has been learned, they are deadly dull—operations which were vital to a community before mechanization and, unlike the sports of the nobility, had no element of danger—you didn't want your peasants injuring themselves and being incapable of work on the Monday!

PREPARATIONS

The competitive element must have been the brainchild of an employer of labour, call him feudal duke, earl, chieftain, baron, seneschal or what have you. You think the peasants originated them? Not on your life!

Picture Jim at harvest time: he has been out in the fields sixteen hours of the day, pitching the hay onto the haywain until every bone in his body is aching; he finishes on Saturday night and goes to the inn for a glass of mead in the blissful knowledge that at least they cannot work him on Sunday. In comes Tom, who has perhaps only done twelve hours.

'Tell you what—I've had an idea. Tomorrow let's go out to Farmer Giles's field and tie up a bundle of hay and see who can throw it the farthest.'

'Have you gone out of your mind?'

'Not really. We'll put up two hop-poles and tie a bit of string across. Then——*ouch*!'

And another reason why these clever games must have originated in the minds of the labour employer is that the things needed to carry them out were the property not of the peasant but of the overlord.

I said that the vintage was never as glamorous as it was cracked up to be, but now that mechanization is the rage it is deadly dull. None the less, for the owner-grower and also the owner-grower-cum-buyer-in and wholesaler (I will elaborate on this later), it is a period of long hours of hard work, coupled with great anxiety.

And so anyone who calls on viticultors in harvest-time with the serious purpose of tasting their wares and doing a deal is an ass. He is merely getting a much-grudged half of their attention.

The best time to visit anyone is surely when the creative mood is on; not before (vintage-time) or after (when the wine is bottled). I should like to guess that the time when Shakespeare would have been most enjoyable to talk to was when he was nearing the end of *Macbeth*, had got over the gestation period, sensed he had written a good play and yet had sufficiently more to do to know he couldn't slack off or lose interest and be thinking of the next play.

So let it be with a viticultor: he has done his best to make a good wine, but he is naturally interested to see how good *you*, and other callers, think it is. Is it better than his friendly competitors' in the next village? What is the sugar-content of their wine? And so on.

Give him a couple of weeks after the picking of the last grapes to get his cellars straight and put away his grape-crushing machinery and have a rest, and then from November to the beginning of the spring racking* you have him at his least busy and most interested in his wine.

* Pouring of wine from one cask to another to take it off its lees, or murk, or grape residue.

2

THE CELLARS OF REIMS

The furious wind was whipping up the waves, even inside the harbour, and these were tossing huge wooden sleepers back onto the landing-stage being so feverishly built to take the new giant hovercraft which were to be ready the following year. I watched lazily, and contentedly went on with writing my article snugly in my little car while I waited—half an hour early—to go aboard the ferry. When it got colder I would turn on the engine, open up the heater vent, warm my feet, and go on writing, and, in between, thinking of the pleasant dinner I should be having at Reims that evening.

I finished my article: it did not seem to have taken long; I looked at my watch. The boat should have left an hour ago. Then I saw that the queue of cars in front of me had half vanished, but that another, hitherto empty, part of the huge parking tarmac outside the Dover Harbour Car Terminal was now full.

I jumped out into the blistering rain and ran a hundred yards forward to the first car left in my vanished queue; it was a huge red Mercedes, with a *Wü* registration.

'What's happening?' I asked.

'The boat's not going,' said the German.

'Nonsense!' I said, with a sinking feeling, and ran forward to the next occupied car. It was huge, sleek, shining and opulent. Inside was a very, very pretty girl, reading relaxedly. She had all the answers: the morning boat had been cancelled, and one had the option of taking, there and then, the Ostend boat—three hours extra at sea, but it was definitely going—or waiting for the afternoon boat to Boulogne, which might not go at all if the weather got worse.

It was one o'clock by the time all the cars got onto the Ostend boat, and the next disaster was that five seconds later it was two o'clock—I had forgotten Continental hours.

We docked at about six. All hopes of getting to Reims in time for dinner were out, but if I drove like mad I could at least get to the guest-house in reasonable time. Then followed one of my nastiest-ever car journeys. It was a question of taking sideroads—I'm too lazy to use a map, I always end up on sideroads—in a blizzard to the French border. This was made double hell by the fact that no one seemed to understand my quite adequate French. I supposed I was in Flemingland. An hour later a chatty barman in France explained, 'They *understand* French all right, and speak it perfectly, but they hate doing it and always pretend they can't.'

At last I got to Lille, but I came in, inevitably, from a sideroad and there wasn't the sign of a sign. Next I found myself in a tiny round *place*, with five exits and not a direction-indicator anywhere. I saw a woman standing in a doorway and opened the window.

'Excuse me, madame, but——'

'Fifty francs.'

'Look, I really am lost, can——'

'That includes the hire of the room; there are no extras.'

'Oh, go to blazes!'

As I escaped down one of the streets I noticed that most of the arches were occupied by shadowy waiting prostitutes—surprisingly well dressed.

My next encounter was with two huge, red-faced sailors, and nearly ended in my getting a broken nose or having to go to the police station.

Something I cannot abide is to ask the way and then be told by the askee, 'Sorry, I'm a stranger here'; and so I have got into the habit of inquiring first if the person is a native of the place. If only I had said, 'Do you come from Lille?' all would have been well, but I used the adjective instead.

'*Êtes-vous liliaux?*' I said, in excellent French.

The two men stopped as if shot.

'*Messieurs*,' I repeated, with exceptional clarity, and trying to put a question-mark in my voice, '*vous êtes liliaux?*'

This galvanized the two men. One put his hand through the window and held the steering-wheel, while the other in a flash opened the off-side door and got in. I was by now very frightened, was beginning to have an inkling of what had happened and jumped out of the car.

The men, being half drunk, had not realized I was foreign. I quickly made up for this by pointing to my GB plate and then using the most English of French accents I could. When the two sailors realized what had happened they laughed so much they were quite unable to direct me.

THE CELLARS OF REIMS

I had to wait until I got back home to get the (nearly) full answer to the mix-up, for the two quite decent-sized dictionaries I carry in the car were unable to cope. But in my big Harrap I found that an inhabitant of Lille was a *lillois, m.*, or *lilloise, f.*, and that *lilial* in the singular was lily-like or (of complexion) lilied, and then came some telling words in brackets: (*m. pl.* form usu. avoided).

The hold-up at Lille meant that I had missed not only my meal with Jean Couvreur but my bed for the night in Reims as well. I had tried to phone once, but there was no answer. Now I made another effort from a café—still no answer, so I had supper off a bowl of onion soup and then just reached Saint-Quentin by eleven thirty and got the very last room in the very last place where there was a bed: the Buffet-Hôtel at the station.

The next morning there occurred one of those little acts of kindness which mean so much when one is alone.

What with dining off soup and leaving Dover with a full tank of petrol, I had only dipped into a few reserve francs which I always save from my last trip abroad. Not only were my Barclays Bank francs intact, but I had not even undone them. I gave the cashier a suitable note, and then looked at another which, for a second, seemed like a new design I had not seen for the fifty-franc note. While I was puzzling over it, the cashier said, 'You want to take care of that, it is a five-hundred-franc note.'

'Mercy!' I replied. 'I'm very glad you told me, I have never seen one before.'

'I'm not surprised,' the girl replied, 'they are very scarce.'

Traveller's joy!

From Saint-Quentin down to Laon and right through to Reims this lovely climber was growing in more uninterrupted profusion than I have ever seen. It is in fact a wild clematis (*C. vitalba*), and it was our great herbalist John Gerard who gave it its popular name—prettier than the alternative Old Man's Beard—from the way it trails and adorns the hedges by the wayside. Anne Pratt, that remarkably prolific and pleasant writer of the last century, tells us why it must have delighted the wayfarer.

> Nor when its blossoms are over does it cease to ornament the wayside; for long after the green leaves have withered into brownness, the clematis bough presents some verdant spray on which the eye loves to rest. So too, on barren soils and in spots far from

refreshing streams, it often delights us with its greenness amidst the withered aspects of the vegetation around.

She goes on to say that the green stalks become so hard that farmers bind their gates and hurdles with them 'and country boys smoke portions of them in imitation of tobacco pipes'.

Be that as it may, there is a minor problem which is not so clear. I thought that Traveller's Joy got its name less because it adorned the wayside than because it reminded the wayfarer of home. Now, surely, this climber is at its most lovely when the 'feathery awns lengthen on the seed vessels which afterwards elongate into plumy tails and jointly form the Old Man's Beard'. But this gorgeous profusion only takes place in late October and November when all travelling in medieval days had closed down for the winter.

I thought it was wonderful; the sun shone, the roads were smooth and straight as a die; I stepped on the juice, the petrol-gauge showed empty, but life was too good to stop; there would be another station soon; and then, on the longest stretch, with nothing in sight, I ran out. Nothing. Draw in to the side, quick, to avoid an accident, and wait. But in two minutes along came a minute Peugeot with the local doctor; four minutes down the road a petrol station, back to the car with a half-gallon, and in ten minutes I was driving into the station which had lent it to me. A charming woman, the wife of the proprietor, served me, and as I pulled out my wallet to pay I again nearly gave her the five-hundred-franc note instead of the fifty.

'Blast!' I said. 'This is too big for the likes of me. I suppose you can't change it for me?'

'Jean!' shouted the woman.

'Yes?' came a voice from under a car.

'The Englishman who ran out of petrol wants to change a five-hundred-franc note.'

'That's all right if you've got it.'

She pulled out the till drawer and frowned.

'I haven't got any large notes, I'm afraid.'

'Never mind,' I said. 'Anything to get rid of this beastly thing.'

She had a few fifties which were quickly counted into my hand. Then came the tens. 'Ten . . . forty, fifty, sixty . . . a hundred and sixty, and seventy, and eighty . . . two hundred. . . .' Eventually it was done. I looked at my huge fistful of notes woefully.

The woman looked at me.

THE CELLARS OF REIMS

'I can change them back, if you like.'
'Please,' I said.

I got to Reims at about eleven o'clock.

So much has been written about the half-blind monk who 'invented' Champagne, about the *remuage* or shaking the sediment of the young wine onto the cork and the blending with red and white grapes, about the great cathedral of Reims, that another newsworthy thing tends to be forgotten: and that is the sheer size of the underground Champagne cellars and the part they played, sometimes military, sometimes civil, and often amusing, in the First World War.

The reason why Champagne cellars have to be so much larger than others is that space must be found for bottles stored not neatly in bins but in the very space-wasting, sloping wooden racks into which the young Champagne bottles go. And I have a feeling that they also had to be made larger because of the potential danger of exploding bottles. At the beginning of the last century M. Moët's cellars (which in 1822 contained half a million bottles; now two and a half million) must have resembled a battlefield, the reason being that, in those days, they never tested to see how much unfermented sugar was left in the wine before it was bottled. As the bottles were then made by hand they varied enormously, and one could not easily tell how they would take the pressure. In fact they were tested in the most unscientific manner, merely being scrutinized to see if there were any air bubbles left in the glass, and then, says a contemporary writer, 'jingled together in pairs or against the others', and those that cracked or burst went back to the poor maker. Those that came through this amateurish ordeal, however, could be used for bottling the young wine, and this started in April.

If contemporary accounts are to be believed, no one seems to have had the faintest idea how much fermentation would take place. The soil where the vines grew, the depth at which the wine was lying in the cellars, the types of wine blended, even the interior surface of the bottles, all these had unknown effects on the in-bottle fermentation pressure of the wine. Sometimes it was recorded that a current of air would set a bin of wine fermenting furiously, while another bin of identical wine, bottled on the same day but put away in another part of the cellar, would be quite flat. Year in, year out, the maker was faced with a choice between wine too powerful for the bottles and wine which had not developed a 'fizz'. And to keep up his reputation he preferred to take the former risk.

The breakage rate was stupendous: no less than eight per cent of the wine bottled, compared with today's tiny rate of less than one bottle in two thousand. August was the peak fermentation month, and during this time the workmen were obliged to go round the cellars wearing wicker masks, so forcible were the explosions.

Almost exactly one hundred years later corks-a-popping had ceased below, but a worse popping was taking place above, for after intensive shelling the Germans entered Reims on 4 September 1914. Here they collected a hundred hostages and a hundred thousand francs from M. Charles Heidsieck, the Mayor, and other Champagne merchants, because they had not supplied sufficient rations for the German troops.

The Germans were chased out again nine days later, but not far enough for the inhabitants of Reims, who, for the next four years, under continual threat of bombardment, settled down to an extraordinary troglodyte existence in the vast chalk cellars of the town. Soon, side by side with the routine work of bottling and the *remuage*, a complete civilian underground life got under way. Children thought they were in for a permanent holiday, but they were disappointed. Every above-ground school had been requisitioned by the army, but it was not long before a schoolmaster called Foumann had started classes in nearly every one of the large Champagne cellars. There, with their gas-masks around their necks, and cheek by jowl with the underground tailor, watch-repairer and cobbler, the young of Reims were educated. Although people soon became acclimatized, it is recorded that 'several of the women did not see the light of day for two years'. Surprisingly, although the air was saturated with humidity, and the smell of petrol cookers and food was frightful, there were no epidemics at all.

The Protestant chapel was installed in the cellars of Krug, while the Cardinal's altar, surrounded by a hundred thousand bottles of Vintage 1911, was erected in those of Pommery and Gréno, and other smaller ones in Roederer and Mumm. Here the faithful came to pray.

Here, too, they came to pilfer great quantities of Champagne. However thirsty the Germans were, in nine days they can have made little inroad into that vast store compared with four years' systematic theft by soldier and civilian alike. The military made quite a business of it. When a negro soldier was killed by falling through one of the deep air-holes on his way down for his nightly basketful of bottles he received a posthumous medal, though the citation was somewhat vague.

If the many remaining citizens found safety in the Champagne cellars, it is impossible to exaggerate their value to the military. 'The stabilization of the front line of battle around the outskirts of Reims meant that, as a result, the vast underground galleries where Champagne merchants had their cellars suddenly became of the greatest though unexpected importance,' writes an official historian of the war. Pommery's cellars were by far the largest and most suitable, and one wonders whether the sudden smart popularity the wine enjoyed in the twenties was due to its famous agent André Simon or to the hosts of visitors and weary soldiers who found rest there. However that may be, thirty-five yards below ground 'it was possible to house a battalion and a half, i.e. 1,500 men, together with three-quarters of a mile of benches and sixty latrine buckets'.

In March 1916 the military circulated an official but highly secret memorandum on the potentialities of the Champagne cellars, in which it was stated that thirty-four battalions could be housed therein. The memorandum throws an interesting sidelight on the ups and downs of Champagne names. Who today, for instance, has heard of Rogeron, Werle, Abélé or Chauvet? Yet their cellars offered to take in a total of 4,700 men—as many as Krug, Heidsieck, Roederer and Irroy.

In 1916 GHQ gave permission for Champagne houses to bring back the gathered harvest into Reims itself—the 1916 was one of the finest ever, and twenty-one years had to elapse until it was equalled. From September 1914 to the great evacuation in 1918 no less than twenty million bottles were sent off, one firm contributing on its own no less than six million of this total.

The 'great evacuation', as it was called, took place in March 1918, and was a tragedy. After living for so long in such warlike conditions, the inhabitants were more than loth to leave the personal belongings they had held on to through it all. But the shelling became worse, and everything had to be abandoned, even livestock. An official notice, which could be seen on the walls for many months afterwards, read: *Poultry: persons leaving the town who possess poultry should go, in order to liquidate them, to the municipal soup kitchens.*

Seven months later the big German retreat started. In the early hours of the morning of 5 October 1918 the last shell fell upon Reims. Champagne, Dom Pérignon's elixir, was free to enliven the world again.

Messrs (Cordon Rouge) Mumm have the most palatial offices in the rue du Champ-de-Mars. If the guest-house is on these lines, I reflected, what have I not missed in comfort? And I was pondering over the probable delights of the meal, too, when I was ushered in to Jean Couvreur.

'Whatever——' he started.

'Let me explain,' I said, and told the whole story.

'And,' I finished, 'I did try to phone you. Here is the number.'

'Yes, but that is the office,' said M. Couvreur. 'Oh, well, but you missed some very nice '55 Champagne, followed by——'

'Stop!' I cried. 'I can't bear any more. All I had was cheese and onion soup.'

'Well, what will you have now? An old Champagne?' said M. Couvreur.

'Yes, but could I have one which is still *sur pointe*?'*

Jean Couvreur's eyebrows shot up.

'That's an unusual request,' he said. 'Are you sure you won't find the wine too dry?'

'I haven't tried it since I was with Moira Campbell at Moët, nearly ten years ago,' I replied. 'It's just that I wanted to see.'

'We had better hurry, then. The cellars shut in ten minutes.'

We quickly went out of the office, down a passageway giving onto a garden, and at the far end, some two hundred yards away, was another large building. We shall never get across that lawn and down to the cellars by midday, I thought. But as we got to the end of the passage a lift appeared in the right wall—used for taking the directors from their own private suite of offices direct down to the cellars. Very civilized, I thought.

The wine, a 1952, was quickly got out of its bin, but, of course, it had to be disgorged by hand, as there was clearly not time to freeze the little bit of sediment into a solid block of ice, as is done when several thousand bottles have to have their first cork taken out, the wine is given its *dosage* (whether this tiny tot of liquid contains a proportion of brandy often, rarely or very rarely I still cannot fathom) and the second cork put in.

---

* This means one that has been placed quite perpendicular, but with the neck downwards and with no *dosage* added. Bollinger are offering one on somewhat different and delectable lines: this is their R.D. (*récemment dégorgé*) Champagne. They have a bin (it will only work with really fine years) lying on its *side* so that the wine can feed on the lees inside the bottle for some twelve to thirteen years. Then they shake the deposit down, add a tiny *dosage* and recork. Thus you get a wine with the wonderful bouquet of an old Champagne, but tasting much fresher.

People love making out how difficult certain old manual crafts are, generally because it gives the workman a sense of pride in a terribly monotonous job, but this task of loosening the metal clamp (usually rusty) which holds the first cork in place, then letting it blow out (with tremendous force) and then, with the thumb, stopping more Champagne coming out than is necessary to get rid of that dirty eggcupful really is one of the hardest things to perform I have ever seen.

All this had only taken a few minutes, and we walked down a long gallery until we came to another gigantic, spotless lift, in which there were some twenty workmen, all in neat blue uniforms with huge open pockets in the front. In his pocket every man had a bottle of red wine; they were all off to their two-hour lunch break at home, and with their free ration. It was still not midday.

'They get away pretty promptly, you note,' said Couvreur, in his excellent English.

Seconds later we were in Mumm's elegant reception- and tasting-room (the really big Champagne firms show thousands upon thousands round their premises, and in the tourist season several highly paid staff are employed solely in conducting groups around), the *sur pointe* Champagne, having come up by yet another lift, being already there.

We sipped. And looked at each other.

Then we drank deeply; and looked at each other again.

'Well, what do you think? Honestly, now.'

'Superb,' I replied, 'but, honestly, probably even superber with a very, very light *dosage*.'

'*D'accord!*' said M. Couvreur, and we sallied forth to lunch at Reims's chic-est restaurant, Le Florence, run by an Italian, Zoboli, where M. Couvreur and I had *Pâté maison*, followed by grilled fresh sardines, but his other guests, just because it was an Italian restaurant, had some stodgy pasta.

A few hours later I had crossed into Vosges: the wine quest had started.

3

ÉPINAL

One of the few satisfactory replies I had had to my letters asking for accommodation was from M. Cleuvenot, the proprietor of the Relais des Ducs de Lorraine, at Épinal; so thither I wended my weary way at about half-past eight that winter's evening after my lunch at Reims. The place was in a quiet part of the town, overlooking the river, and looked so like a private house that for a moment I wondered if I had been misdirected. But the walls of this rather palatial establishment were plastered with all the smartest plaques, so I walked up a flight of steps and started to push at a massive wrought-iron and frosted-glass door. As I did so it was opened from the other side by a distinguished-looking man in immaculately creased new black trousers, but wearing above them a very well cut, spotless white chef's jacket.

'Good evening, Mr Layton.'

God's thunder! I thought: I had no idea I looked as British as all that. He knew I was coming, but not when—I had told him only to within a fortnight.

'Let me see to your bags,' said mine host, and without his clapping his hands there appeared—it seemed as if they had materialized from behind a giant aspidistra—two neatly attired, buxom girls, the sort whose heftiness is such that you do not mind if they carry your largest suitcase.

Up went my bags, and I found myself seated in M. and Mme Cleuvenot's office-cum-sitting-room. Madame was attractive, very placid, and was knitting what looked like a travelling-rug for an elephant. No matter, no room ever seemed more—elegantly—like being at home.

But I dared not sit so comfily—I was so tired I should have fallen asleep; so after a lightning wash and brush-up I sallied forth to renew my acquaintance with Alsace wine.

I landed up at the Grande Taverne, which, as the name implies, was one of those enormous great brasseries, with marble-topped tables in the front half and laid up *couverts* in the rear.

ÉPINAL

There was a pleasant three-course set meal, and one of the choices for the main course was whiting. An aside about this delicious fish: the Victorians loved it, served it a lot fried, with the tail put into the mouth, and called it *Merlan en colère* (whiting in a temper). One of the very few places you can get it in London is the Causerie at Claridge's, where you help yourself to one of the biggest selections of hors d'œuvre in the country and then go on to another dish if you feel like it. But why has this fish fallen so totally into disrepute? Within the same week recently I went to buy whiting both at Overton's at Victoria and at Selfridges, and in each instance the fishmonger took it for granted that I was making the purchase for the cat. In fact at Overton's the man, one of the old school, said, 'Why not have rock-salmon, sir? It's cheaper.'

'I don't think it's quite the same.'

'I always think whiting are too good to feed to animals. I like to eat them myself.'

'That's what I am going to do,' I said.

Surprise and pleasure of elderly fishmonger.

I like my whiting well grilled or fried and then served with browned butter into which capers have been macerated. Nice, too, is a rich parsley sauce. The fact that the fish on its own is a little insipid is not the main reason for its decline in popularity; it is also very low in protein value. This typifies for me, personally, the disastrous trend manifesting itself in eating out these days: fewer and fewer courses but more and more giant helpings of any one course; exactly the opposite of what I seek, which is many courses and tiny helpings of each.

As for those slabs of steak (that's why I don't really want to go to America), I am developing quite a nervous tic when I see one on my plate. I ask for it to be taken away and one-fifth brought back, which results either in a warning that I cannot have a reduction or in the manager's being called to ask what my 'complaint' is about. I have tried tipping in advance to get the waiter to put a tiny helping of meat on my plate; this invariably brings either a double ration or treble the amount of tomatoes or other vegetables.

So all the foods I love are easily assimilated and without too many carbohydrates—asparagus, oysters, braised endives, caviare, eggs, calves' liver, *quenelles*, fresh cod, cheese soufflés and whiting.

The wine-list at the Taverne was surprisingly weak in Alsatian wines, considering how near we were to the region. I chose a Riesling from a *cave coopérative* from a district in the Bas-Rhin, which does not make anything like such good wine as the Haut-Rhin, and when I saw the scruffy label I expected the worst.

The waiter poured; I sipped. An excellent, elegant, clear wine, though positively not a Riesling but a Gewürztraminer, which is more costly. This was cheating in reverse. But, on reflection, I felt this was not helping Alsace wines. True, one was getting a bargain in one sense, but after all a Gewürz is a much more pungent, heavy, sweet wine than a Riesling, and anyone first trying this particular wine and thinking it was a Riesling would get his standards all wrong.

I ordered another half-bottle. There were but two choices left in halves: the most expensive on the list, a Gewürztraminer, and the cheapest, a Sylvaner. I chose the latter. It was from the same Co-op farm, and when I tasted it yet another mistake was obvious. Yet again a 'bargain', in that what was in the bottle was obviously a wine made with the Riesling grape and not the coarser Sylvaner.

With two muddles I thought it would be worth while telling the waiter. To pave the way, though, I decided to tell him how excellently cooked and fresh (both true) was the *merlan*. His reply was polite but platitudinous.

While I was finishing my wine, the woman who was indubitably the owner's wife (which, in France, means she does all the work) started making preparations for typing the next day's menu. The café part of the brasserie was quite empty now, and out from a cubbyhole two waiters struggled to carry onto one of the marble tables a typewriter of gigantic proportions and of such antiquity that it would have looked old-fashioned in Noah's Ark. Without putting a felt underneath they heaved this ludicrous contraption onto the table; another waiter placed a jumbo-sized drink beside it; and then Madame came along with the menus and a copy of what was to go on them the following day.

If dishes are changed daily in a restaurant the problem of presenting an appetizing menu quickly without ruinous expense is difficult. I have been a minor expert on this subject all my restaurant life, and there is no perfect answer. If you are the Savoy your own printing-department does it; if the Wayside Caff, you write one menu only, spelling everything wrong and calling all vegetables 'veg.', and stick it into a scratched, greasy cellophane holder, which is taken around by a greasy, scrabby waitress. In between, you employ a typist to do them individually (ruinous); use a tiny hand duplicator (girls won't stand for dirtying their clothes with the ink-tubes for long); or do one only

ÉPINAL

and hand it round (puts the waitresses and customers in a foul mood and wrecks speedy service).

There is a last way which is quick, very cheap and appetizingly attractive: to use a jelly-graph, where you can even have a three-colour job looking a real work of art. The snags are almost too minor to mention: you may lose all your staff while the jelly is being melted each week on account of the foul smell, and it is a terrific art to see that it sets smoothly and without a number of bubbles—if not, you have to boil up all over again. You need a paper which is of the right size and not too shiny or too mat, which, though cheap, is very hard to find. You need special pens, special inks and, ultimately, a girl with splendid handwriting and a fine sense of timing (when to take the master copy off the jelly—too late and all the copies are blurred, too soon and you don't get your quota of copies), who cannot possibly master all these knacks under a twelvemonth. None the less, I felt that what Madame was about to do was the most time-wasting, most expensive and least efficient of all methods.

The menus were of immense, thick board, seemingly two feet down by one across, and were nicely printed with the permanent *à la carte* dishes, but with a space in the top right-hand corner for the dishes of the day. Obviously the menus had to be thrown away each day, and of course they were so thick that only one could be done at a time. What I should have done would have been to type the daily dishes on thin, good-quality paper, getting a top and at least three carbons, and then paste these onto the main board.

Madame scrutinized the hand-written menu, and then inserted a board; she then turned the platen to get it in place. This sounded like the old policeman's rattle. Then she started to type.

By the guns of Sebastopol! I nearly jumped clean out of my *banquette*. No wonder she waited until all the customers had gone; the noise was terrific.

My waiter was now elegantly laying up a table close to mine and, having gone to Madame to find out what she wanted to drink, put a half-bottle of red wine at what was to be her table. Since she would be well within earshot I thought I would cunningly tell the waiter my complaint about the muddled wines in such a way that Madame could not fail to hear.

This I did, with all the wine know-how I possessed, concluding, 'So you see, you are really misleading the poor public.' And I handed the man an extra tip. He took the money, but made no comment;

Madame, who couldn't have failed to hear, didn't even look up.
Back at the Relais M. Cleuvenot was still up when I returned, and kindly offered me a drink.

'Please,' I said, feeling now that I could talk all night. 'An *eau-de-vie de poire Williams*, if you will.'

'Oho! so you like that too,' he said. 'It's very popular.'

'It's hardly known in England at all.'

M. Cleuvenot was not too tired to be talkative, and I soon found out how it was that his hotel, which was highly marked up in the *Guide Michelin*, looked and felt so much like a private house.

'It was a private house before I bought it and I have done all I can to keep it looking like one. Come upstairs and look at the other bedrooms.'

Up he jumped, and I then had a conducted tour. I must say, he had not exaggerated, for my room, big as it was, appeared dwarfed by some of the others which had been left, regardless of potential lettings, just as they had been taken over. And in all the bedrooms, just as in the restaurant, up the stairs, and in every café and bar in the town, the walls were plastered with black-framed drawings in four or five vivid colours of historical and mythological scenes and characters from fairy-tales. I asked M. Cleuvenot why they were so popular in the town. 'But didn't you know?' said my host in genuine astonishment. 'Épinal is the home of the printing of the famous *images*, founded by Pellerin in 1792.'

I said this was news to me, but that if it was started just at that time it explained why there were so many scenes of Napoleon winning battles. M. Cleuvenot was shocked at my ignorance, jumped up and came back with a Christmas-card *image* of Little Red Riding-Hood, which he thrust into my hand as a souvenir.

My bedroom was as full of these red, black and green daubs, and all were of scenes connected with the Emperor. One remarkable one was of his death on St Helena. Could the British really have given him such a grotesque bed? It makes the Great Bed of Ware look like a child's cot. There is, of course, the inevitable eagle in the centre, but this ferocious bird is flanked on either side by gargoyle faces so hideous that even the victor of Marengo must have been given bad dreams. Dying Bonaparte may have been, but he was not wanting in company. There are six soldiers in the room, which has been so foreshortened that it looks like a chicken-coop: all in full-dress uniform; all wearing various, and enormous, Field-Marshals' plumed hats; and all but one, who is kneeling, standing to attention.

ÉPINAL

The most bizarre picture of the lot was entitled 'Eve of Austerlitz', and was so badly drawn and out of perspective as to be nearly funny. It reminded me of 'Tall Agrippa', 'Harriet and the Matches' and 'The Scissors Man' in *Struwelpeter*.

Napoleon is seated in the open in front of a camp-fire and resting. One leg is thrust forward on a stool, which appears to be right over the fire, so that it looks exactly as though the leg is being fired before amputation. By the side is a huge battle-plan. In front are two soldiers asleep, with a rug over them, and a curious black poodle, whose hind half is very closely clipped while the front is exaggeratedly shaggy. The picture was rather high up on the wall, but I could see that, unlike the others, it had a lot of explanatory print underneath. I got on a chair and took the picture off its pin to see what it said.

On 1 December 1805 the Army was camped near Austerlitz. The next day was to take place the famous battle when Napoleon destroyed, in a few hours, one of the most formidable armies he had ever had to fight. Tomorrow the sun would shine radiantly; the famous Sun of Austerlitz! Napoleon had walked through the lines giving encouragement and then, suddenly, everyone remembered that this was the anniversary date of the Emperor's Coronation. Soon fifty thousand straw torches placed on the end of bayonets made a fabulous illumination. The generals went to look for Napoleon to offer their love and enthusiasm, but found him in front of a bivouac fire with arms crossed, head lowered, and in a profound sleep. Near by was a map showing the disposition of the armies the following day. Thus the man in whose hands were the fortunes of Europe, on the eve of a decisive battle, gave himself to calmness and repose, so certain was he of the outcome. They awake him! The entire army lets out its accustomed cry, *'Vive l'Empereur!'* which must have been heard in the Russian camp like an artillery barrage. Tremendous joy reigns in all the bivouacs, and while the enemy pass the night in prayers and religious solemnities, the French sing gay songs and promise to offer to Napoleon a bouquet worthy of him.

When I had finished this translation I fell into the deepest sleep, and if anyone had woken me I'd have given them Austerlitz!

When I did awake there was the Emperor lying on the double bed beside me.

And today was my Austerlitz: my first day of calling on the introductions I had taken so long to obtain.

4

THE GROWERS

The vineyards of Alsace are split up into more minute parcels of land, and worked by a larger number of peasant growers, than those of almost any other wine area of France.

To give proof of this statement we may look at a breakdown of production in 1962—a low-yielding year, incidentally, making only 450,000 hectolitres,* as against a yearly average of 700,000.

Making from	1– 50 hectolitres were	50,000 growers
,, ,,	51– 100	,, ,,	1,500 ,,
,, ,,	101– 200	,, ,,	470 ,,
,, ,,	201– 300	,, ,,	30 ,,
,, ,,	301– 400	,, ,,	8 ,,
,, ,,	401–1,000	,, ,,	7 ,,
,, ,,	1,001–5,000	,, ,,	1 ,,

An analysis of these statistics shows that there are a vast number of tiny producers who are only *vignerons* in that they simply make what they consider enough for family use.

Those who carry out the commercialization of Alsatian wines fall into three distinct categories, and it so happens that the total cellar capacity of each section is the same—each can hold and store forty million litres of wine.

The first group of growers are too small to be able to sell their wine individually, or cannot be bothered, or think they can employ their time in some more profitable way; for any of these reasons they will send their fresh grapes to the vast co-op cellars, where huge blends are made of a Zwicker or Edelzwicker or Sylvaner or whatever grape-variety or varieties the soil of the commune most favours. The wines made will be sound, good value, but never really great.

The grower-wholesaler will own a far, far larger acreage of vines

---

* A hundred and twenty-five ordinary bottles of wine, or 22 gallons.

than the small grower mentioned above, but what he gets from these vineyards will only be a tiny fraction of what he buys in, either in grapes or in practically fermenting wine, from other much smaller growers. For the foreign wine-merchant from, say, England, Belgium or America, he will be by far the best person to deal with. His labels will be better designed, he will have a range of fine wines which the co-op will not have, and he will have sufficient clerical staff to deal with the complicated paperwork entailed in shipping wine abroad, which the little man funks handling.

Finally we have the grower-individual-producer. Of these there are countless thousands. They and their families will do all the cultivating, spraying, pruning, bottling and labelling, perhaps employing one or two full-time hands. They make quite a song and dance and are genuinely proud of the fact that they 'only sell [wines] from their own vineyards', which message is often proudly printed at the bottom of their notepaper. Their vineyards are not all that small, for they range, over the Haut-Rhin, from seven and a half to nearly ten acres. The good individual grower will make splendid wine.

As I have said, the average annual production is of the order of seventy million litres of wine, of which between fifty and sixty million finds its way onto the markets, the balance being consumed by the peasants themselves. And of this amount only some six per cent is sold abroad.

The first firm I selected was that of a small owner-grower by the name of Arthur Neymeyer-Petitdemange, at Ingersheim—virtually a suburb of Colmar—who was a personal introduction from my great wine-loving, wine-growing French friend Jean Baumard, of Rochefort on the Loire. And he had written an extra-welcoming letter, too.

I am not all that hot on the phone in France (except to order my breakfast), but Mme Cleuvenot put me through, which is the worst part.

A very un-come-hither voice answered.

'Yes, come along, but I must go punctually at midday, because of *la payée*.'

'The what?' I said politely.

'*La payée*. The workmen, you know.'

Then I got it. It was the end of the vintage, and just about the time that owners give the workmen an annual lunch. And not only that, but today was Saturday, and obviously *la payée* was the Alsatian equivalent of the Burgundian *paulée*, although this has now developed into a super blow-out at Meurseult—the only tradition remaining is that all the ticket-buyers (frightfully expensive) buy their own wines.

There are two ways to get from Épinal to Colmar, and I chose the more southerly route, via Gérardmer, because I had heard so much about the scenery around here, and about the lakes. Both are lovely: no wonder some two hundred thousand people visit the region annually for the hundreds of different scenic walks (with guides available if necessary). As for the lakes—you choose the adjective, I'll accept it.

The lakes and pools of the Vosges have always fascinated geologists and historians. Some would have it that the entire valley of the Rhine, from the Vosges to the Black Forest, was in remote times a huge inland sea, which ultimately wore away an outlet in bursting its barriers to the north.

I saw enough, on my way through the area, to want to pay it a more leisurely return visit; and this I was later able to do with my daughter, Alice, when she came out to join me at Colmar.

The largest of the lakes is Gérardmer itself, half a mile wide and over one and a quarter long, which has earned for the town of Gérardmer the title of 'the Interlaken of the Vosges'. While this may be overstating the case, it is certainly a lovely town, and a very popular resort, abounding with hotels of every class and offering a wide range of sports and pastimes to suit all tastes. The name of the town, incidentally, seems certain to be derived from *meix de Gérard*, *meix* being a *patois* word for 'an enclosed garden near to a dwelling-place' and Gérard being Gérard d'Alsace, Duke of Lorraine.

A few miles east of Gérardmer is the Lac de Longemer, which owes its name—originally *Longuemer*—to the fact that it is nearly a mile and a half in length but less than a third of a mile wide. Here the water is always calm, the scene tranquil; the wooded mountains which cast their reflection on the deep waters are magnificent. The lake is fed by the Vologne, on which, between Longemer and Gérardmer, north of the main road, lies one of the most beautiful spots in all France, where, flanked by giant spruces, some as much as a hundred and fifty feet high, this bouncing little river tumbles and bubbles down a series of cascades and craggy rocks; the noise of these miniature falls—the best known of which is the Saut des Cuves—can be heard from a considerable distance.

Farther west along the Vologne from Longemer is the Lac de

Retournemer, small in comparison to many of the others but compensating for it by having the bluest of clear blue water. Its name is derived from its position: before the road was built, the path ended here, below the bald, arid vastness of the Hohneck, one of the highest summits of the Vosges at 4,423 feet.

North of the Col de la Schlucht are four more small lakes: the Lac Noir, the Étang des Truites, the Lac Blanc—known for the exceptional purity and transparency of its waters—and the Lac Vert. The level of this last—superbly situated at more than three thousand feet above sea-level—was raised in 1860, to allow the building of a canal terminating at the rock called the Tanet, or Tanneckfels, from which there is a magnificent view of the vast green mirror, so coloured by the weed suspended in the water.

The last lake we visited, the Lac de Blanchemer, is also spectacularly situated, among the mountains south of the Col de la Schlucht. It is rarely visited by tourists, however; perhaps because it is shrinking rapidly, being swallowed up by peat, as has already happened with other lakes in the area.

In spite of the name, the Petitdemanges were not all that easy to find, as there were others of the same name in the village—deadly rivals, I found out later, as was hinted at by M. Arthur's brochure, which says: *Christian Name and Exact Address are Indispensable on Account of the Namesake.*

No one was about when I went into the office and so, after a few moments, I let out a gentle little 'Yoo-hoo', which caused a lady to materialize. Her appearance startled me so that I nearly stepped backwards into the stove.

Her bright red hair was parted dead in the middle and was so cut and arranged that it covered most of her cheeks and seemed almost to join up under her chin. The small part of the lady's face that did remain was heavily powdered chalk-white, save around the eyes, which were circled with a black make-up. I suppose it sounds an Irishism to say that black can shine, but the whole effect was such that when Mme Neymeyer-Petitdemange cast a look upon one it seemed that two powerful pitch-black fog-lamps were probing the innermost secrets of one's soul. I suddenly felt I had been stripped naked.

'Have you come to make purchases?' said Madame, very flatly.

'Well, er . . .'

'I'll take you down to my husband; he is in the cellars, working.'

But before the reader follows me with Madame down the steps to the cellars, a little aside about medium-size and smaller French wine-growers. There are, particularly in the industrial towns of the north, a good number of trade fairs at which viticultors can rent a booth and then sell or give away sample glasses of their wine, and thus get orders, obviously cutting out all middlemen. Jean Baumard does this at the big trade fair at Lille, his booth being next to that of the Petitdemanges, hence my introduction. Clearly, then, over the years one builds up a good private clientèle, and people like those I was visiting, who were past middle age, would not have the slightest financial need to get into the English market, especially with all the complicated paperwork it involves.

M. Petitdemange was indeed working when we got down into his cellars. He was labelling some bottles, and doing it beautifully.

I introduced myself, and said my piece about wanting to take up an agency. Monsieur wiped his hand on his smock, shook mine and said, 'All my vineyards are on the finest calcareous soils; I have over fifteen acres.'*

'I'm sure of it,' I replied.

M. Petitdemange then repeated the same remark, more or less word for word, eight times in the next quarter of an hour. At the end of the fifth time, Madame, who was far from given to garrulity, said, 'Monsieur Layton has heard that before, he won't want to hear it again,' and walked away upstairs. But he did.

I was wondering, as it was now getting on to midday, if I would be offered a tasting before the *payée*. This was the moment when I would have liked to show some erudite vinous knowledge which would have pulled my host up with a jolt. Usually I can take the stuffing out of a bumptious grower in many a subtle way and without being rude. One is hinting that I have just come from a better vineyard; another is wondering, ever so casually, if offered a taste, if it won't blow up in bottle, or if some other fell disaster will not overtake it. But this was

---

* There are many renowned European wine districts where what is aimed at is not only body but body with lightness. Among these districts are Montilla-Moriles, near Córdoba, for Montilla (Sherry-type) wines; Jerez de la Frontera for Sherries; Armagnac and Cognac for wines to be distilled to make brandies; Champagne; and Alsace. In all of these regions there are favoured vineyards which make wines which have more finesse than the others. There is no pattern to determine which, in fact, they are; they can be at any point of the compass around the region, in the centre (Cognac) or at the edge. But they all have one thing in common: the finest parts are on calcareous, or chalky, soil.

my first day in the region and I *hadn't* got a glass in my hand. At last we made a move, and in no time we were in a little sitting-room in front of a bottle of Riesling. I took a sip, but I had not been in the district long enough to say anything profound.

'Tell me,' I said, 'won't all the form-filling and endless paperwork connected with exportation to England be rather a bore?'

M. Petitdemange appeared to me to breathe a sigh of relief. 'I think it will,' he said, and after that all the tension went.

It was past twelve now, but M. Petitdemange did not seem in the slightest hurry to end our talk, as evidenced by the fact that he was rapidly opening fresh bottles of Rieslings and Traminers. Perhaps he expected me to make the first move, I thought.

'I think I ought to be going,' I said.

'Whatever for?' said my host. 'There's plenty of time.'

'I was thinking about your staff luncheon,' I said.

'Staff luncheon?'

'Yes; you said you had to see to the workmen's *payée*,' I replied.

'Oh, the men's weekly pay-packet. I arranged for my son to see to that.'

The other person I had phoned from Épinal was someone with another tongue-twisting name, M. Zind-Humbrecht.

The first time I had written to him my secretary had called him M. *Fino*-Humbrecht, and on looking at the notepaper I realized that it was by no means carelessness on her part, since the curious *Z* did look more like an *F*, and that went for the *d* looking like an *o* too; and thereby hangs a tale. A tragic tale, which started just one hundred years ago.

But let us quickly go back a few centuries.

Some fifty years B.C. Alsace and Lorraine were inhabited by the Celts; then Julius Caesar conquered the district and Alsace knew the benefits of the splendid Pax Romana for over five hundred years. Then came the breaking-up of the Roman Empire, and the region was invaded by hordes of Huns, Teutons and Vandals. Slowly, mainly as a means of self-protection, the people would permit themselves to be ruled by some feudal duke. After this came Charlemagne, and after him his son, Louis le Débonnaire, who had the bright idea of splitting up his father's empire into three sections, giving Alsace to his son Lothaire. This was in A.D. 817, but towards the end of this century a successor of Lothaire, Charles the Bald, traded the province to a German prince, Louis le Germanique, and Alsace stayed under the indirect or direct rule of his descendants for seven hundred and fifty years.

During this time the most important political event occurred in the fourteenth century. Although the Alsatian people had, centuries earlier, put themselves voluntarily under certain overlords, they found that, as time passed, they had not been all that clever. Peace of a sort they might have, but the price to be paid in taxes and forced labour was not worth it. Thus it was that ten Alsatian cities—Colmar, Haguenau, Kaysersberg, Landau, Munster, Obernai, Rosheim, Sélestat, Turckheim and Wissembourg—formed themselves into a sort of republic, called the Decapolis.

The next important date is 1678, when, by the Treaty of Nijmegen, France, which had acquired certain rights over the province by the Treaty of Westphalia in 1648, definitely re-attached Alsace to her kingdom.

Then—most dramatic date of all—1870. Germany marches on France and conquers it completely. The 1st and 2nd German Armies invade Lorraine between 6 and 18 August, and Metz is taken by 27 October. The 3rd Army invades Alsace between 4 and 8 August; Strasbourg is surrounded by the 9th and capitulates on 28 September. On 10 May 1871 is signed the Treaty of Frankfurt, which gives Germany all of Alsace and part of Lorraine. It stays German for half a century, when it goes back to France after the First World War for twenty-two years, is German and subject to intense Germanization for four years and now has been back with France for twenty-four years.

So there you have it: bumbled backwards and forwards between two great nations like a puppet on a string, Alsace has had a dramatic, troubled history which pervades everything.

Two ideals are supposed to account for this incessant to-ing and fro-ing. The first is the language: it is maintained that the Alsace *patois* is much more German than French. So what? A Chinese born in London doesn't become British, and at that rate parts of Belgium and Holland should belong to Germany and the USA to England, or vice versa.

The other ideal is geographical: some maintain that the Vosges mountains are the 'natural' frontier; others say the Rhine.

I wouldn't like to pontificate, but I know one thing: every history book, every travel book, every work on Alsace is full of the subject, and I tell the reader with as much vehemence as I can command that it affects people's clothes, their architecture, their food, their politics, their thoughts, their wine and—to get back to our subject—their printed notepaper, for the character of the letters and the general layout are inevitably half-German and half-French.

Young 'Fino-Humbrecht' welcomed me on the steps of his house-cum-office-cum-cellars in Wintzenheim, another country suburb of Colmar. In front was a spacious courtyard with a lorry, two cars and, at the far end, the huge stack of new bottles in open cages ready for use (usually after another sterilized wash) when the occasion arose. The courtyard itself was attractively sanded over, and dotted here and there were neat beds of flowers.

By the time I had got up the steps to shake hands with my host-to-be, he had been joined by his young wife, who, I found, had contributed the *Zind* part of the name, and a prettier woman I had not seen in a month of harvest moons. Madame soon disappeared to continue her housewifely work, but she would, I was sure, join us later and offer me little sweet wafer biscuits when the sweeter wines were offered at the end of our inevitable tasting.

In Alsace, more than in other French wine-growing regions, the grower's house, office, cellars, bottling-outfit and delivery-bay will all be in one (usually harmonious) whole. Often the compactness is surprising, and it is not rare to find six or seven neat staff in an office with the boss's office adjoining, and yet on the other side of a narrow passage will be the private dining- and drawing-rooms. But this latter is also part of the office side of the business, for when you have finished with your talking you will taste the wines not in the office but in the drawing-room parlour.

There was nothing half-hearted about M. Humbrecht's welcome, and before long we were descending to the cellars to inspect the new wine. Half-way down the steps my ears were assailed by a noise louder of its kind than I had ever heard before. This was the bubbling of the must through the bungholes of the huge oak vats.

Wine has several enemies; perhaps its worst is oxygen—remember this when you deal with it. I suppose that what wine-merchants are most asked, by those who take their great vintages seriously, is how long one should draw the cork before drinking and whether or no one should decant.

There can be no absolute guide: a ten-year-old Claret of a first-rate growth of a mediocre to bad year would be so thin you would draw the cork just before serving, whereas a twenty-year-old Claret of a great year could do with three hours' breathing; to give perfect advice one would have to know the state of readiness or robustness of every wine asked about, and if this was *only* the classified growths and one took *only* the quite good years of *only* this century, you would have (shall we say there is a quite good year for practical purposes every six years from 1900 to 1936 and then one every four years thereafter) eleven hundred or so different flavours to know about.

This inevitably brings me to the question of perfect cellars and ideal cellar temperatures. When someone has bought a half-dozen bottles of some red plonk and, knowing he will drink it all up inside a month, asks if it matters if it goes under the stairs by the boiler, one tends to think it just isn't worth while teaching the public any more. Anyway, it would probably be the better for being stored in a sauna bath and sent around the world in a ketch.

But if two rich young men bought some 1961 Claret of a First Classified Growth to drink thirty years later, and one put it in the stables and the other stored it in an 'ideal' cellar, there would be a marked difference by the turn of the millennium. An even temperature and, possibly as important, the right degree of humidity do make differences. John Michael Broadbent, of Christie's, has proved this with some of the Clarets he has caused the nobility to unearth from their cellars and the prices they have justly fetched.

So much for wine breathing through its cork when in bottle after all fermentation is over; what of wine in cask in full spate after the vintage?

With really big casks the amount of gas coming off the must is tremendous, and it is not sufficient just to put in a bung and let nature take its course, as is done with small casks. What is used is a glass contraption which fits into the bunghole, with a sort of water-lock that permits the gas to escape but does not let the air enter and harm the wine.

'What a fantastic noise!' I said.

'This will be one of the greatest years of the century,' replied M. Humbrecht, somewhat inconsequentially.

'I'll bet you say that every year.'

'No, no,' he retorted. 'Just try this Riesling.' And before I could protest, a glass of the turgid, bubbling liquid was thrust into my hand.

Now, apart from tasting disgusting, these new wines have the most powerful laxative properties, and, furthermore, only those viticultors who have tasted them year in, year out, can possibly estimate how good they will be when bottled; still, all growers think their callers are experts, so one accepts, and makes suitable comments.

M. Humbrecht was extremely proud of the season's wine, and indeed it was so good that only a few days beforehand a journalist had descended upon the firm and given them a write-up:

THE FIRM OF ZIND-HUMBRECHT

16 Hectares of Wines, a Cellar Capacity of 1,500 Hectolitres and a Wine of Great Quality

A refractometer riveted to his eye, M. Humbrecht announces, 'Ninety-one degrees Oechslé for a Riesling.'* We are in the cellars of Messrs Zind-Humbrecht, viticultors, at Wintzenheim, in the rue Maréchal-Joffre; in a vast cellar where the casks, exclusively of oak, are in three well aligned rows.

And in spite of the tremendous amount of work which has gone on here during the vintage-time, the most perfect order reigns in this temple of Bacchus, where the only noise to be heard is the bubbling of the musts as they indulge in fast and furious fermentation.

'1967 is in the process of giving us one of the great vintages of the century, and especially in the Gewürztraminers, where the musts show 107° Oechslé, equivalent to 14° Baumé,' says M. Humbrecht in offering us a glass filled with Riesling only a few days old. A delight, this new wine.†

But this was only the beginning. Next there followed a Gewürztraminer—this is the great speciality of the firm—which was infinitely more revealing. In fact in this nectar, the colour of a golden-yellow pear, we were able to understand how the firm of Zind-Humbrecht has managed to put its business on such a sound commercial footing, and what a vast store of vinous knowledge there is here. . . .‡

Humbrecht and I lunched at the new Shooting restaurant—décor motif: field sports of every description—which forms a part of

* The Oechslé scale is for measuring the specific gravity of a wine before fermentation; the Baumé is used after.
† Did he really think so?
‡ How on earth you can detect this by simply tasting a wine is beyond me.

Colmar's largest, most luxurious and beautifully renovated hotel, the Terminus-Bristol, opposite the station.

My next appointment I was anticipating keenly. M. Thoman, of the Croix d'Or at Orbey, was another of the hoteliers who had answered my room-for-publicity letter; he had said how much he appreciated my stamps, as he was a keen collector. This elated me greatly, and I foresaw not only a bed for a night or two but one or two gay drinking-sessions over stamp-collections—not that I had one, but I was sure I could get by.

I had thus written to M. Thoman and said I was off to Spain, would he like any from that country, and should they be franked or mint. He replied, asking for mint, and when I went to Spain I sent him quite a number. I heard no word from him, but assumed that this was because of the summer season, and I pictured my host-to-be fairly pumping my hand when I arrived, with apologies for not having thanked me for the stamps (they cost far more than a night's lodging) and positively insisting that I stayed at his hostelry indefinitely.

The Croix d'Or was also the address I had selected for two very important letters—one containing my legitimate French francs I had left in London, and the other a new green card. I had discovered at the last minute that the one I had on me, a leftover from a previous visit, ran out while I was away.

Orbey is one of the less attractive villages of the Vosges, and merely scrapes into guide-books as the centre of the Val d'Orbey, which for scenery, particularly along the neighbouring valleys of the Béhine and Weiss, is unequalled for loveliness in all the district. It was also the scene of some extremely severe fighting in the First World War.

It was pitch dark and sleeting when I pushed open a dimly lit door which said *Croix d'Or* and found myself in an immense, antiquated café. *Tiens!* I thought. This doesn't resemble the smart sophisticated postcard of the hotel which came with the letter. The café was quite deserted, save for two elderly men playing dominoes. Both were what one finds so often in France, persons who were probably quite affluent but whose sartorial elegance left much to be desired—carpet slippers, an apron and the impression that a new blade in the razor would not have come amiss. Neither was at all young.

'I'm looking for M. Thoman,' I said, approaching.

'That's me,' said one of the men.

I was nonplussed, to put it mildly.

'I'm Mr Layton,' I said. M. Thoman looked blank. 'You know, the man who sends you stamps.'

'Ah!' said M. Thoman. 'That's my son.'

'Could I speak to him, then?'

'He is not here at present.'

'Will he be back soon?' I said, feeling that my bed and breakfast were vanishing.

'It depends on how long you mean by "soon". He has gone off on his honeymoon, skiing; he hasn't said where to, or how many weeks he'll be gone.'

'Well,' I said, putting on a brave face, 'the fact is that your son invited me, more or less, to stay here.'

'My son runs the hotel side of the business,' said M. Thoman calmly, 'and I the café, and he never tells me anything about his arrangements.' The tone was not at all unkind, but I got the message.

'Oh, I see,' I said, and then I thought of my post. 'Well, I did write several times to your son, and also I have had several letters addressed here to myself. Could I please have them?'

Now, for the first time, the old man was a little less placid. This struck me as odd—I was soon to know why.

'Would these letters have foreign stamps on them?'

'Why, yes,' I said, 'of course. They come from England.'

M. Thoman prised himself out of his chair and padded to a recess at the far end of the room, a part which I sensed was hardly ever used. On the left was a huge seven-foot-tall sideboard, with cupboards underneath, then a shelf for dishes, with mirrors at the back, and then a headpiece with drawers therein; on the right was a table on which were four or five large cane baskets with handles. They were the sort, not often seen now, that appear in rural pictures where a buxom wench, with one on her arm and full of lovely brown eggs, is sitting on a stile and talking to a shepherd. They are very large.

The old man approached the baskets—I followed.

'You are sure they were foreign stamps?' he said.

'Definitely,' I said.

'Oh dear,' said M. Thoman.

When I got nearer I understood.

Each basket was filled to the top with envelopes from foreign countries: there must have been several hundred. We managed to dispose of three of the baskets fairly quickly, because by the dust on the top it was clear that they had been there for several years. It was also clear that M. Thoman *fils* went for numbers rather than rarity.

When we got to the final basket with no success, M. Thoman said, 'Perhaps they were not important.'

I told him what they contained.

'Oh dear,' said M. Thoman, and a tiny bead of perspiration appeared on his forehead.

'Let's try the dresser,' said M. Thoman.

I was getting in a panic now; no cash and no possibility of extending my trip: the prospect was disastrous. We opened the cupboards of the great dresser. Here were hundreds upon hundreds more envelopes in great disarray. We then pulled out the drawers above the sideboard cupboards; more envelopes. Not a sign of mine.

We sat down. Father had certainly tried; I stood him a drink.

Then my eye caught the three drawers at the very top of the dresser.

'They couldn't be there?' I said.

'Ah,' said M. Thoman, 'that is indeed where my son does keep special letters.' He fished a key out of his pocket, and in the first drawer there they were.

I sped back to Épinal, where a bottle of Château Lagrange 1961 was awaiting me.

5

THE ROAD TO MULHOUSE

ONE of the things I had resolved to do, when it came to recording my impressions of my journey through Alsace, was to be truthful with myself about the places I visited, not praise them up just because I was writing a book and the guidebooks raved about them. But I nearly cracked here on the first day: Remiremont, Thann, Cernay, Mulhouse —what disappointments!

From Épinal to Mulhouse, where I was to spend the third night of my trip, you go through the loveliest of country, until you reach Remiremont, a dreary little place, to my mind, though some guidebooks draw one's attention to the main street, on account of its 'flower-bedecked arcades, which are charming'. But there were no flowers at this time of year, and all the fussy little arcades badly needed a coat of paint.

Remiremont's only claim to historical fame is that it was the home, and for many centuries, of a convent for nuns who were very far from chaste. The convent was, in effect, a sort of snob school; there were fifty nuns and all of them had to prove noble ancestry going back for at least a century before they were admitted. Only the Mother Superior was obliged to take vows of chastity, and lessons, if such we may call them, 'consisted of discussing not the Commandments of God but love and how to become more charming', says a twelfth-century chronicler; he went on to say, 'These ladies soon ceased to call themselves nuns, but were *tantes* instead, and the novices became *nièces*.' He finally added that they even designed themselves a costume which would best show off the most curvaceous parts of their figures.

After Remiremont comes a bleak, beautiful stretch, where at one point I saw a pretty little terraced garden by the side of the road with a sign announcing that *Here rises the Moselle*. Let into a granite wall was a bronze panorama of the river's course until it meets the mighty Rhine at Koblenz. Underneath was a busy, bubbling spring, which made a sudden sally a few yards farther down the garden and then proceeded to bicker turbulently down the valleyside. I seem to have seen the 'veritable source' of many a French river in my wine wanderings, and I find it almost awe-inspiring to watch a little trickle spurting out of the ground and to know that five hundred miles away this same trickle will be a mighty river capable of carrying even small liners down to the sea. My awe, however, is somewhat dampened by a nagging query: why was that particular spring chosen by the authorities as the true source? Surely there must be scores of little springs in the immediate neighbourhood, all with as good a claim. Later I heard a possible solution to this: other things being equal, the distance of each spring from the mouth of the river is taken as the deciding factor.

After this the road got even more desolate; here and there were a few scattered villages, deserted because it was lunchtime and more deserted again because it was Sunday—why is the sabbath such a gloomily depressing day? I was very glad when I at last reached Mulhouse, even though my advance knowledge of that city was far from encouraging.

Mulhouse.
'This town has been described as the Manchester, or even the Wigan, of Alsace.' Thus Bernard Newman in his *The Sisters Alsace-Lorraine*.*
'The tourist need not expect to find much of the picturesque in Mulhouse,' says the Michelin Green Guide *Vosges*.

Both statements are accurate, but neither points out that although, compared to Strasbourg and Colmar, Mulhouse is hideous, it is still a graceful town if you set it against many other towns of comparable size all over the rest of France—for example, Montpellier, Calais, Clermont-Ferrand, Rennes—which, in my opinion, are far worse.

And because it is so ugly, its one building worthy of note stands out like a gem—the sixteenth-century Town Hall, whose beauty lies in its elegant double outside staircase and its outdoor mural paintings.

My hotel in the town was the Strasbourg, in the Avenue de Colmar, which was most comfortable, cheap and warm, and unusual in that, though they did not 'make the restauration', as the French say when you go into a café where they do not serve proper hot dishes, there was a large, quiet, usually empty café tucked away up on the first floor, where you could have breakfast, and cups of coffee at all hours of the day.

This (not having to eat at the hotel where I was sleeping) suited me,

* Jenkins, 1950.

because I wanted to eat at the Guillaume Tell restaurant, opposite the Town Hall, first because it had been warmly recommended and secondly because the proprietor had written me a mystifying letter about accommodation.

As usual, on my way, I looked into several cafés—*Weinstuben*, as they call them in Alsace—and tried, with varying success, to order a tiny glass of Alsatian wine.

It is, I know, a nasty trait, but I have an absolute 'thing'—and therefore I imagine it happening more often than it really does—about being charged a fraction more money for a glass of vino on account of having a foreign accent. I also dislike being given a glass of above-average wine, albeit at a fair price, when I have distinctly asked for *vin ordinaire*. Thirdly, and perhaps less nasty, I hate being given a double measure when I have clearly—at least, I fondly think so—asked for the smallest possible measure.

This question of the mental barrier which certain people erect in their own heads when they hear a foreign accent fascinates me when I am calmly writing, but exasperates me when it occurs abroad. In those I.Q. tests where one has to marry up one set of squiggles with another it is said that sometimes primitive races who cannot read or write show a remarkably high level of intelligence, whereas exam-passing scholars fail totally. If you changed the squiggles for the degree of understanding of a person speaking with a foreign accent, you can also detect a pattern of intelligence which knows no class barriers.

I have been playing little experimental games abroad for years. One of my older ones, if a Frenchman, say, aggressively just doesn't want to understand, is to ask him, in his own language of course, if he speaks French. Before you have ended the final syllable of '*français*' he will reply emphatically, 'No,' and then, literally half a second later, he realizes what you have said—'but of course I speak French!'—and, believe it or not, the question you have previously put is remembered *and* answered.

My newer ploy is the long pause. I stumbled on this one in a café in Nancy. I ordered a black coffee. When it came, thinking it would be nice to pour in a little spirit, I said, '*Et un eau-de-vie.*'

'*Quoi?*' said the man.

Now, I know I was pronouncing the water of life reasonably well: perhaps I didn't purse my lips enough when I said 'oh' and possibly when I said 'de vee' I didn't run the two words fast enough. But it was good enough; I could have repeated myself and to have made my request doubly clear have added, '*eau-de-vie*, you know, *un Cognac*'. Then the man might have *given* me the latter instead of a Calvados or a *marc*, and Cognac is now as expensive in an ordinary French café as it is in the West End of London.

So I said nothing and just looked the man in the face.

'Oh, an *eau-de-vie*,' he said.

'Oh, and you know what you can do with it,' I replied.

But all I have said applies to the rest of France. In Mulhouse, and indeed the rest of Alsace-Lorraine, I am presented with quite another problem in my café-trotting—the trilingualism of many of the inhabitants.

Strasbourg, Colmar and Mulhouse have a joint population of well over four hundred thousand. Here, and in the rest of the towns and villages of Alsace-Lorraine, there are three languages: the Alsatian *patois*; German; and French.

Now, the *patois* has no parallel with, say, the Welsh language, which is spoken only by a handful of people, rather ostentatiously, in pubs, and is regarded as a fine, interesting language with its own grammar which must on no account die out.

Nobody cares about Alsatian grammar, children are certainly not taught it, most people would like to see it die out: it is just that it is the mother tongue—its roots are eighty per cent German—of probably half the population over the age of thirty. If there are any official figures which are at variance with the guesses I am going to make I, personally, would not give too much credence to them, because French is now so much *dans le vent* that many Alsatians would not like to admit to being ignorant of it.

For those readers, then, who know French and German, or French only, or German only, and who want to communicate in Alsace, here are my own statistics.

First, assuming that it would have taken at least three years to frenchify Alsace after the 1918 Armistice, everyone who is now aged fifty or over will be able to speak and understand German, Alsatian and French. Such people would have been around ten when French became *de rigueur*, and even if they had never heard a word of the language until then they could not possibly have failed to learn a great deal from 1921 to 1940.

Secondly, thousands of people between seventy and eighty-five can hardly speak any French, and there are pockets where it is not understood at all.

Thirdly, one hundred per cent of the population under twenty-five will speak French, read French, and know French grammar perfectly. Probably half will be able to talk the patois with their parents if need be; none will know German proper.

Finally, probably a third (low estimate) of the population speak *patois* in their own homes in preference to French.

My first *Weinstube* was called the Black Bear, and I asked, in French, for a small glass of Alsatian wine. Two elderly women were sitting in the middle of the room. They were of huge proportions. One was tatting, and against her ample bosom the little square looked like a bedspread for a dormouse. The other was reading a paper—a German one—suspended on those bamboo holders, so reminiscent of cafés in Vienna. She was really big: her vast, bulbous, elephantine legs were encased in yards of wound-round muttoncloth and her breasts were veritable cannonballs. I repeated my request; she looked at me with contempt and fake misunderstanding.

I asked again—now in German.

Slowly she heaved herself from her chair and waddled to the bar, and I had more than enough time to look around. The room was typically Alsatian and cosily charming. Comfortable wooden benches around the wall, sturdy plain wooden tables, covered with the warm, glowing red tablecloths which are a feature of the region, and, most attractive of all, slightly yellow-tinted electric lamps set in old-fashioned holders and suspended from chains at some considerable distance from the ceiling, so that one got a good light over the table but the ceiling was in semi-darkness. Why on earth was the place dead empty? I thought.

My wine had now been poured out at the counter—in a miniature hock-type glass with a green stem and a white bowl, which only held a toothful.

'How much?' I said, in German.

'One franc.'

'Damn that! The local rate is only sixty centimes, and for a bigger measure, at that.'

'You don't get Traminer for sixty centimes,' said the woman. 'That's our best wine.'

'But,' I said, and had to go back into French because I couldn't cope with it in German, 'you have no right to give the best wine when a person just asks for a glass of wine.'

'You didn't say you wanted the cheapest,' said the woman, now in French. She understood, all right.

'But I didn't say I wanted the most expensive,' I retorted angrily.

'Sorry,' said the woman, and she pocketed the franc.

I cut off my nose by only taking a quarter-sip—it was delicious, dash it!—and stormed out.

In the next place I asked for my glass in German—they answered in French.

At the third, called the White Bear, I switched back—wrong again.

I wandered, dazed, into the street, and now wanted to find my restaurant.

'Excuse me, sir,' I said to the nearest passer-by, 'but what language do you speak best?'

'What has that got to do with you?' said the man, who clearly thought I was attempting to pick him up.

I fled, to ask the nearest policeman.

The Guillaume Tell is much photographed by tourists on account of its pretty façade. It stands on a corner and is all black wooden beams with white plaster in between. And under the roof are several excellently carved painted wooden figures.

The establishment was a *Weinstube* and restaurant (with a very varied, all-prices menu) combined, where I could quaff glasses of Alsatian wine until I was hungry, and then eat. But I had lunched so well that all I could manage was two fried eggs and some Munster cheese to follow; and, of course, wine.

The management ran a hotel as well as a restaurant, and I had received a curiously worded letter in response to my request for a room, to the effect that it was not considered that the place was quite my type. I knew what was meant, but I had written back and said that if they meant that the hotel was not good enough for me, I was prepared to sleep in an attic, but that if they thought I was not good enough for the hotel, my feelings were greatly hurt. There had been no reply. So when I had finished I paid the bill, fished out the letter and asked a buxom German waitress if I could have a word with the proprietor. When he came up we shook hands.

He was clearly disappointed I had eaten so little, and said he wished I could have started, say, with his speciality of mixed sliced meats *à la Mulhouse*, followed by a little fried whiting and then grilled entrecôte, rice and salad.

'With an elephant steak to follow, perhaps?' I said.

M. Tell looked puzzled, but I let it pass.

I now repeated the gist of his letter and laid it on thick. M. Tell took it seriously.

'We really are very modest as far as the hotel side of the business goes. We have ten very small rooms and they have been booked by the same commercial travellers at the same time of the season for twenty years now. Very occasionally one is free, but there is never any guarantee.'

'I liked your wine,' I said, and walked back to the hotel.

Have you ever had, and for no good reason, unaccountable attacks of insomnia? I had one that night, and after about three hours of the deepest sleep I woke up, feeling very wide awake, then listened with the greatest enjoyment to some excellent vibrant dance music.

Mulhouse with a night club? Funny, I thought, but that did not send me to sleep again.

I got out of bed and opened the window. The band was loud and clear and gave me terribly itchy feet. I felt I must go and dance, and got as far as putting a vest and pants on; then I went to the wash-basin and looked in the mirror. 'Not at your age, surely!' I said to myself, and went back to bed. . . .

Car-drivers are lucky if they stay at the Hotel Strasbourg in that the place owns a huge freehold square behind the hotel, where motorists park free. This derelict square in the very centre of the town will be worth a fortune when it is redeveloped, but at the moment there is nothing more there than a few outbuildings. When I went to get my car out the next morning I looked into one, which turned out to be a laundry where a youth was finishing work and preparing to go home.

'It's an all-night laundry,' he said. 'Some people think I am lonely,' he continued, 'but I've got my wireless.' And he turned on a powerful transistor. That was my night club band.

6

ABOUT ALSATIAN WINES

I SEEM to have come a pretty fair way without saying much about the wines of Alsace themselves, and this must now be remedied.

The vine was brought to the region by the Roman legionaries, who came up the Rhône in the first century A.D., then occupied the entire left bank of the Rhine down to its mouth. Recent archaeological probings into the question of the sitings of vineyards have shown that there were some hundred and fifty in A.D. 900, rising to three times that number five hundred years later. The vineyards then extended a little farther to both south and north than they do now, from Altkirch up to Wissembourg. By the twelfth century it was these Vosges vineyards that produced the most esteemed wines of the entire Rhine–Moselle region. Since then the pattern has changed, and the most sought-after vineyards are now farther north, in the Rheingau and on the middle Moselle.

We have some slight indication of the importance of Alsace wines, compared to Rhenish, in the Middle Ages from quotations in the *Oxford English Dictionary*. In the first place, the Old French word for Alsatian [wine] was *aussay*, and this became, when it crossed the Channel in the twelfth or thirteenth century, *Osey* (other forms: *Ossey, Osseye, Osay, Ozey*). In those two centuries the spelling for the rival wine was *Ryne* or *Ruyne*, and not *Rhenish*, which only became accepted a good two centuries later. And when the lexicographers of the greatest dictionary of the world, a treasure-house of words more important than the Bible and Shakespeare put together, got down to work, they decided that *Osey* was a main word at the relevant time, and *Ryne* merely a subordinate one.

My theory is that around, say, 1400 *Osey* was such an important wine and so well known that no one thought of changing the spelling, while *Ryne* was so much less known that changes could be made.

Of note, too, is that *Osey* just pips *Ryne* on the post for the distinction of being first quoted in the English language. In its preface the *Oxford English Dictionary* says: 'In this Dictionary words which are native are traced to their earliest known English.'

ABOUT ALSATIAN WINES

Here are the two relevant quotes:

'Good wyn of Gaskoyne, and wyn of Osey.'

William Langland. 'Piers Plowman', 1362 manuscript.

'Ryniswyne.'

Extract from the Account Rolls of Durham Abbey, 1375.

And, finally, be it noted that by the mid-seventeenth century *Osey* has disappeared from the language as a day-to-day drink, whereas *Rhenish* is coming along fast.

This little aside is intended to dramatize the statement of so many French historians that in the Middle Ages the wines of Alsace enjoyed a far greater reputation than what we now call Rhine wines, and were indeed Big Business.

The three towns where the young wine was warehoused, ready for export, were Colmar (still by far the most vinous town of Alsace), Sélestat (between Colmar and Strasbourg, and today with no wine associations whatever) and Strasbourg (by far the biggest then, but now very little occupied with wine).

The wine first went by barge down the Ill via Colmar and Sélestat to Strasbourg, whence, in great thousand-litre *fuders* (oak casks), it went on down the Rhine to Cologne, Mainz and Frankfurt; and to England, which country was 'especially fond of these wines', says one chronicler.

A rosily bibulous position; and this lasted happily until that cruellest of all religious scraps, the Thirty Years' War, which ravaged central Europe from 1618 to 1648. During this time the vineyards were destroyed and all the villages pitilessly sacked. Again, to show that this statement is not exaggerated, it is a fact that whereas between 1530 and 1590 wine was exported from Colmar to the volume of twelve million bottles, between 1630 and 1690 this figure fell to two million.

And as the decades passed things got worse, not better: by 1720 England had entirely ceased to make purchases from Alsace, and near the end of this same century the final blow came when Baden and Switzerland both closed their frontiers to the wine; Alsatians were for many years to drink what they made all on their own.

Around 1820, however, things suddenly started looking up, and quite quickly too; there was prosperity for just on half a century. Then came the disastrous and sudden defeat of the French armies in the Franco-Prussian war of 1870 and . . . back to square one.

Actually, this is an over-simplification: it was indeed back to the beginning so far as the production of fine-quality wines for the vineyards of the region as a whole went, but for individual growers the position varied greatly from one to another, and is worth examining in detail.

In the treaty which followed soon after the French defeat, Alsace (with Lorraine) became German and, of course, came under Teutonic law. Now, at that time the Germans were making a lot of bad wine, but at the same time they were trying desperately to export good vintages abroad. The fate, then, that Alsatian vineyards suffered was that legislation was immediately brought in which virtually forced growers to make wines from the less good varieties of grapes for blending purposes, to be shipped to Germany to bolster up their home market, while German growers concentrated on finer types.

For those who cared only about how much cash they could make out of their métier, this was a godsend; for others, who cared about the quality of what they sold, it was a disaster—though they did benefit in the long run from their efforts not to lower their sights.

In 1918 they were free from the German yoke again, and once more French. And here comes the most paradoxical and ironic twist of all: you would naturally imagine that from now on all would be plain sailing, but oh, no! For now, having been forced to specialize in wines for blending purposes, the Alsace vineyards found themselves at a disadvantage in competition with *other French vineyards* which had been free to make great wine.

Still Alsace struggled: hundreds of acres of vineyards planted with Chasselas, Knipperlé, Goldriesling and Müller-Thurgau (not in themselves really bad grapes, merely not very good ones) and hybrids (which do make atrocious brews) were grubbed up and the land replanted with Sylvaner, Riesling and Traminer.

The process was slow, but progress was indeed made for just about twenty-one years; then the Second World War broke out, the Maginot Line (which in fact ran through Alsatian vineyards) was overrun, France collapsed, and another grave setback to Alsace wines of quality took place.

But the seeds of good wine-making had been sown between 1918 and 1939, and in the five years the Germans occupied Alsace for a second time they were unable to put the clock back as much as they had previously.

But this talk of debasing the quality and so forth is a little oversimplified, for when freedom to plant improved species returned in 1918 by no means every grower wanted to change what was probably a tolerably profitable and certainly less troublesome way of life—the grapes which make poor-quality wines are the ones which ripen early, and so you do not risk losing the best part of your crop from bad weather at the end of vintage time.

Nor can you entirely blame the older growers: they would have been making some passable little wine and finding a ready outlet for it in Paris cafés as *vin blanc*, when some official came along and said, in effect, 'Grub up your old vines and plant these—they'll give you a third less wine, but wine which you will be able to sell at double the price to the Glory of Alsace.' The answer would surely have been, 'Yes, but who is going to buy it?'

The turning-point came in 1925; this was the year when the big decision was made. But how many heart-searchings, how many quarrels and, indeed, how many breakings-up of families did it entail?

The decision was that the growers (unanimously, says one writer, though I do not believe this for a moment) persuaded the French Government to bring in a wine law which, in effect, pledged the growers themselves—and forced their less honourable brethren—to make better wines. The planting of hybrids and *gros producteurs* was legally prohibited.

What happened in this region in that year is often quoted as a text-book example: a vineyard region will never disappear if the growers maintain high and, perhaps more important, traditional standards.

But the troubles I have mentioned, as well as the 1925 triumph, have had the inevitable effect of considerably reducing the area planted. In 1871 there were over seventy thousand acres of vineyards under cultivation—now there are just on thirty thousand. And this is by no means entirely on account of falling consumption; it comes about also from the gradual suppression of areas of 'doubtful quality', says the *Code du Vin Manual*.

Today, more people are drinking more wine in this country than ever before, *but* the percentage of new-to-wine drinkers who make it a hobby as well is dropping. Can you wonder? The wine trade in Britain is an utterly divided industry. The big money is made by firms—of the highest probity—who sell vast tanker-loads of blended brand-names from the Mediterranean seaboard. At the other end of the scale are the purveyors of fine wines, whose turnover is minute, but whose propaganda efforts in the cause of vinous appreciation are immense. They 'spread the gospel' of good wine; the others benefit.

Asking these two groups to contribute a voluntary levy of so much per gallon sold is akin to asking the makers of *foie gras* to share in a billing with the manufacturers of soap-flakes. The latest joint venture is an advertisement showing wine being poured out of a teapot, the implication being that it is just as easy to serve. Needless to say, the firms who deal in Gewürztraminer rather than Zwicker, in Manzanilla rather than Cyprus 'cream', Meursault rather than Empire Sauternes, Clos de Vougeot rather than Spanish Red, aren't going to get more business through a campaign like this. But the teapot stunt is merely carrying to its extreme something about which the tanker suppliers of plonk to the public do feel strongly—namely, that too much what-wine-with-what-dish propaganda and over-long, complicated names do put people off; and this is where Alsace wines come in. Those who sell them in England make much of their simplicity of nomenclature compared with, say, the absurd complications fostered so mistakenly on the Rhine and Moselle.

This region is the only one in France, of those with *appellation contrôlée* rights, where the wines are legally sold only by the name of the grape. It is worth expanding this statement.

The reader will often see on the labels of the more expensive Alsatian wines *Grand Cru*, or *Grande Réserve* or *Réserve Exceptionelle*, after the grape name of Riesling, Traminer, Muscat or whatever it may be. These three descriptions—in ascending order of merit—are merely traditional ones and have no legal definition whatever, whereas if they were given these fancy names in other parts of France they would be subjected to a number of improving restrictions, one of which would be that the increase in quality would have to be accompanied by a progressively higher degree (admittedly only half a degree each time) of alcoholic strength.

The Decree of the Code du Vin, which fixes the types of grapes that may be used in Alsatian vineyards, was promulgated on 2 November 1945, and enacts that there shall be two categories for white wine: (*a*) grapes making day-to-day carafe wines using the species Knipperlé, Chasselas, Goldriesling and Müller-Thurgau; and (*b*) 'noble' grapes—the Sylvaner, Pinot, Tokay d'Alsace, Riesling, Muscat and Traminer, and their varieties.*

Before I deal with the flavours of the wines coming from these grapes I shall dispose of two small exceptions.

---

* Hardly worth the printer's ink to mention that some woebegone growers try to make a red wine with the ubiquitous Pinot Noir grape. The wine, which I find terrible, represents less than 0·5 per cent of the total output.

ABOUT ALSATIAN WINES

By far the less important is that there are a very few placenames, or officially 'named' vineyards (equivalent to a single vineyard—like Clos des Chênes in Volnay on the Côte d'Or) such as Kaefferkopf at Ammerschwihr and Sonnenglanz at Beblenheim.

The other, more important thing concerns two additional names— trade-names which have nothing to do with grapes. They used, up to fifteen years ago, to be seen on Alsatian wines in England, but, with the usual process of upgrading names and the public's becoming more knowledgeable through travel, they have been dropped. *Zwicker* is the name given to an Alsatian wine made from a blend of two or more mediocre grape species, which can, however, have a 'noble' grape with it. *Edelzwicker* (meaning merely 'noble' Zwicker) is a wine made from a mixture of two (or more) 'noble' grape species.

Let me make one thing clear: until Britain is bound by the terms of the Common Market and it is no longer legal to sell a wine labelled *Sylvaner* which has one-third genuine Alsatian Sylvaner blended with two-thirds of a white wine from the North African Mediterranean, I would rather drink an honest-to-goodness Zwicker in Alsace than a self-styled Sylvaner in England.

Zwicker and Edelzwicker are the bread-and-butter lines of all grower-merchants, and the proportion of the sales these two represent is certainly far higher than they like to admit to visiting foreigners. Both are marketed in litre as distinct from three-quarter-litre bottles, and ninety-five per cent plus is sold in France, most of it probably to the café trade.

A glass of Edelzwicker will be robust and clean, and I find it the best-value apéritif in a café in France today.

Chasselas: This variety is the best of the ordinary wine-making grapes, and, furthermore, forms the base of vineyards planted in the Bas-Rhin. The wine made is described as being 'light, agreeable and half dry', and recommended as a thirst-quencher or with a *casse-croûte*.

Pinot Blanc: This variety is being planted more and more in the better vineyards of Europe; it was formerly called the *Clevener* (or, in German, *Klevner*).

Sylvaner: This grape is the bridge between the very mediocre and the 'noble' varieties, and its quality depends in part on just where it is grown. In the Bas-Rhin it produces *rince-bouche*, but on the finer slopes near Colmar it yields a near-fine wine, with a much more 'spritely' and 'racy' character than the Chasselas. One feels that the vine is being grown because of a possible change—or rather what the growers think will be a change—in public taste. It can best be described as being much closer in flavour to a crisp, full-bodied, dry white Burgundy than to an Alsace wine. My own feelings about it are mixed: when you take the first sip you reject it as something so different from what you are used to, but after a few more glasses you recognize a sort of firmness on the palate which the others do not possess, and which you enjoy more and more.

Now we come to the 'nobility', and it is hard to know in which order they should be presented. Three of the four books and brochures class them as all equal among greats, but the fourth gives the Muscat a slightly lower rating than the other three, so we will start with that.

Muscat: The Alsatians are adamant about one thing concerning this wine which to us less bibulous northerners comes as a surprise—they say it cannot be drunk with a meal, like that, full stop. As a preprandial apéritif, yes, they say, splendid. And yet, in spite of the sweetness associated with the Muscat grape, this is the driest wine of the four, though the smell of the grape is so pronounced you think it is less so.

Tokay d'Alsace: We must get one thing right here: although the grape came from Hungary (brought by the Imperial general Lazare de Schwendi) in the mid-sixteenth century, it is not related to the Furmint grape, from which is made the super-sweet Tokay *Essenz* reputed to have saved so many royal lives in Europe in the last century. The grape, actually, is a variety of Pinot, called the Pinot Gris, and the wine made is perhaps the most full-bodied, alcoholic and robust of the region, recommended as an excellent accompaniment to a *foie gras*, a roast or a country *terrine*.

Riesling:

> Du Riesling dans le verre,
> C'est le ciel sur la terre,
> Un breuvage de roi,
> Une chanson de foi;
> Que la gorge se rince:
> Buvons, chantons le prince!

ABOUT ALSATIAN WINES

This pathetic little jingle could be termed the official song of praise for this, by far the best liked of all Alsatian wines by those who live in the region. Freely translated, it says:

> When God gave the Riesling birth
> Paradise came down to earth.
> This is nectar fit for kings,
> Joy and happiness it brings.
> Quaff this truly noble wine,
> Toast this royal prince divine!

Alsace Riesling is by far the most versatile of all the wines of the region: it is highly recommended as an apéritif on its own, and with nearly all foods. The serious Alsatian drinker-grower and connoisseur esteems a fine Riesling far above all the other types, even though he may actually grow and make more Gewürztraminer because of its increasing popularity with the hoi polloi.

You can get some idea of what the inhabitants think of this royal beverage from a little brochure handed out in most of the hotels. The comments made about the other wines are distinctly cool compared to this:

> The Riesling is the most elegant and most popular grape variety of Alsace, always provided that it is grown in vineyards which have an ideal exposure to the sun and that it is allowed to gain full maturity. When this is the case, a Riesling will be a proud, dry, racy wine, with a fruitiness which is elegant but not overpowering. This subtle aroma will be noticeable on the nose, but much more so on the palate or tongue. To drink it on its own is a delight, but it becomes incomparably great in the company of a fine trout, a *matelote* [fish stew with wine], oysters, a delicate *foie gras*, or even with sauerkraut garnished with plump partridges.

Gewürztraminer and *Traminer:* With these two wines we come to a mystery I have been unable to solve. In the first place, thirty years ago the difference in flavour between the Gewürztraminer and Traminer *wines* was much more marked than it is today. The first question which poses itself is, therefore: were the two wines then made with two *different* grape species? Whether this was the case or not, growers certainly gave one to understand that it was. In those days Traminer was the big seller and Gewürztraminer (*Gewürz* is German for 'spice', so the wine is simply a spicy Traminer) tagged a long way behind. Now the situation is reversed, so that there are many growers who are not even offering Traminer any more, but the secrecy regarding the grape itself has mainly disappeared and you will at last find it in print that the two wines do come from the one grape species.

But something is being held back, and it nags at me.

As I write I have by me an assortment of four different booklets published by the Comité Interprofessionnel du Vin d'Alsace, of Colmar; a French Encyclopaedia on the wines of Alsace; the brochure of the Confrérie de Saint-Étienne (about which more later); and two explain-the-grapes pamphlets of the most reputable growers—eight publications in all.

The most detailed account is from *Wines and Vineyards of Alsace*, a four-language periodical published by the Comité Interprofessionnel.

> Gewürztraminer is a selection from an old species—the Traminer. It [the species] has found in Alsatian vineyards an ideal soil for its development and making high quality wines. Each individual grape is rather small; the colour is a reddish-brown, and the skin contains a constituent with a very pronounced musky taste. This taste recurs in the wine, where it develops [in such a way as to engender] a characteristic bouquet very pronounced on the nose. The wine is very robust and agreeably solid, and particularly favoured by people who drink Alsace wine for the first time, since it appears to taste the least dry of Alsatian wines and is the easiest to understand. It will happily accompany the cheeses of Alsace [they probably mean the Munster] and also cakes, provided they are not too sweet, and for this reason it is the wine *par excellence* for formal occasions.

The author of the encyclopaedia has lifted everything he has to say on this wine straight from the Saint-Étienne brochure, and both start: 'The Gewürztraminer, called also Traminer *tout court*, is the best known of the fine-quality varieties, and the one through which one starts to become fond of Alsatian wines.' This is quite a different statement from the first, for here it is clear that the two wines are identical, which makes nonsense of the fact that a large number of growers sell both a Traminer and a Gewürztraminer.

The brochure is a guide to Colmar, and is published by the aforementioned Comité Interprofessionnel. They have a page or so devoted to Alsace wines, describe all the wines which I have, but do *not* mention a Traminer at all.

We come next to the brochures of two most reputable grower-producers. The first is very smooth, for he talks about 'Gewürztraminer-Tokay'. Note that cunning hyphen! As it stands the author can claim in one breath that it is for one and the same wine, and in the next (or perhaps if he decides to make a Traminer) that there are certain differences.

The second brochure is produced by my friends the Kuehns of Ammerschwihr. Gewürztraminer, they say, is robust, fruity, *moelleux* (no perfect translation—the best is 'sweet, full') and powerful. The Traminer is adjudged to be less robust and more *moelleux* than the Gewürztraminer, but more *coulant* (flowing).

The question I now ask is: 'How do growers make two different wines from what appears to be legally and admittedly one and the same grape?'

Do they, when wanting to make a Gewürztraminer wine, pick the Traminer/Gewürztraminer grape at a late stage of its maturity, knowing that an extra 'spicy' flavour will be the result? Or do they know that certain subvarieties in their vineyards will give a more spicy wine? Or that in certain vineyards the grape will give a more tangy flavour than the same grape planted in another vineyard a couple of hundred yards away?

There is one other possibility, which is discussed by Edward Hyams in his excellent book *Le Vin*.*

Edward Hyams has grown grapes in the South of England for many years now, and fervently believes that good wine can come from his vineyards. It is too soon to deride his ambition, because there is always a thousandth chance that he will breed a grape which will stand up to an English winter, but he is certainly England's foremost expert on the botanical names of grapes.

He says:

> There is, by the way, a selected strain of Traminer even better than the parent variety which is called Gewürztraminer or Savagnin Rose Aromatique, and this yields a superior wine, one of the great wines of the world at its best. However, it appears that the name Gewürztraminer on a bottle label does not necessarily, or perhaps even usually, mean that the wine was made from grapes of this

* Newnes, 1959.

strain. According to Dennis Morris... Gewürztraminer wine is made as a rule from selected pickings of the best Traminer grapes (possibly improved by an attack of *pourriture noble*?) and not from the grapes of the Savagnin Rose Aromatique.

This poses a great number of interesting questions, but this does not mean that it gives the full answer to our problem.

Let us study the grapes which are used in the Haut- and Bas-Rhin. First are the 'permitted'* varieties: one with an average yield—Melon (or Muscadet); and four heavy croppers—Bouquetraube, Müller-Thurgau, Abordant Blanc and Goldriesling. Then come the recommended varieties: two with a small yield—*Muscat blanc à petits grains* and Pinot gris; fourteen with an average yield—Aligote, Auxerrois de Laquenexy, Chardonnay (Auvernat), Chasselas, Gamay à jus blanc, Clevener de Heiligenstein, Knipperlé, Muscat rose, Muscat Ottonel, Pinot blanc vrai, Pinot meunier, Pinot noir fin, Riesling, Traminer; and one heavy cropper—Sylvaner.

The reader will see that no Savagnin Rose makes an appearance here, but that does not necessarily mean that it is not planted in Alsace, for some grapes have literally dozens of different synonyms the length and breadth of the land.

I have looked through all my grape-variety reference books and though I have found one reference to a *Savignin blanc*, in the Jura, I can find no reference to one called Rose or Rosé, aromatic or not. But the grape could exist in Alsace under another name—say, Red Traminer?

But the suggestion that the special sought-after flavour is helped along by *pourriture noble* surely will not stand up to critical examination. *Pourriture noble*, or Noble Rot, is a grey mould which goes by the scientific name of *Botrytis cinerea*, from the Greek meaning, loosely, an ash-coloured cluster, which describes it accurately. What happens is that at the end of the grape-harvest, and also when the damp weather sets in, the white, filament-like threads of the fungus penetrate the grape's skin and feed on the juice. This does not affect the flavour of the grape but causes a rapid evaporation of water from the juice, which results in a concentration of the sugar-content. This is what the growers in the Sauternes area and on the Rhine seek, if—and here is the point—they want to make an exceptionally sweet and fine wine. The Germans call the wines thus made *Trockenbeerenauslese* (dried-berries selected)

---

* i.e. 'We don't think much of them but we won't forbid you to plant them.'

ABOUT ALSATIAN WINES

and they can usually be made only when there has been an exceptionally fine and late summer.

But, of course, the reverse of the medal is that the amount of wine thus made per acre is cut by two-thirds, and it becomes fantastically expensive. Now, Alsatian Gewürztraminer is an equal best with a Riesling and a Tokay d'Alsace, and by the time this book appears it will retail, in England, at somewhere around a pound a bottle as against well over three pounds for even a moderate Trockenbeeren Hock. No, Gewürztraminer could not possibly be made this way at its present selling-prices.

But let us study the question of this Savagnin Rose variety in greater depth.

Just suppose that, putting it at its best, this grape *is* a local name for a recommended variety but *not* one of the big four—Riesling, Traminer, Tokay, Muscat. Suppose it is a grape of which one-tenth in a brew-up would be enough to give the required musky, spicy flavour. This sounds eminently plausible to me, save for one snag: if this were the case, the wine could not legally be called Gewürztraminer, but would be an Edelzwicker.

But there is another, more interesting reason why I don't think this can be the answer. Sometimes a wine will be made with several different varieties, not entirely to extend the amount but because, though one grape will give a *temporary* good flavour to the wine these improvements never stand up to the passing of years: in other words, a poorish grape-variety will always show up in the end.

Now, a well made Gewürz will keep, and even improve, for three or more years, and I don't think this would be the case if there had been any hanky-panky business. And for this reason I also discount an evil thought that came into my mind, so much do I want to solve the problem—that a touch of some chemical unguent could have been added.

THE WINE REGIONS AND THE CONFRÉRIE ST-ÉTIENNE

A DECREE promulgated in October 1962 enacted that the only regional *appellation* in the area should be 'Alsace' or 'Vin d'Alsace', and that there were to be very few *appellation* place names. It was also confirmed that the official region should run from Thann in the south right up to Marlenheim in the north, with, in addition, a tiny enclave around Wissembourg, on the German border. Finally it was enacted that fifty-two communes in the Haut-Rhin and fifty-six in the Bas-Rhin could 'benefit from *appellation* "Alsace" '. They are:

HAUT-RHIN

Ammerschwihr
Beblenheim
Bennwihr
Bergheim
Bergholtz
Bergholtzzell
Buhl
Cernay
Colmar
Eguisheim
Gueberschwihr
Guebwiller
Hartmannswiller
Hattstatt
Herrlisheim
Hunawihr
Husseren-les-Châteaux
Ingersheim
Jungholtz
Katzenthal

Kaysersberg
Kientzheim
Laimbach
Mittelwihr
Niedermorschwihr
Obermorschwihr
Orschwihr
Osenbach
Pfaffenheim
Ribeauvillé
Riquewihr
Rodern
Rohrschwihr
Rouffach
St-Hippolyte
Sigolsheim
Soultz
Soultzmatt
Steinbach
Thann/Vieux-Thann

THE WINE REGIONS AND THE CONFRÉRIE ST-ÉTIENNE

Turckheim
Uffholtz
Voegtlingshoffen
Walback
Wattwiller
Westhalten

Wettolsheim
Wihr-au-Val
Wintzenheim
Wuenheim
Zellenberg
Zimmerbach

BAS-RHIN

Albe
Andlau
Avolsheim
Balbronn
Barr
Bergbieten
Bernardswiller
Bernardville
Blienswiller
Boersch
Bourgheim
Chatenois
Cleebourg
Dahlenheim
Dambach-la-Ville
Dangolsheim
Dieffenthal
Dorlisheim
Eichhoffen
Epfig
Ergerheim
Flexbourg
Furdenheim
Gertwiller
Goxwiller
Heiligenstein
Irmstett
Itterswiller

Kintzheim
Kirchheim
Marlenheim
Mittelbergheim
Molsheim
Mutzig
Nordheim
Nothalten
Oberhoffen
Obernai
Odratzheim
Orschwiller
Osthoffen
Ottrott
Reichsfeld
Rosenwiller
Rosheim
Rott
Scharrachbergheim
Saint-Nabor
Saint-Pierre
Scherrwiller
Soultz-les-Bains
Steinseltz/Riedseltz
Traenheim
Wangen
Westhoffen
Wolxheim

Those are the official communes and that is the official area. Now let us see where in fact the main part of the wine is made.

This is not quite such a large area. In the Haut-Rhin it starts well to the north of Thann at Guebwiller and goes on up to Bergheim, only a few miles north of Ribeauvillé. Then there is quite a break and the Bas-Rhin vineyards (that is, the ones you can take seriously) start at Dambach-la-Ville and end at Barr. The number of effectively wine-producing communes is around thirty in each region.

Over the length and breadth of the vineyards of France, those responsible for propaganda have hit upon an idea which is effective, dignified, sincere and, above all, cheap, and although certain details vary from region to region the basic conception is always the same.

To understand its origin let us briefly see how commerce was organized (and how much better than today!) in both England and France in the Middle Ages.

After the Dark Ages ended, and business started going again, people needed saddles, bread, coaches, fans, wine, houses and so forth—you name it, they wanted it. And of course with the population growing apace there were young men who, wanting to earn a living and get married, were prepared to knuckle down and learn how to do whatever was needed to supply such services and earn a living.

They prospered. Thus, by providing what was sound they inevitably created a demand. Inevitably, too, when this happened layabouts saw a way of getting in on the act but, because they had not troubled to learn the know-how, started spoiling the market.

To take two trades of which I have some knowledge: when the genuine Tavern-keepers and Bakers saw their livelihood in jeopardy they were furious. They forgathered in strength and went round London and Paris with cudgels literally beating up their rivals. At this point I should like to make a guess at what happened next.

After the 'baddies' had got beaten up and were licking their sores they would have said to themselves, 'Look, we are onto a good racket. True, we took quite a knock last time, but we surely know how to defend ourselves better the next time. We'd better get in some bigger cudgels and have them ready.'

At the same time the 'goodies' had gone home to their wives and recounted their success, and the wives surely must have said something very like this.

'What children you are! Playing cops and robbers at your age! The next time you go along they will be ready, and as they are so much younger than you they will trounce you.'

'Well, if we don't do something we will be out of business. They are not only undercutting us but supplying such sour wine, and bread which is such short weight, that people will stop taking either.'*

'Why don't you ask the King?'

And in due course a Guild was formed, and henceforth it was illegal for anyone to trade unless he was a member, and of course members saw to it that no one joined unless he was a craftsman. From there on it was an easy step to taking on apprentices, who were bound by very strong legal ties to their masters, who, in turn, saw to their spiritual, mental and physical well-being. (As an example, when I was apprenticed to a member of the Worshipful Company of Vintners I signed a document which was the same as youths had signed in the early fourteenth century, swearing that I would not commit adultery or play at dice—without permission!—until my indentures were over.)

Gradually, as the centuries passed, these guilds lost their legal powers and also their valuable privileges, but they have remained in being on what one might call the social side.

What has happened, then, is that in certain wine regions of France clever *vignerons* have reactivated genuine old guilds which had their origins between the thirteenth and sixteenth centuries. And the publicity thus engendered was so successful that other wine-growing districts started to *invent* names for guilds which hitherto had not existed.

But the Confrérie Saint-Étienne of Alsace is not such a one: it is one of the oldest *bona fide* guilds in France. It was restarted soon after the Second World War, and a few years later had a great stroke of luck in acquiring the Méquillet Collection, one of the finest assortments of vinous documents in France. The papers were stacked away for several years, but in 1963 a selection was presented in a little booklet, and very interesting reading it makes, too.

What fascinates me is the importance attached to the type of grape even in those far-off days. The first document (1551) gives the names of vines permitted in the Haut-Rhin, where Muscat and Traminer are mentioned for the first time. Nearly a century later, a most important

* There are several references in the Annals of the Rolls Patent of London in the fifteenth century of bakers supplying short weight and being heavily fined for so doing. The bread was served from an open table and the swindling bakers seem to have invented a most ingenious contraption whereby, as the bread was slid over to the customer, a knife sliced off a small portion which fell into a secret receptacle underneath the table.

event occurs, for in 1644, by special proclamation, the Riesling grape is granted the Freedom of Riquewihr.

Then in 1750 there are details of a vineyard planted in the walled garden adjoining the monastery of Weinbach at Kientzheim.

The walls of the enclosure are between eleven and twelve feet high and two feet thick. The well and the water-supply from the reservoir are contained in a building that is entirely of cut stone. The walls of the house itself are no less than three feet thick, and so is that of the terrace, which is eighteen feet high. The cellar is fifty-two feet long, thirty-two feet wide and fifteen feet high. The vineyard contains some seventeen thousand individual vines, viz: three thousand *gentil rouge*, two thousand red, three thousand Muscat, seven hundred Riesselieu,* five hundred Toquer,† five hundred Chasselas, seven thousand seven hundred Little Richelieu, and about fifty red grapes with red juice.‡ There are also a hundred fruit trees all of species which produce the finest fruits.

Forty years later one of the first vine seedsmen issued his first catalogue; the same family is still in the same business.

1789 CATALOGUE OF VINES
of
J. Michel Ortlieb

Notice to the public concerning different types of vines that are offered by me:

1. The Little Reuschlinger
2. Val Ordinary
3. Green Gentil
4. Chasselas
5. The Great Raeschlinger
6. The Riesling
7. The Payan
    A very red-juiced grape which is used to give a wine a deep colour.
8. The Common One
    At only five pounds a hundred and very well wrapped
9. Val Red

* Or Richelieu.   † Old spelling of Tokay.
‡ Red-juice grapes are now exceedingly rare.

THE WINE REGIONS AND THE CONFRÉRIE ST-ÉTIENNE

10. Tokay
11. Les Dames
12. The Great Italian
13. The St James
14. The Red Gentil
15. The White Gentil
16. Burgundy
17. White Muscat
18. The Grey Grape
19. The Red Grape
20. The Black Grape
    At fifteen pounds the hundred

Customers are asked to pay in advance for what they order and we will try to serve them with care and fidelity.

One hundred and ten years later the number of grape-varieties in the region had grown enormously. Here is a selection of semi-noble grapes which were relatively new to the region in 1900: Knipperlé, Lamper, Kleinberger, Trollinger, Frankenthaler, Olber, Veltliner, Thalburger, Farbtraube; and the new varieties: Meumir, Gewürztraminer, Portuguese, Lasea, Rotgipfler, Muscat Ottonel, White Morillon, Malvoisie, Limberger, St-Laurent and Sauvignon.

But the Confrérie obviously wanted to do something more lasting and more profitable than showing the public a collection of interesting documents, and in 1957 all the 'brethren' under Grand Master Jean Hugel unanimously decided on a Wine Museum, with a Seal for Quality. The idea is quite brilliant, since it provides a permanent talking-point for growers amongst themselves, and at the same time keeps up a most healthy sort of rivalry. It also brings in funds to the Confrérie.

The Seal of Quality

The Seal will be attached to a gold ribbon which will be glued down the length of the bottle. This ribbon will go under the capsule and under any neck label and will finish with the Seal itself, which will be just above the label.

In creating this Seal the Confrérie has elected to carry out a wish expressed by a number of members that a large selection of wines of different varieties and also of the finer years could be exhibited amongst themselves, for their own personal interest, and also for those who wish to learn about Alsatian wines.

This aim naturally imposes certain most strict duties upon the Confrérie Saint-Étienne, most especially that of seeing that the wines are chosen completely impartially and without any favouritism. It is also important that the Confrérie keep an eye upon wines which have been granted the seal in order to be quite certain that a fine wine really does come onto the market.

A set of rules (which follow) will permit the Council of the Confrérie to administer the scheme in such a way that quality wines do come forward and do receive due recognition. All owners of wines granted the seal are on their honour to respect the rules made.

If the creation of this Seal does involve the Confrérie in considerable expense, there will be considerable compensation in the fact that it will have increased the reputation of the great wines of Alsace.

Finally, the Confrérie wishes to say that in inaugurating this seal it in no way wishes to become involved in the day-to-day commercial sale of wines, but merely to give a certain cachet to the most typical varieties.

Rules for the Wines

Article 1

The Confrérie will each year organize a special *Tasting of Wines* in order to choose growths which, by their incontestable quality, deserve to be to honoured representatives of the produce of the Alsatian vineyards.

These wines will:

(a) be inscribed in the Registry of the Wines Library [*Oenothèque*— good word!] of the Confrérie;

(b) be served as often as possible at banquets and similar functions of the Confrérie;

(c) be permitted to benefit from the Seal especially created by the Confrérie, which will guarantee the quality of the wine selected.

Article 2

Wines which may be submitted for the special tasting will be bottled [i.e., not cask] wines:

(a) which come from the wine-production area of Alsace during the year before the last vintage;

(b) which come from traditional Alsatian grape-varieties such as the Riesling, Gewürztraminer, Tokay d'Alsace, Muscat, as well as the Pinot blanc and the Sylvaner;
(c) which belong to a paid-up member of the Confrérie Saint-Étienne;
(d) whose total production is not less than 2,000 bottles.

Article 3

The wines which will be suitable for tasting will be drawn at the cellars of the owner by members of the Junior Council, who have been especially commissioned for this task. These latter, who are under the obligation of strict professional secrecy, will:
(a) satisfy themselves that the stock is sufficiently large;
(b) obtain confirmation of this in writing from the owner;
(c) take away four samples.

Article 4

These samples will be handed to the special Tasting Receiver, who will be responsible for seeing that when the wines are tasted it is impossible to tell from whom they come.

Article 5

Tasting will take place in two stages:
(a) *First Stage:* the wines will be classed in order of quality by a jury consisting of one or two Grand Councillors, two Junior Councillors and two professionals. Provision is made for them to be joined by others in a consultative capacity;
(b) *Second Stage:* in the week following, the best growths will be submitted to the Senior Alsatian Wine Commission, comprising six to eight Grand Councillors chosen annually by the senior members of the Confrérie. This Commission will concern itself with judging the quality of wines selected, which should be especially typical of the grape-species used and of the stated year.*
The Commission will also decide upon the number of wines which shall be selected.

Article 6

The results of the tasting will be analysed by the Secretary in the presence of the Council, and will then be announced to both

---

* What this means, I am pretty certain, is that if a wine was presented as 1961 vintage, tasted positively exquisite but was not particularly typical of 1961, then the judge should turn it down.

Councils and to the owners of the wines submitted within a fortnight of the tasting. These latter must, within a week, give a firm reply if they wish to accept the honour and agree to abide by the regulations.*

Article 7

The selection of a wine by the Confrérie Saint-Étienne confers on it the right to a seal, which is actually numbered, and it is important that the owner of a wine so 'sealed' should do all he can to control and defend this valuable privilege.

He will each year, in furtherance of this aim, tell the Secretary of the Confrérie what his stocks were on 1 January, and will at all times allow a commission of specialists in the sale of such wine to have a say in the disposal. The proprietor will also send a dozen bottles free to the Oenothèque for reference purposes.

Article 8

The Grand Council of the Confrérie remain owners of the Seal until the stock of wine 'sealed' has been exhausted. Only this Council can authorize its use.

Article 9

The honour of the Seal is reserved for the wine that was actually put in to the special tasting, and can only be used for the sale of this particular wine; it must not be used for general publicity of the grower's other wines.

Article 10

The use of the Seal is given for a duration of two years, but extended if, after a fresh tasting by the High Commission, it is decided the wine is worthy to continue with the Seal.

The duration of two years can be cut on the grower's application, for genuine and important reasons, or if the special Control Commission considers it necessary.

Article 11

The owner of a 'sealed' wine promises to receive from the Con-

---

* It is a little difficult to see why a grower would go to the trouble of putting in samples if he did not wish to have the Seal awarded him. If there were several grades of Seal, one could understand a grower putting in a wine he was confident would win a top rating and feeling honour-bound to withdraw it if it was only put in second place. Possibly a grower puts in a wine simply to see if he is making something good.

frérie as many seals as correspond to the number of bottles declared and known to be held (maximum fifteen thousand), two thousand on his agreeing to abide by these regulations and the balance in yearly amounts of thirty per cent of the quantity still to be taken. Exceptions to this rule can be authorized by the High Commission of the Confrérie.

The price of the seals is fixed at ten [old] francs each.*

Article 12
Any infraction of the rules will cause the case to be heard by the Council of Municipal Magistrates who, after listening to the Wine Seal Control Commission and to the Grand Councillor responsible for the defence of the indicted grower will be able to pronounce as sanctions:
(a) the immediate withdrawal of the Seal;
(b) removal from the Register of the Confrérie;
(c) notification of the other members of the Confrérie;
(d) publication of details of the offence in the Press;
(e) civil proceedings in the Law Courts.

Article 13
In offering their wine to be selected, grower members of the Confrérie promise on their honour to abide wholeheartedly by the rules above laid down and to submit to all decisions taken under these rules.

Such, then, is the main part of the work of the Confrérie, which is certainly doing a splendid publicity job for Alsatian wines.

The Confrérie gets its name from the tradition that the culminating point of its year is a Grand Banquet over which the Master presides, which takes place on Boxing Day evening, the feast of St Stephen. These bean-feasts are no less than five hundred years old, or perhaps one should say that they are five centuries old with a break of a hundred

---

* Articles 10 and 11 should be read together, and contain a lot of meat. Taking the charge for the Seal first, this could be called the hub around which the whole Confrérie works. The price today is a little higher; to say nothing of the cost to the grower—not negligible—of affixing it to the bottle.

As for the rest of the rules in these two Articles, it would appear that the Confrérie is most anxious to ensure that once a grower has been granted a Seal for a wine it should not all be sold in one fell swoop. But it is clear that the members do not want to have hanging about a wine which, for all their good tasting, is not going to stand up to many years in bottle.

years. The reason is that the banquets became more and more costly until finally, in 1848, they became bankrupt and slid quietly into oblivion until they were resurrected in 1947.

The Regional Committee of Experts on Alsatian Wines may not have such a glamorous time as the others, but what it says has the force of law.

The organization came into being under Ordinance 2675 in November 1945, known as the 'Statute of Alsatian Wines', when twenty-seven members were nominated by the Ministry of Agriculture, of whom eighteen were to be growers and grower-merchants and nine 'technical councillors' and full-time officials.

Their very long-term job is to do with decisions as to which land and which vineyards shall have *appellation* rights. True, the main areas are delimited, but it is not as simple as that, for their task over the next half-century, say, will be to downgrade here and upgrade there various vineyards within each commune.

Then there are the grape-varieties to supervise. Here things move incredibly slowly, but some three years ago the twenty-seven did make a big decision (and, one supposes, a painful one, if it meant putting some peasants out of business) and enacted that the planting of two species—the Müller-Thurgau and the Pinot-Meunier, which in any case have been less and less planted—should be forbidden, and that as from 1975 they would lose their *appellation* rights.

A quiet life, you will say. But what about vintage-time? Then the Committee earns its keep, for it has two most important decisions to make: the date that the vintage shall start; and the minimum degree of alcohol the wine must have to be allowed the *appellation* 'Vin d'Alsace'.

Still this is not all. If you overmanure your vines you may get a lot of grapes, and in turn a lot of juice, but the resultant wine will be pawky and thin; worse, the wine can often take on a smell of the manure, which has been known to remain with it for years. Hence the Committee has legal powers to prevent overfertilization of the vines.

The Oberlin Institute, at Colmar, was founded by the renowned eponymous ampelographer in 1893, and now belongs to the town of Colmar. Its work there, and at the Viticultural Research Station, falls into several categories. Its long-term concern is with the selection of new varieties which will ripen late, produce a commercially worthwhile quantity, be tolerant of diseases, not get eaten up by bugs and, over-riding all that, make a wine which will stand up to a couple of years in bottle.

M. P. Huglin, present director of the Viticultural Research Station, is a particular specialist on this subject. He points out that the Gewürztraminer, Riesling and Sylvaner grapes have been planted for so long in Alsace that there are acres upon acres where these grapes have interbred and lost their individual characteristics. The task before M. Huglin, then, is to resort to the *Clonal* selection technique, whereby the propagation of the individual vines is carried out by grafts and cuttings from an original and true-to-type stock.

That for the present; for the future, 'A study of genetics which involve a great number of crossings will perhaps allow, at some distant future date, the happy possibility of obtaining better varieties without losing the Alsatian vine-stock characteristics.'

M. Huglin continues:

> The best choice of grape-varieties and their optimum use cannot be effected without a deep knowledge of the vineyard areas, the soil and the climate, and this will be helped along by the work of delimiting the vineyards, to which I have already referred, by the Committee of Experts on the Wines of Alsace, who have already begun what will be an invaluable job.

Poor M. Huglin! You know as well as I do how unbelievably conservative all growers are and that, while the going is good, they are loth to make a change. And even when disaster seems not far round the corner they will not take the bull by the horns.

But it is not only so with wine. Some years ago I bought a pub right in the hop-growing country of the Weald of Kent and met a number of wealthy hop-farmers in the region.* At that time a fungus disease of the bines was causing a great deal of anxiety. When growers found they had got it they tended to whisper it not among the hop-poles, mainly, I think, because they dreaded to feel that they had been hit, like the patient who will not admit he has cancer. This soil fungus is called Verticillium Wilt (*V. albo-atrum*) to distinguish it from Fluctuating Wilt, which has been known for many years wherever hops are grown in England, and is rarely serious. Verticillium, according to a Ministry of Agriculture leaflet, is 'practically confined to the Weald of

---

* See *A Year at the Peacock* (Cassell, 1964).

Kent and neighbouring parts of Sussex and is most prevalent and severe in an area around Paddock Wood, where it was discovered and from which it has gradually spread'. The first signs of the disease, which is also called 'Progressive Wilt', appear towards the end of May. The bottom leaves on the bines turn yellow, dead patches develop on the leaves and within a week half the leaves on an affected bine will be dead. In three weeks the hop bine is doomed. A great deal of research into wilt-tolerant and also wilt-resistant varieties has been done in the East Malling Research Station in Kent, where an eighty-strong staff of qualified research workers are studying the problems of hop diseases on a five-hundred-acre farm. But what is so unrewarding is their difficulty in persuading brewers that the new varieties will make good beer. As one expert says in an article, 'In the long-term view, an unprogressive brewing industry could represent a greater hazard to the hop-growing industry than Progressive Wilt.'

But we will leave the hop-farmers to their affluent fate and return to the Viticultural Research Station. Let M. Huglin continue.

Cultural Techniques

The possession of fine species alone is not by any means all, since they must be grown in first-rate conditions. And there is little doubt that our ancestors were conscious of this need, if one is to judge by the rules more or less imposed in the Middle Ages.

The evolution of certain techniques, such as pruning, was extremely slow until the beginning of this century, and the chief change [in cultivation] was from the training of the vines on a single footing to a system of propping them up along wire strands, which was very favourable so far as good ripening of the grapes was concerned.

But the situation in which we now find ourselves, of the shortage and high cost of manual labour, coupled with tremendous technical progress, obliges the grower, whether he wishes it or not, to adapt himself to the exigencies of the second half of the century we live in.

In these circumstances it is to be understood that a whole programme of research, combined with numerous experiments, has been carried out with such thoughts in view: chemical weed-clearance, better spacing (from the tractor point of view) of the vines, and so on. And if our experiments are primarily aimed at making work easier for the grower it must be remembered that everything is also done to avoid making unworthy wines.

THE WINE REGIONS AND THE CONFRÉRIE ST-ÉTIENNE

M. Huglin then goes on to mention the work carried out in 'the struggle against diseases and parasites which attack the vines'. Here he makes a claim which I feel will surprise the reader.

Thanks to studies relatively old in France and abroad, the majority of parasitical maladies of the vines are sufficiently well known to be able to be fought efficaciously. It is, however, our duty always to be testing out new chemicals which are put out by firms who supply growers. . . . On the other hand, virus infections of the vine, which can devastate a vineyard, are much less understood, and experiments carried out in this sphere have been interesting.

One of the least understood things about vines is how they will fare in different latitudes, and it is to be noted that a grape which will produce a wine with an exquisite bouquet in Alsace will make one with hardly any at all if grown on the Mediterranean. The reason is that in the hot south the fermentation is turbulent and fast, whereas in the north it is horribly slow. And of course the grapes come very much later to *full* ripeness, and this is where M. Huglin's establishment is of far more practical use, value and help to the grower every single vintage-time than, in his modest way, he likes to admit.

In former times the viticultor may well have got up at dawn to see what the weather was to be like; he may have taken note of how and when the starlings and other birds started their terrible depredations; he may have squeezed a handful of grapes and tasted them; all very picturesque, but totally amateurish and unreliable compared to M. Huglin's exact scientific appraisal of the data which tell the grower the ideal moment to gather.

To get some idea of the importance of weather to a viticultor, think of him as a farmer—not, as are most farmers in Britain, of many crops, but of one. In Britain you may find one or two people making a livelihood from a single crop—strawberries, hops, asparagus—but even this is extremely rare; and certainly in none of those I have mentioned do you find up to ten thousand people within a very small area all specializing in the same crop. What, you may say, about the farmers of potatoes, peas and sugar-beet in East Anglia? This is a closer parallel, in that all these growers rely on a single crop which could be entirely wiped out by a blight, but to none of them is the weather so important that twenty-four hours of heavy rain just before the harvest can take all the guts out of the crop (as happened on the Moselle in the middle of September 1967), while ten days of sunshine at the right time can turn a poor harvest into a first-rate one.

Several things follow from this unique reliance on weather in the intensive wine-growing districts—excluding only those southern climates where there is sunshine more or less all the time. One is that the most detailed meteorological reports are available and issued; a second is that a freak rainstorm in the north of, shall we say, the Médoc or Alsace, may cause a slight discrepancy in these issued reports. And a third, I am afraid, is that it may be in the interests of certain large firms to bend the truth when transmitting reports from France or Spain for publication in England. It is not only a question of making the weather out to have been less bad than it has. The reverse, too, can be advisable —not in minor districts like Alsace, where the wine is not made, or wanted, to last for many years—but in, say, Bordeaux, a gentle hint that all is not well in the weather world could just nudge a buyer who might otherwise have hung on for something better into taking ten thousand pounds' worth of the previous year.

As for the freak discrepancies, these, as I say, can be genuine, but they are still useful things to cultivate. You see, if you own a château in the Médoc, and it has been pouring off and on for weeks before the vintage, it makes wonderful sales talk if you can recall that by some happy freak it was quite fine in Pauillac just the ten days you did the harvest, and that's why you have the only good wine of the year.

Most large growers in Alsace, Jerez, Champagne, Bordeaux and the Côte d'Or get out weather reports, vintage reports and, later, vintage appraisals; these are sent to the London agents or shippers, who bring them in to the wine papers. The shipper gets free publicity; the wine journals get free copy; it is up to the reader to sort things out. If he has been out to each region and personally called on the growers, as I have, then he can assess how much each one is telling the truth.

From Alsace, reports come from about a dozen firms. The example which follows is a consolidation of them all, as at October 1967.

> Following the worries over the spring frosts which affected many vineyards, the summer, especially in June, was nearly perfect.
> Towards the end of June the flowering took place under ideal conditions, and the grapes developed well during the succeeding weeks, so that hopes were already high for a fine-quality wine.

THE WINE REGIONS AND THE CONFRÉRIE ST-ÉTIENNE

There was a fortnight's wet and cold weather in the middle of September, but the adverse effects were not anything like as bad as anticipated.

Then followed a period of virtually continuous hot sunshine, right up to vintage-time, which allowed the harvest to take place exceptionally late, with the result that the musts have a sugar-content rarely attained.

While the majority of the wines can be classed as 'very good', a fair quantity (about 25%) can be rated 'exceptional', and these wines will surpass anything made for about twenty years. Some examples: the Sylvaner wines showed Oechslé readings of between 82° and 90°, and some even approach 98°. The weight of the Riesling musts was very high, while with the Gewürztraminers 100° was commonplace, and some verged on 125°.

As for the Pinot blanc and Pinot gris [the Tokay d'Alsace] these suffered here and there from *pourriture*, but even they will be well above average.

It cannot be overstressed how vastly different is the job of the winemaker in northern, potentially rainy districts from that of his counterpart in the sunny south. From the drinker's point of view, the most important difference is that one northern region can produce a vintage in complete contrast to that of its next-door neighbour. It does not always happen; it does not often happen; but in the very region we are dealing with, in 1967, a remarkable variation occurred.

At the same time as the Alsatian reports were pouring into the wine-trade papers, so too, only in vastly greater volume, were those from Germany.

The great German districts of the Rheinhessen, Rheingau, Palatinate and Moselle are all within a bare hundred and fifty miles of Alsace, and yet here the weather ruined everything. The grape which suffered most was the Müller-Thurgau, and the vintage was disastrous in the Rheinhessen. Here the harvest started about 22 September, but, because of previous bad weather and the fact that the grapes were already ripe, they were often rotten when gathered. At some places along the Moselle it rained continously for thirty hours around 19 September, this representing three weeks' average rainfall in the region. In the Rheingau the main harvesting of Riesling grapes took place between 7 and 10 October, by which time a number of grapes had fallen to the ground.

I mentioned above the depredations of the birds; let me end this chapter with a story to illustrate the point.

M. Jean 'Papa' Hugel, one of the Grand Old Men of Riquewihr, has three sons, all of whom help in the centuries-old business. Georges does the 'admin', Jean *fils* looks after the vineyards, while André takes care of the cellars.

It is Jean *fils*'s story, and he confesses he has told it many a time.

It was the end of the vintage, and 'Papa' Hugel had decided that one of the vineyards of Traminer grapes (which the birds love extra much) at Riquewihr should be picked extremely late, so as to make a superb wine. As the other vineyards would have been stripped by the pickers the starlings would be extra keen to get at this last one, and so, as had happened several times before, Hugel organized a roster of his work staff, so that a bird-scarer could be on duty every single hour of daylight.

The picking was almost certain to start on the Monday, but already, by mid-day on Saturday, the Hugel family knew that nothing, apart from the supernatural, could prevent a great wine from being made. The Hugels' gamble looked like paying off handsomely.

Although he was tired, Hugel again looked over his human bird-scaring roster: on Saturday afternoon Pierre was on till six in the evening; then, as he had to go into Colmar to see someone in hospital, Claude was taking over till darkness fell. Sunday morning Jean was on duty from a half an hour before dawn until ten a.m. Then old Luc would take over for the rest of the day. So on Saturday afternoon he felt that, as the rest of the vintage had been taken care of, he could give himself the treat of an hour or two with his family.

Sunday dawned; a wonderful day, there was no *need* to go and look at those grapes, but it would be rather pleasant just to see those bursting skins and he could kill two birds—how he'd like to kill the lot!—with one stone by discussing with Luc what work should be done in the vineyards when the harvest was over, for Luc was really a foreman and one of the most intelligent of men. But Jean was intelligent, too, and terribly reliable; and when Luc retired, as he would shortly have to, Jean could take over. And Jean obviously didn't intend to leave the district, for was he not getting married——

Hugel stopped walking with a jolt. Getting married? *Getting married!* Wasn't the wedding today? Wasn't it this very morning? And hadn't Jean asked specially if he could be relieved at half-past nine instead of ten o'clock? And hadn't Hugel said, but of course, and anyway it was decent of him to volunteer? Good grief! *Had* he asked Luc if he would mind coming along just that half an hour earlier? No! He hadn't. He broke into a run. Then he slowed down again; there was no need to worry; Luc was always ten minutes early for appointments, and Jean would probably wait for five. That gave those starlings just fifteen minutes to do their worst.

But he was wrong—in that quarter of an hour the entire vineyard had had every bursting berry pecked to the ground.

8

ROUTE DU VIN

Like other wine-districts of Europe, Alsace has its Route du Vin, and it is certainly one of the most beautiful of all. There are fifty-seven villages and towns actually on the route, and thirty-five marked 'by the side of the route'. The distinction is worth explaining for those who might actually want to make this beautiful car run. The route at times goes half up into the mountains, and certainly into the byways, but the mappers have played very fair, in that if you follow the excellently printed map you can always be sure of being able to motor through a village and on to the next one—in other words, you never get to a dead end. Most of the 'side-of-the-route' villages, however, are culs-de-sac.

I planned to do the route from Thann in the south, not far from Mulhouse, to Marlenheim, near Strasbourg. My little map-measurer, having been run backwards and forwards several times over the terrain, gave a reading of a hundred and fifteen miles (sixty-five as the stork flies)—a journey you could do twice on your head in one day, *if* you were strong-willed enough not to stop and accept a glass of wine with every grower you met and at every *cave coopérative* and *cave de dégustation* en route. So I set off from Mulhouse to Thann, armed with yet more introductions and swearing to be extra firm with myself. Yet my very first encounter with a grower was to be the result neither of my advertisement nor of a London introduction, but of my talent for getting lost.

From Thann, the Route runs via Cernay and Wuenheim to Soultz, a charming little olde-worlde village where the old houses have been beautifully preserved, and boasting a lovely Renaissance Town Hall and a small Gothic church.

Next comes the eleven-thousand-strong town of Guebwiller, which deserves a mention as a summer tourist resort of note, an industrial centre, and a wine town of importance.

It has had two moments of history. The first was in 1445, on St Valentine's Day, or rather night. Obliged to defend themselves against the tyrannies of their suzerains, the Prince-Abbots of Murbach,* the inhabitants of Guebwiller had built themselves a splendid rampart around the town, and also a fine moat. Both came in useful against a later enemy, the Armagnacs. On the night of 14 February 1445 it was so cold that the moat froze and these Armagnacs assailed the town. But a woman, one Brigitte Schick, who was probably suffering from insomnia, heard the men coming and kicked up such a shindig that the attack was called off. This sort of thing must have taken place countless times in the Middle Ages, but what makes this particular incident stand out is that the Armagnacs fled so precipitatately that they left their scaling-ladders behind, and these have been preserved in the romanesque-veering-to-gothic church of Saint-Léger.

The other event is much closer to our time. In November 1944 the news that Mulhouse had been recaptured from the Germans filled the hearts of the inhabitants of Guebwiller with high hope that their turn would soon come. But this was not to be the case, as the Germans were still holding out, and even counterattacking dangerously, in the famous 'Colmar Pocket'. So important was this that the Gauleiter for Alsace, Wagner, came personally to Guebwiller in January 1945 to stiffen and galvanize the troops. But the offensive of the French 1st Army Corps was now irresistible: at four thirty on 4 February the town was declared free, and on the nineteenth General de Lattre de Tassigny arrived to the acclamations of delirious crowds. Note that it was exactly five hundred years to the month after the earlier deliverance.

Beyond Guebwiller come Bergholtz, Bergholtzzell and Orschwihr.

It was at Orschwihr that I took a wrong turning and found myself going up a sandy lane which then led directly into the courtyard of a largish house, and I had no alternative but to drive right in to turn round. No sooner had my bonnet poked its nose past the gate than a huge Alsatian dog bounded out and barked fit to wake the dead. This brought out a pleasant-faced man, to whom I explained my trouble. He re-routed me, and then said, 'Are you on holiday?'

'Certainly not,' I replied, and explained my dual mission.

* Only ten minutes by car off the Route and in a charming wooded valley, the remarkable romanesque church which is all that remains of the famous Abbey of Murbach is worth a visit. It reached the height of its power in the ninth century, and Charlemagne was one of the benefactors. 'As proud as the dog of Murbach' was a popular saying of later centuries on account of the silver greyhound on the arms of the Abbey; only those with sixteen quarterings of nobility on their escutcheons were allowed to enter it.

'I wish you would take me on,' said the man.

I looked around the courtyard; it could not have been spicker or spanner. Two or three dozen casks of many sizes were stacked against one wall, and an enormous mound of clean, neatly arranged green bottles against another. The set-up seemed just about the right size for me, not too big and not too small. A fine sign on the wrought-iron gates told me his name—Louis Albrecht.

During the pause that occurred while I was thinking things out he spoke again.

'I think I had better warn you,' he said, 'that I cannot let you have anything in bulk.'

This was meant to be a little off-putting. A fair amount of cheap Alsatian wine which is sold in England is a blend of Sylvaner and white Bordeaux, with little resemblance to the real thing, and Alsatian growers are a proud lot who do not like to see the wines of their region thus debased. However, some merchants do insist on bulk shipments and, of course, the grower who refuses risks losing a deal and the chance of selling the bottled wine with his name on it.

To me, however, this meant he was entirely to be trusted.

'Tell me,' I said, 'have you ever sent any wine to England before?'*

'No, never,' said M. Albrecht.

'You are quite sure?' I said, thinking how rude I was.

'Positive.'

I weakened. 'May I see round?' I said.

It was only ten o'clock, and the tour of the place would take half an hour, after which I should be invited to taste; and if you have accepted the invitation to look round you cannot refuse to *goûter*, still less so if you have invited yourself. Tasting wine at ten-thirty! It is virtually impossible not to swallow a certain amount, and if you are unlikely to eat before two o'clock it is very fatiguing.

I was very impressed with the general set-up, and more so with the wines, especially a Riesling Grande Réserve 1961, which had been brought out as a *bonne bouche* at the end and was truly remarkable.

While we were 'discussing' this bottle Mme Albrecht came in; the conversation became more animated and more general, and I quickly gathered that neither of the Albrechts had been far out of Alsace. Then one said something polite about wishing they had been to England.

---

* This was a very important question. There are a number of grower-merchants who grant their principal agency to a London firm and then continue to trade direct with other firms, using another and fictitious name. I detest the practice.

This gave me the opportunity to say—as a way of finding out what other English had called—'But then you must have formed certain impressions of England from talking to those Englishmen who call on you here.'

'But no Englishmen have ever been to this house before,' said M. Albrecht emphatically.

When the bottle was finished I got up to go. Walking down a dark passage to get my macintosh I saw, hanging from an adjacent peg, a six-inch square of celluloid with a large plain red L in the middle.

An L-plate! Obviously some happy English taster had left this as a souvenir. I must say, I was furious, and confess to hinting rather too forcefully that they had misled me. Both the Albrechts were completely mystified. I explained again, more frankly still.

'Oh, that L,' said M. Albrecht. 'That is given to us by our carriers, Laval, and we hang it on the gate when we want them to call for cases of wine to go to Paris; it's cheaper than by rail.'

Realizing how terribly bad-mannered I had been, I remembered that in tidying out the car that morning I had come across two L-plates left there by Alice before she had passed her test. I went out to the car and brought them in.

'Here are two more,' I said, 'as a present.'

After Orschwihr comes Soultzmatt, a delightful little town built along the banks of the Ombach, and noted for its mineral water.

At Westhalten, beyond Soultzmatt, I had a contact which looked promising, but I thought I would 'do' the little place first, and I am very glad I did, for its picturesque charm is considerably heightened by its two lovely fountains, which are one of the most enchanting features of many villages along the Route. One pleasant feature of the more picturesque villages is that the façades of the wine-growers' houses have not spoiled their charms by huge signs announcing their existence. Another thing is that in such villages it is very hard to get any idea of how large a firm is by looking at the outside of the house.

The premises of M. Heim of Heim & Co. at Westhalten were a particularly good example of both these observations, for the whole of a very large business is done from what appears to be quite a small house in an attractively deserted, winding, narrow lane in a medieval village.

In Alsace the cellars for storing the bottled and bulk wine, the machinery for crushing the grapes, all the *hottes* (wooden containers strapped to the backs of those who carry the grapes from the pickers to the waiting vats on a horsedrawn cart or lorry by the roadside), all the spraying equipment, all the labelling-department and dispatch, the offices as well as the private dwelling of the owner and probably his parents or in-laws, will all, in the great majority of instances, be under one roof—or, more accurately, give onto a single open courtyard. While it is intriguing the first time, it gets very irritating after a while to drive into such a courtyard at lunchtime when everyone is absent, look around and have no idea whether a certain door will lead you to the labelling- and dispatch-room, down to the cellars, up to a private house, along to the lavatories, or to what you are looking for—the offices. And when the courtyards are as large as some are, it means a lot of walking.

M. Heim, as it happened, was at the doorway when I called, and so we sat in his spacious office—overlooking one of the prettiest little gardens in Alsace—and then, inevitably, went on to taste his wines in the tasting *salon*. I say *salon* advisedly, because these charming and restful rooms are again part of the Alsatian grower-wholesaler's way of life. You don't taste in the boss's office, but in a ground-floor sitting-room which is nearly always situated between the private part of the house and the offices; so the wife and family do not have to pass through the latter, nor do the owner and his clients need to invade the privacy of the family home. There will be minor variations, of course, and if the owner is aggressively sales-minded the place may have rather a lot of calendars, table-mats, ashtrays, corkscrews and glasses with the firm's name, whereas if he is particularly *not* so, then the room really will look just like the drawing-room of a private house, even down to deep armchairs.

The *salon* of M. Heim was about mid-way between the two extremes, though it did have in one corner a lovely, large-spotted and freshly painted rocking-horse, and in another a very large, opulent-looking refrigerator from which, deliciously cool, came the wine. When we had finished tasting I was waiting for the inevitable invitation to look over the cellars, but, to my delight, after calling down Mme Heim to invite her to join us in a bottle of bubbly and to tell her he would be out for lunch (poor wives!) my host whisked me off to one of Alsace's best restaurants, Meisterman, in Colmar. Here I cheerfully accepted my host's choice of the first course—excellent *foie gras*—and just as I was being handed the menu to choose the main dish proprietor Meisterman, a pleasant, middle-aged bachelor, came up to see if all was well.

'Ah! You hesitate, I see,' he said to me. 'But you cannot today, for we have fresh frogs' legs in a béchamel sauce.'

I had had frogs' legs on occasion, and thought them nondescript.

'Aren't they rather gimmicky?' I said.*

'No! No! They are a *pièce de résistance*,' replied Meisterman. 'The frogs don't come from Alsace, of course.'

'Why not?'

'Because they are the staple food of the storks, which are coming to the region less and less, and it is therefore strictly illegal to catch them.'

The frogs were quite good, the sauce was exquisite and so was the Gewürztraminer.

It is amazing how a little alcohol loosens the tongue; as we were motoring into Colmar I had wanted to make some wisecrack about Heim's huge car and his business. Now I found tongue.

'You must do pretty nicely by the wines of Alsace if you can run a bus like this,' I said, referring to his colossal, gleaming silver Mercedes.

'I get by,' said Heim. 'Most growers have a part of France where they are particularly strong, and ours is Brittany. There is enough business there for us to send our own lorry direct.'

'What do you send mostly?' I said.

'Blended wine in litres,' replied Heim. 'Edelzwicker, chiefly, for sale by the glass in cafés. That's the bread-and-butter side of the business. The wines you have tasted are only the tip, though quite a large one, of the iceberg, and if any other grower tells you to the contrary he is deceitful.'

I knew this, but was grateful for his frankness.

Back at Westhalten the great doors to the courtyard were now shut, and I made to get out, but before I could open them M. Heim had pulled out a little circular gadget from the pocket of the car and pointed it at the doors, which at once opened. I was most impressed. 'It's really for the lorry-drivers,' said M. Heim. 'Quite a lot of time is saved.'

Madame had coffee and liqueurs ready for us before the tour around the cellars, and when we had finished we walked slowly through the garden. In the far corner I noticed a huge brown hut with dozens of curious apertures in it, of a design I had never seen before. It was far

---

* As I didn't know a good French phrase for this I had to twist things round to say, 'Aren't they for the rubberneck [*badaud* is a fine sonorous word meaning 'gaper', and *badaud de Londres* is a cockney] who doesn't know his food?'

larger than a potting-shed or henhouse, and yet not quite big enough to be a small house.

'That,' said my genial host, interpreting my quizzical looks, 'was my uncle's beehive.'

The eleventh place along the Route is the flourishing little agricultural town of Rouffach, remembered in a sixteenth-century saying: 'The gibbet of Rouffach is made of good oak, be afraid of the gallows of Rouffach.' It seems that the community had just constructed its gibbet when the inhabitants of the neighbouring village of Pfaffenheim asked if they could borrow it to hang one of their wrong-doers. They received the magnificent reply: 'Our gallows belongs to us; it was paid for by our money and it was made for us and our children and not for strangers.'

Next comes Gueberschwihr, with the tower which is all that remains of its magnificent twelfth-century romanesque church. Then Hattstatt, a very ancient little town, formerly fortified, Obermorschwihr and Husseren-les-Châteaux, interesting as the highest place for growing Alsatian vines, at over twelve hundred feet.

Eguisheim is an ancient little town, where you positively must get into the little sidestreets and alleyways, for they are every bit as picturesque as in the far more famous villages of Riquewihr and Ribeauvillé. But Eguisheim is actually more famous for its *trois châteaux*. These huge square, red sandstone dungeon-keeps dominate the skyline from miles around. What interested me was the way in which, as one drove along the road below, the apparent distances between each pair would so suddenly and dramatically change.

Wettolsheim, the last village before Colmar, is very special, for it claims to be the commune where the first vines were planted in Roman times.

9

COLMAR

The nicest *place de la Gare* in Alsace is certainly that of Colmar. I am certain I am not giving the place ideas above its station when I make the claim, because bang opposite the station itself, with its Buffet Gare, is the Hotel Terminus-Bristol, by far the smartest hotel in the town and now modernized to even higher standards than before. Travellers here are also fortunate in that the son of the owner, resident there as manager after a tour of hotel duty in New York, has brought with him several neat little touches from hotels in that metropolis which add to the friendly comfort of his Colmar place. He has also a very pretty young wife with (when I was there) a striking hair-style, who also lives on the premises. Madame is an additional attraction to the hotel, because to the jaded businessman the sight of her walking through the reception hall is, to put it mildly, galvanizing.

I had been given a superb, freshly decorated room overlooking the square and the gigantic station clock. There was an external telephone in the room, which I liked using because the telephonist, whom I had noticed downstairs as being very pretty, did not keep one waiting and had complimented me twice on my accent.

The call I now had to make was an extra important one—to the Chief Inspector to the repression of wine frauds in Alsace, and I determined to excel myself in choice of phrase and limpidity of diction.

The contact had come from the full-time secretary of C.I.V.A., the Comité Interprofessionnel du Vin d'Alsace, a neat, earnest and alert young man, newly appointed, and the last person I should have pictured as playing practical jokes. I had located him with some difficulty, and though the many introductions I had to him were truly impressive he clearly—though politely—was not terribly interested in my book, and the name and phone-number of the Wine Frauds Inspector was not the sort of thing he wanted to impart. I feared that the Inspector wouldn't have much use for me either.

I got through to his office though without much difficulty.

'Good morning,' I said in my best Jack de Manio voice—honeyed, but forcefully compelling. 'I am an English writer from London.'
Not a word.
So I added my usual 'and I have come a thousand miles just to see you'. This is meant to get men reaching for their hats, telling their secretaries they won't be back for the day and hurling themselves into a taxi. It has never remotely had this effect.
There was now a distinct chuckle on the other end of the line, which I thought terribly rude. Still no speech.
'Did you not hear me aright?' I went on, icily calm but furious.
This time there was a big laugh and a man's voice said, 'Say it all again.'
'I said,' I said, my accent and grammar now going completely haywire, 'that . . .' And I started all over again.
Again a hearty laugh.
'Very good,' said the man. 'Do it all again.'
'Do what again, you——' and I just curbed myself. 'Look,' I went on, 'don't you bloody well understand French? I want to come round and see you.'
'To paint the ceiling?'
'What?' I shouted.
'Or to mend the electric lights? Or to sew up the carpet? Or to bring along a new chair?'
These last three queries were not spoken in the ordinary Parisian accent the man had previously used but in the broken French of an Italian or Spanish workman who hardly knew the language.
'Oh, go to blazes!' I said, beside myself with fury. 'I'm leaving the Terminus-Bristol this moment, and if you don't see me there will be hell to pay.'
And I was as good as my word. I stormed out of the hotel, jumped into my car and drove along straight away to the administrative offices on the outskirts of the town. Like a cross between a barracks and a prison, but attractively laid out and not so ugly as all that, the various sub-departments' offices were quite easy to find. My quarry was M. Muller. His name was on the door, and as my anger was by now abated I only gave a mouselike knock. The door was opened instantly by a pleasant-looking man who then stood back and gave me a long, searching look. And if it is possible for a face to express: 'My God! He is the real thing. Now I'm for it. Please accept my apologies,' and a moment later, 'But it's really rather funny and I won't get the sack

and I hope this little English bloke has a sense of humour,' then M. Muller's face did at this time.

'Come in, Mr Layton,' said the real inspector, 'and let me take your coat. Ah! That's better. Do sit down. Will you have a cigarette? They are Virginian.'

'I only smoke black tobacco,' I said coolly. Then I waited.

'Mr Layton, I really am very sorry. Actually, it wasn't me you spoke to a short while ago but my young assistant, and when he phoned the Terminus-Bristol and found that there was a genuine wine-merchant there I fear he fled as he didn't dare face you.'

At this moment Muller clearly wanted to laugh his head off and only managed to keep a straight face by a supreme effort.

'I hope I look genuine,' I said.

'Yes, yes, very,' said Muller, looking at my red face. 'You see, my assistant and Pierre Bouard are old school chums; well, Bouard has quite a gift for mimicry and often on Saturdays he phones this office and pretends to be all sorts of different people, an electrician, a meter-reader...'

Muller saw by my face that I understood and was equally amused. It was clearly such a relief to him that he rushed on. 'We had heard vaguely that you were coming to Alsace because Pierre had dropped one or two hints about it, but the thing was that Jean, that's my assistant, thought that this was a clever build-up so that he would fall into the trap. I really am very sorry....'

He paused to light his Virginian. 'Six months ago he caught Jean very badly. He found out somehow that on a certain Saturday morning he—that is, Jean—would be in the office all alone, and so he phoned up and said he had come to patch up a hole in the carpet under my desk. "Couldn't you come on Monday?" said Jean. "No," said Pierre, "it has to be this morning," and he hinted that some very high-up official had laid this on for me as a special favour. Poor Jean, he had to lug my desk out into the corridor all on his own, and then put it back when nobody turned up!'

M. Muller leaned back in his chair and breathed the quietest-ever sigh of relief; he felt that the crisis was over.

'Well now, Mr Layton,' said the inspector, 'what can I now do for you?'

Again I read into the tone perhaps more than I ought. Did it say, 'You have put me in a spot, with your being the butt of a hoax. I would have been distantly polite anyhow, but now I suppose I shall have to divulge certain things I would rather a foreign writer didn't know'?

If so, here was my big moment. But the devil was that I hadn't much of an idea as to what frauds had to be suppressed! I knew that it was a prison offence to put glycerine into a wine to make it appear more unctuous and mellow; that you mustn't secretly bring in wines from another country or district to blend in, even if it did make the wine appear better to the uninitiated; and that it was forbidden to allow any wine to leave one's cellars without a certificate. I went through all these things rather like a schoolboy who, having failed to do his lessons, tries to soft-soap his form-master.

M. Muller listened with extreme politeness, but there was no possible doubt that he wanted to imply that if I had spent all my adult life visiting vineyards and at the end of it all I could talk to him about was that hoary old story of glycerine, I was a bit of a numskull.

'Well, what other things do you do?' I eventually said, lamely.

He told me.

In certain sunless years grower-producers are given permission (after local experts have testified that it is needed) by the Ministry of Agriculture to add a certain quantity of sugar to the musts to bring up the alcoholic strength. This is called *chaptalisation*, after Jean-Antoine Chaptal, a very great chemist, and Minister of Agriculture in Napoleon's day.

When the sugar is so added a relatively high tax is levied on it, and one of the wine fraud-squad's tasks was to see that payment was not evaded. M. Muller explained that the big grower would need so much sugar that if he started to punt around buying up tax-free supplies here and there he would soon get caught. The little grower could do this very thing, but M. Muller had a hearty contempt for him, not because he was evading the law but because (and he seemed to have worked it out to the nearest centime) what the man saved on the tax he paid for fourfold in wasted petrol.

The other thing they were on the watch for was the planting of forbidden—or perhaps, more accurately, officially frowned-upon—grape-varieties in vineyards where a high standard was demanded. Here again I got the impression that, apart from safeguarding the quality of the wine, they were really as much concerned to see that if a man was claiming a subsidy for planting up with a better-quality grape he did not put in a false return.

I returned to the Terminus-Bristol to meet my daughter, Alice, who was arriving to complete the trip with me, and we set out to 'do' Colmar together.

When Voltaire first came to the town, he wrote, 'I am living in a hideous house in a hideous town, a capital of hottentots governed by jesuits.' He stayed there for thirteen months in 1753-4, and when he left he wrote to the Countess de Lutzelbourg, 'I have got more used to Colmar than anywhere and have a desire to become an Alsatian.'

The reason for the writer's visit was that he had lent the Duke Charles-Eugène de Wurtemberg-Montbéliard, the seigneur of Riquewihr, a large sum of money at interest. The Duke turned out to be an extremely bad payer, and Voltaire journeyed to Alsace to see what he could do to safeguard his investment. And the reason he chose Colmar was because as he was, off and on (and at this moment it was very much on), out of favour with Louis XV, he wanted to be as near the frontier as possible.

Like Voltaire, I started by disliking Colmar and finished up by becoming extremely attracted to it. One of its sons was the great Baron Haussmann who, in tearing down so much of Paris in order to embellish, as he certainly did, has been called the 'great Parisian demolisher'; it is odd that he should have been born in a town where so few old houses have been done away with. That is the great charm of this little headquarters of the Alsatian wine trade (as it indubitably is) which, because industry has bypassed it in favour of Strasbourg and Mulhouse, is still very much as it was in medieval times.

In Roman times the city was one of the many Imperial summer residences. As it prospered there was built in the centre of the settlement, as a sign of its nobility, a *colombier*, or dovecote, and so the place became *Villa Columbaria*, the place of the doves, then *Columbaria*, then *Columbra* and finally *Colmar*.

Unlike that of Voltaire, who was unhappy there at first and wrote picturesquely to a friend that he had come to Colmar to 'dry out my soaking clothes after the shipwreck', my own first visit there was a happy memory.

Alan Sichel and I were on a wine-buying tour of France and, without knowing it was on, we got to Colmar on the opening day of the Annual Wine-tasting and Fair which ranks with that at Angers as the biggest and most varied in all France. When I saw what a splendid building it was housed in I announced that I would stay in the town and have a good day's *dégustation*, while Alan, hinting a little loftily that it was only for boozy locals, said that he would drive out to the various wine villages to call on his contacts.

We parted. I walked smartly along to the fair, paid my Fr. 1.50 entrance, bought myself a little wine-tasting glass and prepared to taste.

How I love these wine fairs! Officially you pay fourpence or so for each wine sampled, but if you are any sort of a buyer, and not even a very genuine one, the payment is waived and anyway, as the day wears on, the growers behind their stalls fill up your proffered glass without bothering to take your money, though they always charge if they have to supply the glass themselves. This is a sort of punishment for putting them to the trouble of having to rinse out a glass, so the one you buy at sixpence pays for itself twenty times over.

I decided to make a royal day of it and to savour the wares of each booth to the full. It was a superb, hot, cloudless day, and to celebrate this glorious burst of weather I had on my pale cream linen suit, in which I rather fancied myself. It could only be worn for one short day because it was very old and thus attracted every particle of dust with extraordinary rapidity.

It was at about eleven o'clock, when the first six or seven tasting-booths were lighter of some thirty-six sips of good Alsatian wine and I was that much more enlightened, that the great thought came to me: why not earn an honest penny by reporting this splendid tasting to some London paper? I felt in my wallet . . . well, if I went without lunch I'd just about have enough for the call, and so I made off at lightning speed to the head post office.

'London?' said the girl, in a tone which meant, Where on earth is that, and if it's where I think it is then it's a terrible bore for me to have to get it.

'Yes, London,' I said, and then, realizing that I did not know the number of the *Daily Express*, which I had selected to print my scoop, 'but I shall want inquiries first.'

'Go into the booth,' said the girl wearily, and in I went, into one of the smallest, dirtiest boxes I have ever seen.

A quarter of an hour later, after coming out three times to ask the girl to hurry up, I got the number; after a further half an hour and at least a dozen poppings in and out of the booth—for you couldn't stay in it for long without suffocation—I got on to the *Express*, and as I started to talk to the News Editor the line went blank.

The telephonist, then her superior, then the head of the post office all refused both to refund my money and to put me through again, and so I went back to the fair, paid another franc and a half, and started tasting again.

Some four booths and twenty-four sips—most growers were showing six wines—later, I felt that some food, mainly to act as blotting-paper to the wine, was indicated, and so I thought I would do just one more before I went back again into the town. I must explain that every booth had, behind the stall itself, an inner sanctum, partitioned off by a curtain, where the growers themselves entertained their personal friends. At this stall I was just about to proffer my glass when an eye was put to the curtain, which was then drawn, and much to my surprise I was asked to step inside.

And there to my astonishment was Alan Sichel.

'You were quite right, Tommy,' he said, noting my surprise. 'Everyone I called upon was at the fair, so I came back.' Then he looked at me. 'But *wherever* have you been?'

I looked down at my suit. Fifty sips cannot always be spat out without some stains resulting, a dozen visits to a filthy telephone-box aren't helpful, but over and above all that, in my eagerness to phone London I had put my tasting-glass in my pocket without rinsing it.

Someone has called Colmar an architect's nightmare, but none the less it is a delightful town to wander around. Listen to André Hallays at the turn of the century (what he said holds true today).

> By its capriciousness, by the variety of the construction of the buildings, the old part of this Alsatian village is a delight. Everything is irregular; none of the houses are of the same design or the same height. All the squares show an obstinate lack of symmetry while the streets twist and turn in a remarkably snake-like way. All these angles and all these curves produce on days of sunshine shafts of light which are as unexpected as they are beautiful.
>
> Large doors with wide arches interlaced with mullioned windows, galleries of wood with exquisite carved balustrades, turrets, bell-turrets, belvederes and little minarets; here is the essence of the Renaissance. At the first glance one is tempted to say that it is the German Renaissance. But if one looks at the buildings of the town a little more closely and, especially, if one recalls the houses in Nürnberg and Rothenburg-ob-der-Tauber, one quickly understands that the Colmar

decorations are quite individual and entirely Alsatian. Neither the architects who built the houses nor the sculptors who decorated them were perhaps very illustrious, but their work reflects a striking sense of *rhythm*, and, although it is hard to explain exactly, if one looks at the Maison Pfister in the rue des Marchands, or stands in front of the Maison des Têtes or the graceful Renaissance Gendarmerie, it is clear that the style is not German Renaissance but Alsatian Renaissance.

The three houses described by André Hallays are still there, and well worth a visit. The Maison des Têtes, now a luxury restaurant whose home-made *foie gras*, *Coq au Riesling* and *Selle de chevreuil* have earned it a rosette in the *Guide Michelin*, gets its name from the multitude of little wooden heads carved on the wooden exterior of the building.

The most remarkable house in the old town was built in 1537 and was then called the *Haus zum Hut*, but later came into the hands of the Pfister family from whom the place takes its present name. And standing as it does on the corner of two ancient streets it is doubly arresting. Its glory lies in its first-floor with its beautifully carved wooden gallery, broken by a superb loggia, also of carved wood, which juts out on the corner. And on the walls under the gallery are painted religious scenes as well as medallions of several Kings of France.

Another reason for Colmar's charm is that it is dotted all over with fountains and statues, many of which were given by another of the town's famous sons, the sculptor Auguste Bartholdi, who was extremely attached to the town of his birth. It was Bartholdi who, after one of his visits to America, conceived the idea of getting the French Republic to present the United States with that vast statue of 'La Liberté éclairant le monde' which now stands in New York harbour—some idea of its size can be deduced from the fact that when the *head* of the statue alone was exhibited in Paris in 1878 an official banquet was served in the inside.

But Bartholdi always thought big: at the Musée Bartholdi, in the house where he was born, the main exhibits are great concrete chunks of arms and legs, the size of small treetrunks. And his 'Lion of Belfort', the principal sight in that town and carved out of the pink Vosges sandstone, is thirty-six feet high by seventy-two feet long.

The Musée d'Unterlinden is housed in a former Dominican convent; this, complete with cloister, is a delight to the eye.

Here, in the chapel, is that masterpiece, the pride of the whole town, the Issenheim altarpiece, which is so strikingly magnificent and moving that I feel I must describe it fully.

Towards the end of the thirteenth century the Antonians built a convent and hospital near the village of Issenheim, just north of Colmar, which was on a most important trade route.

The Order of Antonians—St Anthony is the patron saint of swineherds (and that is why the littlest pig of a litter is sometimes called an anthony)—originally grew out of an organization of laymen devoted to the sick, and sprang up around a little chapel at Saint-Didier-de-la-Motte, near Vienne, which enshrined the relics of St Anthony the Hermit. These relics had been brought there by Crusaders returning from Constantinople and were reputed to have miraculous healing powers.

He was supposed to be best able to cure pestilential erysipelas, which towards the end of the eleventh century was a death-bringing disease spreading all over Europe. This was about the time the order was formed, and that was why the brotherhood was recognized as early as 1095 by Pope Urban II and granted a constitution by Pope Boniface VIII in 1298.

Incidentally, erysipelas causes a bright red, burning rash on the skin and so is also called 'St Anthony's Fire' or 'Sacred Fire'.

At any rate, probably because the relics of St Anthony were reputed to have healing properties, the convent at Issenheim grew in reputation and wealth and prospered exceedingly, until by the beginning of the sixteenth century, under the Sicilian Guido Guersi, it was not only dispensing charity but attracting the greatest artists of the day.

And to the convent, bringing with him a great reputation from Germany, came Mathias Grünewald. Or, to get the record straight, that was one of his names, which can be traced back to an unreliable seventeenth-century biographer, Joachim von Sandrart. Twentieth-century researches have given him back his rightful name of Mathis Nithardt, but he is also known as von Gothardt, and sometimes as Mathis von Aschaffenburg, this being the town where the artist, already with a good reputation, had settled down in 1485.

Mathis was born in 1460 in Würzburg, and that really is all you can say about him, except that he happened to be at the convent at Issenheim at the moment when the great church needed a painting behind its altar.

Two steps led up to this altar, where the priests offered the holy sacrifice. The church at Issenheim was never closed to the sick, and even the worst cases were carried to the foot of the altar—a vast, solid construction in hewn stone—by the lay brothers who nursed them.

It was here, then, that Master Mathis hung his great painting, which he executed between 1510 and 1515.

Could it be only because they are in the unusual form of a polyptich that these paintings have caused so much admiration and discussion? You could think so until you have seen them, but once you have cast your eyes on this kaleidoscopic feast of colour you banish the thought as absurd.

The first picture was that of the Crucifixion, and a massive rough-hewn cross is seen with a Christ drained of blood, swollen and blotched, against that background of darkness which descended upon mankind.

But the Church in those days knew how to turn from sorrow to joy, and when the second aspect of the work is unfolded on its hinges we see the Annunciation and Resurrection painted in scenes of colourful, exuberant gaiety.

Then there is a second turn of the heavy wings upon their hinges, and on the two painted wings we see, appropriately, St Anthony visiting St Paul in the Wilderness and, finally, the Temptation of St Anthony.

This tumultuous drama of vivid bestiality is one of the most fantastic pictures I have ever seen, far finer in detail and imagination than anything by Hieronymus Bosch. The whole scene is one of frenzied destruction and corruption. St Anthony has been flung onto the ground and is being trampled and beaten by loathsome animals. Above the gutted hut of the hermit a shining angel can just be seen in the clouds—an angel attacking a black flying demon with a golden lance fashioned in the form of a cross.

In the foreground is a hideous figure of the demon of the plague; his skin is vermilion, his belly is swollen and all over his body are blotches and pustules. His hands are mere stumps, and the picture is so lifelike that it is almost certain it was taken from life—a patient being treated in the convent hospital at Issenheim. But far worse are the demons trying to pluck at St Anthony's blue gown. In the centre is Gluttony, represented by a bat-winged hippopotamus whose open jaws reveal its horrible fangs. Beside it is Adultery, an evil rat-faced animal with antlers for ears and two rabbit-like teeth. Farther back is Anger, an eagle with human hands brandishing a bludgeon. On the other side of St Anthony, on the ground, is a beast with a dragon's feet, a shell back and the head of a basilisk trying to peck the rosary from the hermit's hand.

The whole scene is thought to have been a symbolic representation of the outbreaks of venereal disease which ravaged the western world during the fifteenth century.

10

CABBAGES AND KUEHN

Leaving Colmar, we rejoined the Route du Vin at Wintzenheim, virtually a suburb of the town.

Wine town number twenty is Turckheim. Ah, Turckheim: if one has used 'picturesque' and 'charming' for earlier places on the route, whatever words remain to sing your praises?

Here is one of the very, very few wine communes along the route to have the right to a vineyard name, Brand; then you have that pretty little High Street, with its shops which twinkle so attractively when the lights go on at dusk. Then there is the famous Deux-Clefs restaurant and inn.

Turckheim is surrounded by a splendid medieval fortified wall, and one enters the town—which is built in the shape of a triangle—by one of the three imposing old gates. But the place's greatest claim to fame is that it was here that the great Henri de la Tour d'Auvergne, Vicomte de Turenne, Marshal of France, won one of his most renowned battles. In 1674 a great Imperial army of sixty thousand men was threatening Alsace, and to defend the area Turenne only had twenty thousand. It was one of the cardinal rules of war that you didn't fight during the winter months, but Turenne did and won hands down, a brilliant victory of which Napoleon said that he admired its tactics better than those of any other battle he had studied.

Beyond the rather uninteresting villages of Ingersheim and Niedermorschwihr, we found ourselves in the sauerkraut country.

An enemy of wine, because of its peppery vinegar flavour, but glorious with the famous local beer, Alsatian *sauerkraut* is made from immense, hard, white cabbages grown on the plains which lie between the vine hills and the Rhine. They are cropped in the winter, the women cutting off the dirty, dark green outside leaves, leaving a luminous, pale, lemon-green ball twice as large as a football and so heavy that it is quite a job to lift. The cabbages are then piled high onto lorries or carts waiting at the roadside. They presented such a remarkable sight that I for one was unable to resist getting out to look.

The two men I spoke to were pleasantly informative, telling me that all their crop was going to a near-by factory; as one of them did part-time work there later on in the year he was able to tell me how they were prepared.

Most Alsatian families, it seems, have their own tub or cask of *sauerkraut* in a shed in the garden, and with care it can be used all the year round. First, a few more outer leaves and also the hard core should be removed; if you don't want the bore of cutting the cabbage up by hand you can purchase a curious contraption where you feed the cabbages into a hopper placed over a tub equipped with cutters. You then slide the cabbage-filled hopper to and fro and the finely shredded cabbage falls down into the tub. The shreds must next be well washed and extra well dried. They now go into another cask or large earthenware crock which—nice vinous touch, this—should be lined with large vine-leaves. Next you pack down a layer of shredded cabbage, then you throw on a thick layer of coarse salt, and on this you sprinkle juniper berries. Continue layer by layer till you have filled the container; your last layer must be of salt. Cover with a linen cloth. Now place on top a round piece of wood (or a square one if your container should by any chance be square), which must be a very little smaller than the opening of the container. On this you put a heavy stone, which must be non-porous.

The next morning, take a look at your *sauerkraut*-to-be; under the pressure of the stone the water from the cabbage should have covered both the stone and the wooden cover. Be sure that this is always the case. After three weeks the froth which appears on the cover will die down and the cabbage is now ready, save that you must replace the salty liquid with fresh water.

I was so grateful for this advice that I went and ferreted about in the car and produced two Voltigeurs de Luxe cigars, which are really only large whiffs made of rather coarse tobacco—France is not very good at cigars. The men received these with evident pleasure and we parted company, but I had only covered ten yards when I heard a shout behind me.

'What can I do?' I said, returning.

'Why not take a couple of these?' said the two men, and each had in his hands the largest cabbage he had been able to find on the lorry. I looked at the monster spheres and calculated. How long would it take me to rearrange the suitcases in my car to accommodate them? Everything was packed so neatly, and the many bottles of various

Alsatian wines were so excellently stacked, that I did not want to re-arrange things.

'May I have just one, please?' I said, and it was dropped on top of everything else.

I was now late for my next appointment at Ammerschwihr, the twenty-third village on the Route du Vin, but the road from the cabbage-fields was fast and straight, and when I saw a fine hotel-cum-restaurant on the highway I could not resist jumping out for a couple of quick drinks. Inside, the whole place was most elegant, with a very open-plan bar, hall and stairs leading up to the first floor, giving the place a curiously maty atmosphere. There were several people around, all chatting away like magpies, roaring with laughter and evidently not going to take any notice of me. By the bar was a sophisticated, well groomed middle-aged man smoking a cigarette, and behind it a pretty girl in Alsatian costume.

'*Bonjour!*' I said, in a tone meant to convey, Here I am, folks; I may look foreign but I understand French and if you'll tell me the joke I'm prepared to join in and laugh as heartily as the rest of you.

No one took the slightest notice of me. The attention of all of them—there were also two women standing by with mops and pails—was taken up by a woman who was kneeling on the close-carpeted stairs, apparently fixing a stair-rod. She had on a dirty cap, which was meant to protect her shining gold hair, and she was wearing an equally dirty, very thin, terribly short nylon overall, which permitted one to guess at a splendid figure, though all one really saw was a pair of shapely legs and a frilly pair of pants.

'*Bonjour!*' I said again. This time the tone was different: it said, Look, I can join in your merry-making, but only after you have served me.

Still no attention. This was too much. I went up to the elegant man.

'*Bonjour, monsieur le patron,*' I said.

The man turned slightly towards me and said, 'Not me, sir. The owner is there.' He pointed to the girl on the staircase, who had now taken the mop from one of the cleaners and was swabbing the marble tiles of the hall with such vigour that both her stockings became badly corkscrewed and a shoe came off.

I was now hopping mad.

'Oh, she's the owner is she?' I shouted. 'Very funny, very witty. There's no need to make fun of me, and if she's the owner I'm King Kong.'

At this the woman turned and came up to me. The laughter died away. She was very lovely. She took off her cap and a cascade of shimmering hair fell onto her shoulders. I now saw that the dress under her nylon overall was of great style, and that those hands, though superficially grubby, had not been used to much manual work.

'You know, monsieur,' she said, 'people who work do sometimes get a little dirty.'

I slunk away embarrassed, thirsty, and even more late for Ammerschwihr. I was driving like a maniac now, and as I approached the village there was a sharp turn which I nearly missed. I swung the car around with a great tug on the steering-wheel. I just made it, but then, immediately, there came a sharper turn to the right. I tugged on the wheel and made the turn, then *crash!* and the tinkle of glass falling about. I looked at the back, and saw that the old shoe which had been placed to hold the cabbage steady had been dislodged by my violent swervings and had sent the green vegetable crashing into the side window.

In 1969 the population of Ammerschwihr was 1,474. This miniature village is one of the most lovely along the Route du Vin, and I think I like its *ambiance* better even than that of Riquewihr or Turckheim. It was terribly bombarded during the German 'Colmar Pocket' resistance in January 1945, but the reconstruction, using the original stones, has been so magnificently done that the place, to my mind, looks nicer than it did before.

Ammerschwihr is surrounded by some of the very finest vineyards in the best wine region of Alsace. The Kaefferkopf vineyards, though far better known than the Brand ones of Turckheim, are enshrined in the *appellation contrôlée* laws.

And because of its importance as a wine centre there are a great number of very fine, immensely large and deep underground cellars in the houses of the village, which proved of great use during the bombardments. These wine vaults have, over the centuries, acquired distinguishing names. One, for example, is called 'Paradise'. The deepest of all is called 'Hell', and the inhabitants never tire of telling visitors that it was in this latter vault that the priest stored all the church treasures, including statues of the saints, when the aerial attack reached its climax.

None of these minimal claims to fame, however, counts anything beside the fact that in the most imposing mansion of the village is the famous Aux Armes de France restaurant, whose specialities of hot *foie gras*, stuffed trout and filleted sole with noodles (and, later, *Coq au vinaigre*) won proprietor Gaertner two rosettes for good cooking in the *Guide Michelin*.

Next door were the imposing offices and cellars of by far the largest wine-growers of the immediate region—Messrs Kuehn, now being run by the young, energetic François Kuehn, whose notepaper, like the tone of his letters, had impressed me greatly. He showed no irritation whatever that I was so late, and soon we were sitting down to the usual *dégustation* in his very elegant room.

Then we went on to lunch at the Armes de France. The restaurant takes up the whole of the first floor, and is vast. It is divided into two parts—a café section with rather bare tables (used as an overflow, I suspect, in the summer), and the restaurant proper, whence there is a wonderful panoramic view of the village and vineyards beyond. What I think surprises and pleases the metropolitan guest most is the extreme amplitude of the tables; one which is here set for four covers would take eight—three on each side and one at each end—in London.

In the middle of the room are the trolleys with the hors d'oeuvre, the sweetmeats and, most important of all, the *foies gras* in their majestic golden crusts—a more appetizing sight it would be hard to find, and I could not resist it when Kuehn and I sat down for a very late lunch after the tasting.

After Ammerschwihr comes Kaysersberg. Bernard Newman, in his book *The Sisters Alsace-Lorraine*, says: 'There are those who claim that Kaysersberg is as picturesque as Rothenburg on the Tauber. I doubt if this claim could be justified, but it is a charming place, almost unspoiled. This is a real corner of Alsace, with every glance revealing a balanced picture.'

Geographically the place is interesting, since in Roman times the layout of the land made it one of the most important passages between Gaul and the Rhine valley—the name Kaysersberg or *mont de l'Empereur*, comes from the Latin *Caesaris mons*.

It was here that Albert Schweitzer, son of the local pastor, was born in 1875. The other important name in Kaysersberg's history was that of Lazare de Schwendi, who is supposed to have given the town its reputation for great wines. According to local tradition the Holy Roman Emperor Maximilian I was at one time the overlord of the town and put in as his bailiff Schwendi, who had previously, while fighting in Hungary, captured the village of Tokay. And from here to Kaysersberg he brought a few vine plants which, as the centuries passed, flourished and gave the locality a tremendous reputation for fine wines.*

To me the place was important because I had here one of my most important introductions—to M. Théo Faller, through Guy (father) and Hervey (son) Prince of Lebègue, of annual underneath-the-arches-tasting fame.

Guy's devotion to Lebègue, and that firm's and his devotion to *only* the wines of France, have been the subject of surprised and admiring discussion in the trade for many a year. Lebègue had their centenary, appropriately enough, in 1961, which has every prospect of being the greatest Claret vintage of this century, outstripping 1928, 1945 and even 1929 in breed, finesse and longevity.

Lebègue's beginnings deserve a mention. On 10 February 1860 Gladstone, speaking in the House of Commons 'from five to nine without great exhaustion, aided by a great stock of egg and wine', as his diary recalls, introduced the French Treaty Act, which removed the duty on 371 articles and greatly reduced the duty on everything else. This dramatic turn of events was duly noted by a twenty-year-old man from the Cognac area, Jean Lebègue, who worked out that if he imported French wines to England in cask and bottled them there he would only be paying twopence a bottle in duty.

With a certain amount of Gallic caution he took a year planning things, and so opened in South Molton Street in 1861. At first he specialized in Cognac, and successfully, but the phylloxera scourge hit the Cognac area so badly that production fell suddenly and dramatically. Lebègue turned his attention to Clarets, and at the same time moved to Fenchurch Street, only a stone's throw from Mark Lane, the great city street for wine-shippers. No sooner was this accomplished in 1869 than Jean Lebègue had another brainwave. The Great Exhibition marked the start of an era of splendid prosperity, and this caused an upsurge in the sale of Champagne. Not everyone could afford the more luxurious brands, however, and so the young Frenchman hit on the bright idea of shipping over a more modest-quality wine and helping buyers in the design and supply of labels of their

* To me this is mystifying: it is always claimed that the excellent Tokay d'Alsace is indubitably *not* made with the grape which makes the Hungarian Tokay. If so, is the Schwendi story a complete myth? Or did he bring a grape which was used to make Tokay *at that time* but ceased to be at a later date? Or have its four hundred years of acclimatization in Vosges mountain soil caused it completely to lose its sweetness? Or could a certain amount of cross-fertilization have taken place over these centuries?

own choosing—and the idea now known as B.O.B. (Buyers' Own Brands) was born.

By the end of the century Lebègue was the doyen of the French colony in London and appointed by Poincaré a Chevalier of the Légion d'Honneur.

Such were the beginnings of the firm which Guy Prince, as managing director, made famous for its annual wine-tasting. *Dégustations* by candlelight had always been a favourite of his, and he had given several in city cellars on upturned casks before the war. But the Lebègue cellars gave him a unique chance.

The first tastings in 1949 lasted the better part of a week, and guests who came on the third day were astonished to see a huge baize-covered board in the foyer, where one has a glass of Champagne before going into lunch, literally covered with clippings from the Press in praise of the event.

As the years passed, and members of the trade realized that it was indeed a unique chance to catch up with their knowledge of wine, the Press, uncharacteristically, did not become blasé, and the number of columns devoted to the tasting grew to such an extent that one famous journalist said, 'The occasion is fast becoming the most eagerly sought engagement in Fleet Street.'

The Times said:

> Though this is only the seventh year of Messrs. Lebègue's annual tastings of French wines, they have already attained a unique place in the oenological calendar, both for the scale of the display and for the grace and amenity of the proceedings.
>
> The atmosphere curiously and pleasantly blends the businesslike and the romantic: in the background of the long crypts under London Bridge Station the dim ranges of casks, bins, and packing cases; along the aisles the hundreds of candles, shedding the only light that does justice to the jewelled red and gold of the juice of the grape; and the quiet progress of the students of the mystery down the long tables, packed three deep with bottles, passing them all under critical review.

The *Telegraph* noted that the French Ambassador had been to the tasting on that day, the American one was going the next day, and the Lord Mayor the day after that.

The *Field* said:

There is nowhere better to compare the quality of wines of varying ages than at a wine-tasting, one of the principal of which is that held annually by J. L. P. Lebègue and Co. in their cellars under the arches of London Bridge railway station.

This year marks the centenary of the 1855 classification of the Grands Crus de Bordeaux shown at the Paris Exhibition of that year. This classification was presented to this year's guests at the tasting. Further, to bring the list to life, as it were, Lebègue's staged a bottle of a post-war vintage of each of the 'classed growths' shown at the exhibition; and it is probably the first time such a comprehensive exhibition has been staged since 1855.

For the first few years Guy had rigorously excluded women from the tastings, mainly because the smell of a powerful scent does indeed detract from the appreciation of the bouquet. This had infuriated the very few women buyers in the trade, and especially one, who was, in fact, a very good taster, and many comic rumours went round the trade as to how many lunches she had to be invited to subsequently to placate her. In 1956 ladies were at last admitted; not only that, but a whole day was set aside for their enjoyment. This caused a remarkable recrudescence of interest in the event, which was astonishingly well covered.

In *Illustrated* Gilbert Harding, true to his forthright self, said:

> Anything that can be done to improve women's taste in drink is to be applauded. Heaven knows, it is generally deplorable.
>
> There are few women who can honestly claim to know anything about drink. It is, after all, women who must bear the blame for such horrible witches' brews as port-and-lemon, gin-and-lime, and many of the more revolting cocktails that seem to be compounded of after-shave lotion, sweet glue and gin.
>
> So I rejoice to hear that more women are drinking wine than ever before and that a large firm of wine merchants now invites women to its candle-lit cellars under London Bridge Station to taste and learn more about the finest wines.

The fact that too much perfume was not a good thing must have gone out on some feminine grapevine, for the publicity story that most reporters thought best was that such charming persons as the Duchess of X, the Countess of Y and actress Z were singularly unsmelly.

Perhaps it was best summed up by my friend Daphne Boutwood in the *Sunday Times*:

> There has been a strong feeling—among men—that wine is a precinct into which women may not enter, like the Athenaeum and the Church; that it is so sacred that women can never appreciate it, or only to a limited degree. 'A nice waite waine for the lady?' waiters will suggest, sickeningly, while one's escort holds the wine-list well away as if it were a secret document or a rude postcard, to be kept from the lady at all costs. Perhaps this is because her eye might wander down the right-hand column instead of the left, but mostly it is considered unthinkable that she should want to see what she is about to drink.
>
> And now, gratifying recognition of feminine influence and taste, last Wednesday was set aside as the first Ladies' Day in Lebègue's famous wine-tasting week. It was a notable occasion, and a suitably impressive sight: as far as the eye could see down the vaulted length of the candlelit cellar, a bobbing of exotic hats, a mingling of unsmoking, unscented ladies—for it was politely indicated that Chanel No. 5 might not agree with a Lafite '54.
>
> After all, wine itself has many feminine qualities. It is graceful, it pleases, it needs great care and attention—and, during its variable lifetime, you never know what it will do next.
>
> One question remains: will women ever accept the mystique which surrounds the drinking of wine, the exaggerated ceremony, the elaborate jargon? Say 'wine' to a woman and she thinks of soft lights and romance. Say 'wine' to a man and he thinks of vintages and districts. It's a matter of approach, and I am not sure that ours is not the better. As our hostess, Mrs Guy Prince, last week said, 'Don't talk about wine, drink it.'

For me the annual tastings never pall; I never fail to be quite moved when I look down that long vista of white tablecloths on which are upwards of a hundred and fifty wines, all lit by thousands of candles set in huge wrought-iron chandeliers which depend from the white-washed arches.

Everyone gets an elaborately printed tasting-booklet, and on page seventeen, in respect of Stand N, it says: *ALSATIAN WINES FALLER FRÈRES: Clos des Capucins, Château Weinbach, Kaysersberg, Haut-Rhin.*

The Château Weinbach (meaning 'Wine stream', probably because the vines grew particularly abundantly there) is a finely kept up medieval mansion, and the car wheels made a pleasantly crunchy noise as they rolled over the thick gravel drive which led to the courtyard. To my knock the door was at once opened by a young, pretty, elegant woman, wearing one of the most lovely full-length fur coats I had ever seen.

Splendid beginning, I thought.

So I doffed my hat a little more deferentially than usual, and said, 'Madame, I have come a thousand miles to see you and your husband, with a special invitation from Hervey Prince of Lebègue.'

You could hardly say that Mme Faller's eyes lit up, but she was certainly polite, and soon we were walking across the courtyard and got into the bottling-room.

I thought that I was being taken to meet M. Faller, but when we got inside Madame merely waved her hands towards the bottles, as if to say, 'See what a nice set-up we have,' and then selected two different bottles and made back towards my car. These bottles she placed in the back in a way that indicated that my visit was over.

I cannot remember feeling more shamed, angry and disappointed in my life. All the Laytons have bad tempers, but there was one thing to do here and that was not to lose it. I went to the back of the car and took out the two bottles.

'You are terribly kind, madame,' I said, 'but I really don't feel I have enough room.'

Madame looked at me and then into the back of the car, where she could easily see a cardboard wine carton partitioned for a dozen and almost empty.

'You see,' said Mme Faller, 'my husband has gone to a convalescent home in Italy. I am running the place, and if I don't get to the tax office by six o'clock to pay in, we will not be allowed to send off the wines for the weekend.'

I looked at my watch and the proximity to Madame's zero hour was nobody's business.

'Can I come with you?' I said. 'This is one of the few wine operations I have never seen.'

In answer Madame waved to a huge car standing in the courtyard, and we were soon driving at Jehu-like speed to Ribeauvillé, where a large lady in a tiny attic-like room took from Mme Faller what seemed to be a great sum of money.

When we got back to Château Weinbach the atmosphere changed; I saw round the cellars, tasted and talked.

Then, as we shook hands by my car and said goodbye, Mme Faller said, 'Are you sure you can't squeeze in those two bottles?' And she looked at the carton.

I opened the back of the Mini Traveller.

'By Jove!' I said, also looking at it. 'I'd forgotten that empty case.'

Place twenty-five on the Route is the ancient little village of Kientzheim, where, in the heavily restored church, is the tomb of Lazare de Schwendi. Then comes Sigolsheim. Here, historians think, is the 'Field of the Lie' where the sons of Louis le Débonnaire captured their father in 833, prior to making him prisoner. Bennwihr comes next; and then Mittelwihr, the district around which has been christened 'the Midi of Alsace', since the climate is so warm that almond trees not only flower but, in some years, even ripen. And then, the twenty-ninth village on the Route, comes the pearl of Alsace: Riquewihr.

11

RIQUEWIHR

I HAVE already run out of superlatives for some of the towns along the Route, and so my only comment is that I have only seen Riquewihr, thank heavens, after the tourists have left, and I think the main street in this little village is of enduring delight. Given a rare three stars as worth a visit by the chary *Guide Michelin*, Riquewihr has also had several books written about it.

Alice had picked up an old secondhand book called *Wayfaring in France*, by Edward Harrison Barker, published in 1890 by Richard Bently, Publisher in Ordinary to Her Majesty the Queen. It is a rambling book: the author goes from the Landes, south of Bordeaux, where he talks to the resin-gatherers who shin up the pine trees, through to Brittany to commiserate with the poor geese there who are plucked several times a year in order to keep up the supply of goose-feathers, and on to Alsace, where, after commenting on the curious wooden trays with teeth employed by the children who collect the wild whortleberries used for making a spirit called Myrte, he gets to Riquewihr.

> The road led me to the little town of Riquewihr, lying in the midst of luxuriant vineyards—an islet in a sea of gold-green foliage. It was once fortified and extensive fragments remain of its ancient walls. The curious gable tower with clock and belfry; the fortified gateway; the rows of windows supported by worm-eaten beams projecting one over the other, their sills abloom with flowers in decaying boxes which the ivy linaria [*or toad-flax*] has been striving for many years to cover with its green leaves—all this and much more made me loth to leave the place.

It looks as though, when Barker visited Riquewihr, it was a little poverty-stricken, and not the prosperous, superbly maintained place it is now. I seem to remember hearing that it had only been 'discovered' as worthy of the full French Tourist Board treatment in the

1930s. But my reason for mentioning Barker's book is that it has an etching of the town showing the fortified gateway, complete with portcullis, taken from exactly the same spot as one of the many photographs of Riquewihr you can buy in any of the many souvenir shops there. The etching is extremely detailed, and Alice and I had the idea of standing where both artist and photographer had and seeing what had changed in the intervening eighty years.

By Jove! Hardly anything. A low stone wall which probably hindered traffic has been removed, and a large outdoor pot plant has made an appearance. But the wooden portcullis is there, and with the same defects in the staves as it showed in the last century.

The annals of Riquewihr are more comprehensive than those of any other Route du Vin village or, indeed, any other medieval village in all France. Wine has played a very large part in the life of the place, and I think that one of the most interesting aspects of all was the struggle which went on over the tithes to be paid (in grapes, not wine) to the various Lords of the Manor. Like all tithes (*dîmes* in French) of grapes, that at Riquewihr had its origin in the Church. It originally belonged to the Bishop of Basle who enfeoffed it, in 1291, to Anselme of Ribeaupierre. And although in both the English and French languages the word means a tenth part, the actual percentage demanded was never fixed at this quantity for many years in succession. In 1689, for example, Christian II de Deux-ponts demanded from the towns of Riquewihr, Ammerschwihr, Kientzheim and Kaysersberg and the village of Sigolsheim that he should have his tenth share of raisins. The inhabitants protested that the traditional amount was only a sixteenth; finally a thirteenth was agreed upon.

The official measuring container then was called a *tendelin*, a rare word in French, although still used in Alsace. It is a sort of huge wooden hod which goes on the men's backs.

But while it was relatively easy to fix the amount, it was much harder to see that the peasants produced what was owed, and there was always a great deal of swindling. Because of this it appears that the vintage was picked not necessarily at the right time from the grape-maturity point of view, but when it best suited the counter-swindlers.

The ban on harvesting could only be pronounced by the Mayor Tithe-collector (*Zehendmeyer* or *Maire-dîmier*), and before it was practicable to do this the Counts of Ribeaupierre had to summon enough men from the surrounding mountains (it was safer than having locals, who might be friends of the peasant growers) to see that the

RIQUEWIHR

tithe was in fact gathered in. These men were called *valets dîmiers assermentés*, or sworn-in valet tithe-collectors. Incidentally, if they did have any grapes growing in their garden plots they were the only people in the community who had the privilege (surely a doubtful one in years when the grapes were late maturing) of gathering their harvest *before* the ban was lifted.

It is to be stressed that the tithe was paid in grapes and not in wine, since, after the apportionment, the bunches were pressed in the Tithe Courtyard of the Counts of Ribeaupierre at Riquewihr.

Every operation was under the direction of the Mayor-Tithe-collector, and he was even responsible for all the equipment. A document of 1573 sets out what he was not to lose in that year: two presses, two vats, a chopper, three buckets and one length of old and one length of new rope. This functionary was paid in kind; he got four casks of the best wine and four of *piquette*,* together with the hay from two small fields situated at Bennwihr.

The official wine-pressers got a salary, paid in silver, a measure of good wine and the right to a share in the *piquette* they were permitted to make.

As the years passed the evasion got worse.

In former days much more red wine was made than now, but the grapes whence it came were even then nothing like as good as the white ones. Now, the tithe had to be paid in white-wine-making grapes, and the thirteenth part was due *in* white-wine-making grapes, even if the grower was growing a lot of red-wine-making grapes. One thing which helped the peasants swindle their overlords was that the 'sworn valets', coming mainly from other parts of the valley, did not understand much about wine and, worse, had no idea which vineyards belonged to which peasants.

If the peasants diddled their overlords, it was often because the latter were greedy; but they also, especially in time of hardship, did things which, if they had not been restrained, could have put them out of business altogether.

One was the planting of poor wine-making species of grapes; another, worse, was using for wine plain land which should have been used for corn.

Ever since Roman times, when the Emperor Diocletian ordered the grubbing-up of that 'disloyal plant the Gamay', officialdom has tried to

---

* *Piquette* was a light, thin wine for home consumption, made by throwing water over the final pressing of the grapes and then re-pressing them.

protect the grower from himself, but then the growers were at times so desperate that they knew not where to turn.

This was exactly the case during the Thirty Years' War, but when it was over the magistrates of Strasbourg and Colmar tried repeatedly to show growers what was good for them.

> It is publicly recognized not only in Alsace but among all the peoples of the Empire that the best wines from Alsace which indeed are better in both strength and flavour than all and every wine from Germany, and which are expedited over land and sea, are those grown in the commune of Riquewihr.

Thus begins an ordinance of 1630, which aimed at encouraging, and, if that was not enough, forcing the growers of the favourite district to revert to ancient (that is, pre-war) and ultimately more profitable ways of wine-growing. The ordinance went on:

> Our ancestors, even from antiquity, have held to the principle of planting great or noble grape varieties, knowing from experience that such varieties, because of the excellent quality of our soil and the sunny exposure of our gentle slopes, will produce grapes which will ripen to perfection. This rule was one which our forebears respected, and indeed helped them to prosperity. But as the years passed by it often happened that, out of curiosity, very ordinary varieties were planted. This happened several times, and especially before the town of Riquewihr had formulated rules prohibiting such disgraceful plantings.

Now comes the sting in the tail:

> So to put a stop to this disgraceful habit it is necessary to restate these ordinances and the Magistracy henceforth condemns the planting of common varieties under pain of a double fine, and also of the offender's being obliged to grub up the offending vine-stock.

During the whole of the seventeenth century the Magistracy was always on its toes to see that its edicts were carried out, and the Strasbourg archives are full of records of fines meted out, and to persons of consequence, too. They themselves had certainly not dug the holes in the vineyards, but their employees had and that was enough.

The beginning of the eighteenth century saw the tragedy (and that is not too strong a word) of the vines descending from the sun-drenched Alsatian slopes and onto the plain. It was a double tragedy. In the first place, the fact that vineyards were ousting the cornfields meant that, as the cost of barley went up because of the inevitable shortage, horse transport went up with it, and that sent all prices up.

It produced a similar situation to what arises when a modern government puts twopence on a gallon of petrol. The non-motorist feels it will not affect his pocket, but it does, for a few months later he will be paying a copper or two more for matches, tinned sardines and bread. Furthermore, the 'vineyards of the plain' were planted with very poor varieties which enabled the wines to be sold at a terribly low price, to the great distress of the growers of fine wines up in the hills, because Alsatian wines quickly earned so evil a reputation that all foreign sales dropped off almost completely.

I have dealt with the problems of making wine in the past; what about the marketing of it? The small vineyard-owner has always had so much manual work to do that he has never been able to be much of a salesman, and this is where the commission agents, or *courtiers*, come in.

In Alsace (as in other wine regions of France) they go back to the Middle Ages, at which period they went by the name of *gourmets*.

These intermediaries became extremely popular in Riquewihr, so much so that the two lovely and very ancient inns in the town (still extant and great tourist attractions) owe their continued existence to them. These *gourmets* clearly needed somewhere to sleep when they visited the town, and also a room wherein to transact their business, and so it was that in 1537 Prince Georg of Württemberg bought a house in the town which he donated to the inhabitants, who, in turn, rented it out to the *courtiers*. It was called the Cerf. There was also an even older inn called the Étoile, still extant in the High Street.

But I am afraid these *gourmets* did not stay 'goodies' for long; indeed they became 'baddies' so fast that laws had to be introduced to stop their greed. So as early as 1505 the first rules were drawn up:

> Henceforth the office shall be a public one and he who wishes to exercise this profession shall be duly sworn in and shall be responsible to the local magistrate for all his activities. He must swear loyalty to his prince and to his town and must sell the wine of any supplier as best he can, whether he be a local citizen or a stranger, rich or poor,

and without being influenced by sentiments of friendship or enmity; nor shall he receive any presents.

When a prospective buyer comes along and asks advice, the *gourmet* must be very sure not to reveal any defect of the wine in question unless the said buyer asks expressly if there are any faults and wants to taste it.

Gourmets are forbidden to over-assess the bourgeois of Riquewihr and also to refuse to pay them the money they have received for their wine.

All moneys received must be genuine [*de bon aloi*].

You may think that a somewhat sad picture of a down-trodden little commission-man emerges from this description, but you would be very wrong, for, in exchange for being sworn in and (theoretically) not taking presents, he was given the trump and all the court cards by being the only person in the town permitted to sell wine; even the church bailiff was, surprisingly, not allowed to deal in wines in any way save through the *courtier*.

These men, as the decades rolled on, became more and more grasping, and gave less and less good service to the people from whom their wealth derived. They were, of course, allowed small vineyards for their own table use, but what caused the greatest resentment was that 'these *gourmets* possess in vineyards four times as much wine as they need, both for their own personal consumption and for their taverns, and they should not be allowed to buy either grapes or wine for their own account'.*

But although they made money on the side by prohibiting dealing, these *gourmets* must, on the whole, have been pretty well trusted. The job became, like that of taster-blender in the big Cognac houses of the Charentes, mainly hereditary, and if a buyer arrived in the town it is astonishing to record that the *gourmet*, if the *vigneron* was among his vines, would know where all the keys of all the cellars were hidden and, opening up, would wander round the casks, offering samples until the prospective client was satisfied.

But there were tricky times ahead. The French Revolution, which swept away nearly every traditional method of trading, temporarily put the *gourmets* out of work, but in 1803 the Municipal Council of Riquewihr, stating that 'their usefulness is generally recognized', set

* From an address by sixty Riquewihr citizens to the Regency in 1778.

them up in business again, though with a new set of regulations which tightened up even more stringently the prohibition against trading in any wine but that from their own vineyards. They also received a commission, amounting to one per cent, at which tiny amount it remained until 1930 when it went up to five per cent.

Once the client had bought his wine from the *gourmet* the latter had no further responsibility for it, or for its ultimate condition. The *tonneliers* (coopers) were similarly sworn in; their main job was to see that the wine left the cellars of the grower in good condition and in casks which were sound, and for this they received a tiny commission in wine. At this stage they in their turn faded out, and yet another man (again officially sworn in) came on the scene. This was the *Leiterer* (porter), and he seems to have been the bad character of the set-up. His task was to take the wine from the cask-makers and carry, roll or otherwise propel it to the wagons. Now yet another person comes onto the scene: the *chargeur*, or spanner. All he had to do was tie up the casks on the wagons (with twine made from pruned vine-stools) so that they did not become dislodged on the journey. For this he received two pitchers of wine (about four litres) for every *fuder* (thousand litres) loaded.

Naturally, all these *courtiers*, cask-makers (by the way, they made casks using chestnut—willow was strictly forbidden), porters and spanners, possessed various implements, gauges and instruments in connection with their calling, and as they all seem to have been somewhat dishonest the townsfolk, and especially the *vignerons*, insisted on giving these various tools a thorough inspection once a year.

And so what a sight it must have been in the town square of little Riquewihr on Easter eve when the great annual inspection took place; and then how pleasant was the dinner afterwards, with free wine all paid for out of the rates!

Most of the really lovely old houses with their criss-cross oak beams, their gay window-boxes and marvellous wrought-iron signs belong to old families of wine-growers, and in one of these lives 'Papa' Hugel, who by years of patient hard work and regular annual visits to Britain has secured for himself and his three hard-working sons by far the largest share of the Alsatian wine-market in this country. If you are in the wine trade and George Dove and Allan Arnold, who handle the firm's sales in London, hear you are off to Alsace they will, in their kind way, see that you do not fail to visit M. Hugel, especially as he speaks excellent English and is one of Riquewihr's most erudite men on the history of the town. If you have personally known him for a number of years you will receive more than an invitation to visit the cellars, and that was why I found myself seated one Sunday in their first-floor dining-room, and in front of a variety of hors d'œuvre made and supervised by Mme Hugel herself.

I had heard she was a fine cook and, frankly, I was just the tiniest bit sceptical. But no! Although during the meal we did have luxury foods, it was her superb touch with simple things like egg mayonnaise, tomato salad and that gorgeous vegetable celeriac* which stand out in my memory.

* *Céléri-rave* in French; also turnip-rooted celery in English.

12

SNAILS AND STORKS

The next, and thirtieth, place on the Route is Ribeauvillé, a much larger town than Riquewihr, with a great reputation for medieval charm which I think is exaggerated, though the main street is pleasant.

The chief draw is the festival which takes place on the first Sunday of September each year. It has its roots in the Crusades, when the soldiers had to be amused and the army was followed by a collection of jugglers, clowns, minstrels and pipers. When the wars were over they became mere vagabonds, though they still had a certain influence with the common people. At this juncture the lords of Ribeauvillé had the bright idea of allowing all these men to form themselves into a Guild and to forgather annually in Ribeauvillé, the lords extracting from the men a tax of oats and chickens (no questions asked where they came from) while their lordships stood all the players free wine from the town's fountain. It was called Pfifferday—*le jour des fifres*, or fife day—and even now you get a free taste if you attend the gay, rather cacophonous procession.

The next places are Bergheim, Rohrschwihr and Saint-Hippolyte, an attractive spot with a lovely fifteenth-century gothic church; followed by Orschwiller (we have now entered the Bas-Rhin *département*) and then Kintzheim, which is an adorable medieval walled village, with several very old houses built into the fortifications.

At Châtenois, the next village, one turns off to the most controversial of Alsace's tourist attractions, the fortress of Haut-Koenigsbourg. I decided not to write about this place on a principle that I hold strongly: there are so many beautiful things to describe in this world, so why describe ugliness?

I would have left out Haut-Koenigsbourg if it had not been for the numerous books which Norman Peterkin had given me. As he started making his collection in the late twenties they were mainly written between 1890 and 1920, and so are much more vivid in memory than those written more recently.

As I dipped into Peterkin's books, written either during or just after the German occupation, I realized that the story of the reconstruction of these once superb ruins crystallized everything that the French disliked about the Germans, and particularly in the matter of taste.

Haut-Koenigsbourg, then, was an immense feudal castle-fortress, dominating the entire plain leading down to Châtenois, Sélestat and the Rhine from its circular mountain-top, so craggy and steep that its curious position was the cause of the strange way the place was formerly built. It had several owners during the Middle Ages, until it was given stability and added grandeur by the Counts of Switzerland in the sixteenth century; and it was one of the great castles of the Vosges until it was set on fire by the Swedish armies in 1693. Thus it stayed, a beautiful ruin, and would have remained so had not the Municipality decided that it looked somewhat derelict and cunningly presented it to Kaiser Wilhelm II at the turn of the century. But people did not often pull the wool over those eyes. The Kaiser accepted the castle graciously, and wrote to the Mayor, 'May this present become a new link between myself and the Empire, and may Haut-Koenigsbourg always see at its feet a peaceful countryside and a happy people.' And then he promptly told the Mayor of Sélestat to do the castle up at the town's expense.

Then the desecration started.

One of the best books on the region is *À travers l'Alsace*, by André Hallays, published in 1910. He was in the Vosges in 1903 and saw what Wilhelm II was doing:

> Monsieur Bodo Ebhart was engaged to re-build Haut-Koenigsbourg—an architect with quite a reputation for this type of work.
>
> Not all Germans at the time approved of this scheme of their Emperor, and many complained that a great deal of somebody's money was being wasted in re-building a place which only needed to be restored.
>
> But work goes ahead apace, the workmen multiply. Never have I seen anything quite so puerile as all this vast amount of money being spent to build a theatrical scene. The beauty, the formidable beauty of which I have seen so many superb photographs some years ago, of these ancient dungeons of the Middle Ages; of these towers, of these fortifications—all being destroyed.
>
> Here we are in 1903. An architect who, in all likelihood, is not devoid of talent, is concentrating all his energy and ingenuity to reconstruct a thirteenth-century dungeon and fifteenth-century walls. Masons are re-building turrets so stupidly inaccurately that all

projectiles would go round in curves and decimate those who fired them; carpenters are putting wooden slats on the stone turrets, and painters are painting them black, with possibly some sane object but which, in my ignorance of the rules of fortifications, I am unable to fathom.

PHOTOGRAPHIEREN VERBOTEN is written on the gate to the entrance to Haut-Koenigsbourg. Why this interdiction? Could it be that the restorers of this castle sensed the laughable situation they had created in installing an electric crane on the top of a medieval tower, and wished to hide it from the public eye?

Or could it be that they wanted to stop some 'powerful foreign country' from learning the secret of the turrets and drawbridges of Haut-Koenigsbourg. One can hardly seriously believe in such modesty nor in such prudence and so one is again constrained to ask why *Photographieren verboten*?

More ink, as the *Guide Michelin* truly says, has been spilled over the pros and cons of the Kaiser's rebuilding of Haut-Koenigsbourg than any other similar project, but I for one do not think the place is anything like as ghastly as is made out. One reason is that the site, with its precipitous crags, is most unusual; another is the astonishing panoramic view; and perhaps the most important thing of all is that the reconstruction is now not far off three-quarters of a century old, and has become mellowed by time.

Returning to the Route du Vin, we pass through Scherwiller, Dambach, Blienschwiller, Nothalten, Itterswiller and then Andlau.

This last is a charming, flower-decked little village, famous in former times for its convent. It was founded by Richarde—possibly an English princess—in 887. After her husband, the Emperor Charles the Fat, had accused her—he claimed after ten years of married life that their 'marriage had not been consummated'—of immorality with a bishop, just because she had been observed kissing his cross, he ordered her to prove her innocence by battle or fire, and Richarde, dressed in a white robe which had been soaked in wax, passed through the fire unhurt. But she was still hurt enough by the slur on her to retire for the rest of her life to found the convent at Andlau, of which now only the church remains.

After Andlau comes Mittelbergheim, an attractive little village where the vine flourished in Roman times; then the little town of Barr, famous for its box-calf tanneries and also a very important commercial wine centre, albeit in the less distinguished Bas-Rhin. Barr has a splendid old Town Hall, where there is held annually a pleasant little Wine Fair. Here we must leave the Route again for a little, because here is the firm of Wilm, who as well as being wine-growers have a very thriving business in marketing edible snails.

In the millions of years since the land snail originated it has made its way over the entire world, subdividing into over seventeen thousand species, to be found in rain forests, on the tops of high mountains and buried in scorching deserts, where it can doze off for the incredible time of two to three years.

But the one that interests us here is small and fragile in appearance, the Bourgogne of gustatory fame, *Helix pomatia* in Latin, as distinct from the garden snail, *H. hortensis*, which is edible but not quite so good.

To this gasteropod the two most important things are moisture and young stools of greenery, and come mid-April when the temperature becomes milder and the showers start he awakens and is at his most voracious. He has two pairs of antennae: the upper ones, which can be elongated to up to an inch in length, are topped by eyes, though the snail is very short-sighted; while the lower ones, much shorter, are the organs (and very sensitive they are) of touch.

The snail, a hermaphrodite, reproduces itself twice a year in spring and autumn, and the courtship lasts for several hours. The genital organs are on the right-hand side of the neck, and twelve to sixteen days after they have united the pregnant snail chooses a damp spot at, say, the foot of a tree, digs a hole some two inches deep and there carefully deposits, over a period of ten hours, up to twenty-five eggs. She then abandons the hole and decamps: she has done her work. Three weeks later the eggs hatch into nearly perfect miniature snails, fully able to cope with life, to crawl out of their nest, find shelter and voraciously feed themselves.

Every year the snail grows by about a tenth of an inch, and although the edible ones are usually harvested when two years old they have a lifespan considerably longer than this—indeed, several snail-dealers in France have exhibits of snails with shells nearly as large as tangerines.

M. Wilm has his snailery in one of the most lovely houses in Barr, which also houses his wine-merchant's business, and it was there that I, glad to get out of the gently falling snow, met him to be shown around the works.

SNAILS AND STORKS

The first thing I learnt, and the most surprising, was that although the snails he marketed were indeed the *Helix pomatia*, only an infinitesimally small number of them came from the vine-clad hills of the Côte d'Or—the rest all came from Turkey or Hungary. They are not dispatched from these countries complete: the shells come in one consignment and the meat in another, deep frozen.

'I suppose then,' I said brightly, 'that the chance of a snail finding himself, albeit cooked, back in his own house is about one in a million?'

'No,' replied M. Wilm, in a voice which hinted that he had been asked that one before, 'one in twenty million.'

As I walked round I asked several more questions, but the query which nagged at me most was why snails came from Turkey and Hungary. I went through several reasons in my head: the hotter sun made the snails grow larger, they would grow faster, the greenery in Hungary made them taste better. Another reason, which seemed the most likely, was that the peasants got paid much less for picking them. I waited until there was a lull in our conversation

'And why,' I said, enunciating each word carefully, 'do you get your snails from Hungary and Turkey?'

'Because people there don't like eating snails,' was the terse reply.

Without their shells the snails weigh out at fifty to a kilo. At Wilm's factory they are first washed and cleaned and then cooked under pressure for an hour and a half, which is a better method than boiling as it conserves the juice. Then they go onto one of the most remarkable automatic machines I have ever seen. The cooked snails are put back by women seated at long tables and are placed on aluminium trays studded with little round holes to take the shells—*upside down*. The trays now go onto a moving belt, which, at a certain moment, passes under a row of feeder tubes which drop into each shell a special liquid sauce. The trays, with the snails on them, now continue along the belt which brings them to a freezing-unit, which freezes the mollusc solid; this is so that the juice or sauce cannot come out.

Now the orifice of the snail-shell is well and truly stuffed with the best-quality garlic butter, again by women, then an even fiercer freezing, and the snails tumble into a hopper feeder which most ingeniously wraps and seals them.

Now M. Wilm's gasteropods are ready for the table, and the lucky housewife has nothing more to do than pop them in the oven. This has to be done carefully, however, and the cooked product is extremely perishable, and so they issue a little advice brochure.

How to preserve our Snails

Snails which have been pre-cooked are exceptionally perishable and must be eaten quickly. To keep them for a maximum of three to four days they must be kept *continuously* in the refrigerator and only taken out dozen by dozen, as required.

How to warm our Snails

To heat snails you should use special plates into which you put the shells, and you should place them with the open buttered end uppermost. Then in an oven which has been well warmed in advance you place your plate so that heat derives from both the bottom and the top. You leave the plate in the oven until such time as it becomes impossible to touch the shells with the fingers, but without letting them simmer so that the sauce dries up and the butter burns.

How to eat Snails done the Alsatian way

Place the snails, really hot, on the table, and to enjoy them graciously tip out the liquid *into a soup-spoon*, then extract the snail with the help of a specially made two-pronged fork. Eat with white bread and wash down with a bottle of Wilm's white Alsatian wine, 'Sea and Snail Special'.

There is a slight danger of being badly poisoned by eating snails, in that they can nibble and digest certain plants which, though quite harmless to them, are not so to us. It is therefore advisable, if preparing your own snails, to cause them to fast for a good twenty-four hours. It is also a good idea to use only those where the operculum (the fibrous plate covered with secretion) is closed ready for the winter sleep.

Anyway, having got your gasteropods, you first cut away the above-mentioned operculum and then soak them for two hours in heavily salted water and vinegar. Then you give them a very good rinse over running water and plunge the snails, still in their shells, into boiling water for five minutes to blanch them. Take them out of the water and drain them again over running water. It is now possible to get the snails from their shells, which you do with a tiny two-pronged fork, and then cut away the portion of black flesh called in zoology the *cloaca*.

Place the snails in a stew-pan with just sufficient liquid to cover them: this should be half wine, half water, with a *bouquet garni*, carrots, onions and shallots. Cook very slowly for two to three hours, and then leave them to get quite cold in the juice in which they have been cooked.

As for the shells, these you boil for half an hour in water which has had washing-soda crystals added. Drain and dry well. Finally put the meat back into the shells and seal the entrance with parsley butter.

There are other things which you can put in snail-shells besides the snails themselves. The super-greedy gourmet and practical joker Grimod de la Régnière, author of that great work the *Almanach des Gourmands*, says, 'In the season when it is impossible to obtain snails, it is possible to deceive ourselves in a most agreeable way. Make a *farce* of game or fish, to which are added anchovy fillets and a grated nutmeg, and bind with yolks of egg. Fill into the heated shells and serve.'

But *Escargots à la comtesse Riguidi* are even better. 'Place in the empty cleaned shell a morsel of fried veal. Stuff onto this a *farce* of game, to which have been added cream and chopped truffles. Bung up the end with buttered breadcrumbs. Place the stuffed snail in a snail dish, cook in a hot oven for five minutes, and serve.' I would infinitely prefer this to the real thing.

Back to the Route du Vin. After Barr comes Heiligenstein: its nineteenth-century Town Hall has a statue of Ehretwantz, who introduced the Clevner grape into the region in 1742; outside is a splendid view across the plain, ending with a sight of Strasbourg Cathedral.

Village number forty-five is Bernardswiller, a charming little place at the foot of Mont Sainte-Odile.

Then comes Obernai. Two stars for atmosphere in the *Guide*, and how well deserved!

There are few small towns so satisfying to the tourist who cares for local colour as Obernai, nestling at the foot of Mont Ste-Odile, with its little streets bristling with pointed gables. Many are those who choose the town as a weekend or holiday resort. In any event, the place deserves the compliment of a leisurely tour of inspection, on foot. . . .

Every year, on the second Sunday after the Fourteenth of July, is celebrated the folklore festival of the 'Marriage of Ami Fritz', based on the novel of Erckmann and Chatrian; on the second Sunday of October comes the vintage festival.

Actually, by far the most attractive thing in this attractive town is the market square, with a splendid fountain and statue of the ubiquitous Ste Odile in the centre.

Ottrott is the next place along the road, and its claim to vinous fame is one I strongly disapprove of—namely, that it is here that one of the very rare red wines—the Rouge d'Ottrott—is made. In all my dozen or so books on wine I have fulminated so vociferously against the folly of trying to make a red wine in a district where the soil and grape-varieties are suitable for white that I will only say that the thin, paltry, silly little red wines made in Germany, Switzerland and Alsace should never leave their respective countries, and should only be drunk even on the spot when politeness to a grower who has shown you around his cellars demands that you taste, without making a grimace, what he proffers.

I remember Ottrott, too, for the incident of the snowball. Alice and I had agreed to write down some little incident or unusual thing we saw in each Route du Vin village, and especially those where there was, so to speak, no official thing of interest. Generally there was some trifling thing like a man with a red nose, a girl with extra-long pigtails, a child sucking sweets and, especially, empty nests waiting the spring return of the much-beloved storks. But at Ottrott, cudgel our brains as we might we could think of nothing.

'I'd better just put a blank,' Alice said.

'It looks——' I started, and at that second a huge snowball came crashing against the windscreen.

As for the empty storks' nests, they are rather a sad sight when one realizes how much the peasants like to see them occupied. Why are the storks leaving Alsace, or rather, why are they failing to return? Of the fifty thousand or so nests known to exist in Europe in 1965, only a hundred and twenty were left in Alsace. The ringing of the birds and careful study have shown that the storks are deserting the west and south of Europe and tending to nest in the east and north. This pattern is borne out by the fact that the rate of nest-desertion is greater in the Haut-Rhin than in the Bas-Rhin which, so confusingly, is the northern-most of the two *départements*.

So worried are the inhabitants of Alsace about the diminishing numbers that some official action has been taken: artificial nests have been built and, in villages where the desertion is specially pronounced, empty nests have been re-populated with baby storks brought over from the Nile.

SNAILS AND STORKS

It is in March that they return, with a loud clacking of their beaks, to Europe, the male arriving first to refurbish with twigs, and, more especially, with vine-prunings. Almost circular, the nests are relined every year with earth, and can easily weigh over two hundred and fifty pounds and measure six feet across and up to three feet high. Between three and six eggs are laid in each nest, and the moment the baby storks appear the father works day and night to feed them, on insects, mice, baby lizards and even small snakes, as well as frogs; while mother teaches them to fly. So efficient are both parents that within two months the young can fend for themselves.

Once they have mated, the fidelity of storks is remarkable, and I believe that, as well as the convenience of the nest's being above the chimney, it is this which has led to the bringing-the-baby legend.

There is one story which has been repeated so often that it may have a ring of truth. A pair of storks settled on their usual nest in a little village near Benfeld, and a well known ornithologist said that he wished to have an egg in order to rear a bird. It was suggested that he should take one and that a chicken's egg should be substituted. This was done, and all was well until the birds were hatched. When the father stork saw the baby chick he suspected the mother of infidelity and collected a number of other males who, on seeing the intruder, agreed about the adultery and pecked the poor mother to death.

The storks leave for warmer climates in mid-August and, like the boojum, they steal secretly and silently away. In Alsace they forgather at Ebersheim and Sélestat, also at Strasbourg Cathedral. There are two routes from Europe to the south: the first, used by the Alsatian storks as well as birds from south Holland and West Germany, is over central France, Spain and Gibraltar; while the second, which is much more popular, takes the birds from north Holland, Denmark, Russia and Poland over the Balkans and the Bosphorus.

As for storks in the rest of France, there are none. I know this because, when the Germans ruled Alsace from 1871 to 1918, 'There are no longer storks in France!' was the sad lament. And I have a feeling that the average Frenchman vaguely feels that while these handsome birds still fly over Strasbourg all is well with his country. Rather like the apes in Gibraltar.

The fiftieth stop is Molsheim, a delightful medieval town of some six thousand souls. Its greatest claim to fame is its Metzig, a superb Renaissance edifice put up in 1525 by the Corps of Butchers, who held their official meetings upstairs and had their butchers' shop on the ground floor. What is so lovely about the building is the outside steps leading to the first floor.

But Molsheim to Alice and myself was memorable on account of a meeting, over a coffee and a Gauloise, with the Cassis traveller. He was obviously dying to get into conversation with us for he first jumped up to light my cigarette while I fumbled for a light and then, seeing that the waiter had forgotten Alice's sugar, went up to the counter and got some for her. With this second visit we could not but invite him to our table—an invitation accepted with alacrity.

He was, of all things, a representative of a firm that sold Cassis—that blackcurrant liqueur so popular in Dijon. What had elated him was that he had just heard over the wireless that the Minister of Finance had partially reprieved the blackcurrant crop from a swingeing tax. In a few minutes briefcase and mackintosh were transferred to our table and the story was told.

Between the two world wars the blackcurrant crop (along with other 'small fruits' which had replaced the vine in the poorer wine-producing slopes of the Côte d'Or after the disaster of the phylloxera) had been a most profitable one, and no less than twelve hundred tons had been gathered annually. Came 1940, and a devastating cut in supplies of sugar, and whatever people might pretend, said our new friend, saccharine gave the liqueur a disagreeable taste. This brought production down to four hundred tons in 1945. When sugar supplies became plentiful again output shot up once more; in 1966 thirteen hundred and fifty tons had been gathered, and at this point the Government thought that a tax would be a good thing. But the Burgundians thought otherwise and they put up their case to Parliament, where it was presented by the flamboyant Senator Poujade. The case for not taxing blackcurrant was that Cassis was classified as a hygienic beverage, the fruit being macerated for exactly two months in the most neutral spirit it is possible to obtain. As such, the liqueur is that industrial fruit which is the most rich in Vitamin C (antiscorbutic acid). And they asked Parliament, 'Didn't the Soviet cosmonauts take blackcurrant-juice on their trip?' The fruit, as grown along the Côte d'Or, they explained, is of a far finer quality than anywhere else in the world and 'it is like comparing a Musigny to a Noah', they continued, pointing out that the Noah was a forbidden grape species.

I doubt if Parliament cared two hoots what the Russians took up in their capsule, and I doubt if much Vitamin C is left after the pure alcohol has attacked the juice, but I do think that what would have swayed them was Senator Poujade's last point, namely that if the tax was slapped on serious unemployment would result.'

More coffee arrived, and I was pressed to pour a Cognac into mine.

'My greatest difficulty,' said our new-found friend, 'is to persuade customers to drink their Cassis up while it is fresh, and certainly in its first year of production. The thing about this liqueur is that it is the only one which loses its wonderful perfume as soon as the liquid begins to oxydize. I tell people that you can tell when a Cassis is at its best by looking at the colour, which should be a brilliant red, almost violet, and that when it has turned a russet-brown it is over the hill.'

When the sweetish Cassis is mixed with the dry white Burgundy of the region (one part of the former to four of the latter) it becomes my favourite apéritif of all. It has been called a 'Kir', after Canon Kir, Mayor of Dijon, and to this day the Mayoralty of Dijon takes no less than three casks of fresh Cassis yearly to offer at its official banquets. I reckon then that if each guest gets two glasses of the apéritif they must entertain some ten thousand people a year.

After Molsheim come Avolsheim, Soultz-les-Bains, Traenheim and Westhoffen; then Wangen, a pretty little village, very much occupied with wine both commercially and aesthetically because on the Sunday following 3 July each year is held the *fête de la fontaine*, when wine, flowing freely from the pump, reminds the villagers that until 1827 they had to pay their overlords a tax of three hundred litres of wine yearly.

The fifty-eighth and last wine village is Marlenheim, an attractive little place, but really more known for its excellent restaurants, being an important stopping-place on the main Strasbourg-Nancy road. I have irritating memories of the place because I came across one of those firms which, not satisfied with owning a flourishing business under one name, have notepaper printed and trade under several banners—a practice I despise. In this instance it took me hours to find them, and when I did I had no desire to pay a call.

13

BEER

DEAR Byron, please forgive me.

> Know you the land where the vines and vineyards
>   mingle together with wavering hops?
> Know you a place where the elegant *foie gras* is
>   eaten along with peasant pork chops?
> Where savoury kraut and tart of the onion is heaped
>   on your plate with the Quiche of Lorraine,
> And you drink and you eat till your belly is bursting,
>   and then in the evening you do it again?

What I am trying to convey in this jingle is that Alsace is the only region in France where wine has to fight for social supremacy against superb beer, and the supremely gastronomic *foie gras* does not have it all its own way in competition with terribly plebeian dishes like onion tart or sauerkraut garnished with gobbets of fatty salt-beef and dumplings.

If wine has partially been ousted by beer in the region in this day and age, the growers have only themselves to blame, since there is a wealth of evidence to show that beer-brewing started on account of the high cost of wine.

The right to brew beer was once held exclusively by those who possessed a licence from the municipality to be *brasseurs*, and the fact that this permit was strictly adhered to is shown by a document in the Strasbourg archives, dated 17 November 1642, in which Nicolas Herst and Daniel Tomas 'on account of the high cost of wine' are given permission 'to brew beer together for their private consumption and that of their families, without the *brasseurs* of the community having the right to take any action against them'.

The Strasbourg *brasserie*—the name by which we know those huge cafés today—started by being the waiting-room or service-hatch from which the peasant came to fetch his daily ration of beer. That would have been the very beginning, but quite soon the waiting-room was made more comfortable and the peasant would linger on for a pint or three before going home. It is important to stress that at this period the *brasseur* brewed only for his own brasserie, and there was no question of the beer's being delivered elsewhere in the town, so there must have been hundreds of different brew-ups all with different flavours, all around the town. This would have been about 1700, but this situation was not to last for long, for there had also sprung up a host of smaller, scruffy bars called officially (at that time) *les petits débitants* where—and this is guesswork—a lot of bad beer was sold, to which the big brasseurs took exception, and where a great deal of the city's disorders took place.

These smaller establishments eventually became known as *cabarets bornés*, one-eyed cafés, and in rather a curious way. In order to bring in further taxes to the city's exchequer the magistrates stipulated that places of a fairly high standard, and paying for a licence, could put two lanterns outside their front door, but smaller bars were allowed to display only one.

But whether the peasant drank his beer in an *estaminet*, a *café*, a *cabaret* or a *brasserie*, the big brewers continued to make better and better beer and seem to have felt that what they were doing was almost of national importance; so much so that in March 1860 they persuaded the Mayor of Strasbourg that the workmen they employed should be subjected to some extraordinary—and extraordinarily stiff—working rules. They warned the Municipality that:

> The brewing of beer entails a series of operations which permit of no delay nor adjournment, and since we are subject to a fiscal surveillance where neglect can lead to a heavy fine, it is imperative to formulate certain regulations so that the master brewer has indisputable and efficacious control over employees, but none the less safeguarding the rights and needs of these latter.

One can understand that this broadside would have shaken the Mayor and his Corporation to the roots. They probably had a mental picture of Strasbourg and the surrounding villages as one huge beerless desert. Whatever they thought, the brewers had their way.

REGULATIONS FOR WORK
In the Breweries of Strasbourg

Article I

When after his period of training a worker has been definitely admitted to an Establishment, he cannot leave it unless he has given notice at least a week in advance.

The owners will fulfil the same conditions if they wish to dismiss a workman. They will, however, be allowed to take action in the case of any serious neglect of the present rules.

Article II

There can be neither fixed days nor fixed hours for work. The workman is expected to conform at all times, to carry out orders which are transmitted to him and to carry them out with zeal and precision.

Article III

Workmen may not, without permission, leave the establishment either during or outside working hours.

Article IV

Each workman is responsible for the materials which are entrusted to him, and also for his tools.

Article V

It is forbidden to enter the stables, shops, grain-lofts, oast-houses and other places with a light which has not been placed in a lantern in good condition.

Article VI

No stranger is permitted to be introduced into the establishment by any workman without permission of the proprietor. This also goes for the cellars and outlying buildings.

People with whom workmen are obliged to have contact, such as tailors, cobblers and laundrymen, etcetera, may only contact them on fixed days and then at times fixed by the brewery owner, and only at a place especially set aside for their reception.

Article VII

Every workman who is taken on at the brewery will engage himself to join a Mutual Assurance Society in case of illness, which the Brewery Syndicate guarantees to maintain in the form laid down.

So much for the workmen in the brewery itself, but at the same time the Corporation approved:

RULES FOR THE BRASSERIE CAFÉ
Agreed by the Brewers of the town of Strasbourg

To have worked in a Strasbourg Brasserie is a recommendation everywhere, and especially in the centre of France. *But*—this recommendation will soon lose its efficacy if the tradition of honour, orderliness and activity, which have given brasserie waiters of this town their reputation, is whittled away by slackness. It is not enough just to know one's job: good conduct, sustained work, a love of orderliness, are qualities which are almost as much sought after as knowledge.

It is to guide waiter-workers in this vocation and to keep them on the straight and narrow path that the Master Brewers of Strasbourg have resolved to keep constantly under the eyes of the aforesaid workers a placard listing the duties they are expected to perform over and above those required by law. The faithful accomplishment of these duties will show they are worthy of their position and, above this, they will get an especially warm welcome when they apply for jobs elsewhere.

The Master Brewers agree henceforward to expel all those workers who would fail to adhere to the strict observance of the rules. These persons are false friends and perfidious counsellors who would drag others down so that they end up in abject misery and hospital.

Here, then, are the rules which the Syndicate of Brasseurs has drawn up and approved, and their strict observance is vital.

Article I
No one shall be idle so long as he has an order to execute or the occasion to occupy himself with gainful work.

A workman sent on an errand in the service of his brasserie shall not be sidetracked under any circumstances.

Article II
All work must be accomplished in silence. It is forbidden to sing, cry out or whistle.

Article III
Waiters are to be docile and respectful towards the customer and correct in their attitude towards their comrades. Quarrels are strictly

forbidden. If there is a disagreement it will be referred to the owner or someone competent to make a pronouncement. All discussion on subjects which have nothing to do with the service of beer is forbidden on the premises.

Article IV

Workers, either alone or jointly, may never open an account with a customer without permission of the owner. It is strictly and severely forbidden to become drunk.

Article V

All unnecessary lights must be put out at once.

Article VI

Proprietors will deduct a fine from the salary of workers for any breaches of these rules.

Article VII

Workers who distinguish themselves in their obedience to these above-mentioned rules will be given by their employer brewers a special testimonial which can be produced to future employers.

Alsace being so close to Germany, it is surprising that the hop was first grown there only in the early nineteenth century, extremely recently considering the fame of the beer, although it was quite common in Germany in the fourteenth century, in the Low Countries in the fifteenth and in England in the sixteenth. The main Alsace hop-growing district at the present time is to the north of Strasbourg; the ones I saw did not seem to be anything like as seriously, neatly, intensively and—above all—tidily grown as those in Kent, and as the poles are even higher than those in the Weald and Herefordshire they present a curious, straggling sight.

But it must not be thought that the only good thing that came from Strasbourg was its beer.

With a hundred lakes in the vicinity, and with the Ill flowing through the town and the Rhine close by, fish, from the Middle Ages, was a staple food. More, it was a delicacy: from the fifteenth century onwards Strasbourg innkeepers had a great reputation for serving meals exclusively of fish. True, the habit was helped along as much on account of the Strasbourgeois' extreme fidelity to the ceremonial Friday fish day as because of the abundance of fish, but it must have been pretty tasty, because in 1492 the Corporation slapped a tax of nine kreutzer on the bill for each fish dinner, two kreutzer more than they extracted for an ordinary repast.

The fish which has made the gastronomic name of the region is, of course, the famous Blue Trout of the Vosges. This is *the* fish to go with the regional wine, and furthermore it is cooked *in* the best wine of all, the Riesling. I have the happiest memories of it because it is the perfect dish after a long day's tasting, in that it is nourishing and, so important, easily assimilated. In Alsace they tend to like it with plain melted butter. In Austria, another place where it is a speciality, they have it with *beurre noisette* (burnt butter) and finely chopped toasted almonds. My own creation is better still; burnt butter with even more finely chopped capers, something which should be used much more in the kitchen.

Some Alsatian dishes of the mid nineteenth century were remarkable in their amplitude. I end this chapter with a few notable recipes.

Waffelpasteta: Take 3 quarts of fresh butter, 16 egg-yolks, 16 tablespoonfuls of flour and 16 tablespoonfuls of sour cream. Work up your butter well and then add 1 egg-yolk, 1 tablespoonful of flour and 1 of sour cream, and so forth, taking care to work your paste thoroughly. Now butter a mould with melted butter, place your paste inside and cook for 1½ hours in an oven which should not be too hot. When it is cooked take it from the oven and cut the top part to make a lid; then with a knife dig out a hole in the mould and fill this with hot *foie gras* and *quenelles* of bread and mushrooms.

Kougloupf: This is still very popular in Alsace. Take 1 lb. of flour, 6 oz. of butter and 1 good tablespoonful of Kirsch or prune brandy, a little sugar and 3 whole eggs; work all these together and then add 4 ounces of seedless Málaga raisins and twopence worth of fresh yeast of beer melted with milk (or, better still, with cream). Go on beating the mixture until it begins to rise above the bowl and until it leaves the hand clean, i.e. ceases to be tacky. Now get moulds made of earthenware in the special traditional shape and rub them with fresh melted butter, sprinkle on peeled almonds in the grooves and now fill the mould with your Kougloupf mixture. Cover the moulds with a very hot napkin which will cause the paste to rise. When this takes place put it in a slow oven, take it out after a while and put it back in a hotter oven for 1 hour. Sprinkle with sugar and serve cold.

Boutmouss: This is made from rose-hips, which should be gathered very red and allowed to soften like medlars. When they are soft enough pass them through a hair sieve and then for each 1 lb. of boutmouss you add ¾ lb. of sugar. Cook both together until the mixture bubbles slowly. Now add vanilla and cook again for 15 minutes, stirring all the time. Add angelica and lemon peel, cut in small pieces, if desired.

Eierküchas: Take 1 spoonful of flour, a little salt, 1 spoonful of cream and 1 egg. Work them all together and then place some melted butter in a casserole. When the butter is really hot pour in 1 ladleful of the mixture and wait until it browns on the underneath. Now turn it over and cook it until brown on the other side; serve with rich gravy. Alternatively, if you want your *eierküchas* as a sweet, substitute sugar for the salt and then fill with a gooseberry fool.

Carpe strasbourgeois: Ingredients—a good large fresh carp; flour; parsley, onions, salt, pepper and garlic; olive-oil.

Cook the flour in the oil until it turns golden brown. See that there are no lumps. Add 3 or 4 onions, cut into quarters, to this *roux*, also 7 or 8 cloves of garlic. Now add water and a goodly sized bunch of parsley and allow to simmer for 20 minutes. At the end of this time put in your carp and simmer for another 30 minutes, or until cooked. Take the fish, and reduce the liquid and pass through a sieve. Cut the carp into portions and pour over the sauce. Wait till it gets cold.

Yes, they eat well in the Vosges.

14

FOIE GRAS AND FEYEL

The rue du Dôme at Strasbourg is narrow, smart and, of course, in the shadow of the giant cathedral. Number 27 is a good deal more dignified than other shops in the street, and far more old-fashioned. The huge window is dressed in such a way as forcibly to remind one of Fortnum and Mason at Christmastime, but perhaps at the turn of the century. It is quite full, but contains only one thing—*foie gras*. There are, admittedly, variations on the same theme—*blocs* for two to a dozen, *terrines* for four, six and eight, and larger ones for the gourmet. These are dotted tastefully around the window, but the eye does not dwell upon them for long, since it is distracted by the sight of innumerable china geese of all sizes.

I ascended the steps to the shop with a sense of pleasurable anticipation. My rendezvous was with a M. Hubert Bijon, who had written warmly to me in London, inviting me to see over his factory. The only snag, so far as I was concerned, was that Messrs Foie Gras F. Feyel (founded 1811, Telegrams FEYPÂTÉ) were in a suburb by the name of Schiltigheim, and the way I get lost driving out to suburbs of foreign towns is nobody's business. Still, this was an invitation not to be missed; besides, there might even be a taste of *foie gras* at the end of the conducted tour.

The Monopole-Métropole was the establishment I had selected for my first night in the town, and a remarkably lucky choice it turned out to be. It is one of those hotels with a large Restaurant-Brasserie attached (the food being excellently cooked and not overpriced), which is so very nice when it is sleeting like mad outside; furthermore, although the exterior looks rather old-fashioned, all the bedrooms have been done up in the most modern and comfortable way. The hotel, which is conveniently situated between the *place de la Gare* and the centre of the town, is owned by the genial Léon Siegel, and it was to him that I explained why I wanted directions to Schiltigheim for the morrow. He must have sensed that I did not relish the journey, for he said, 'But why should you motor out there? Feyel have got a shop right in the middle of Strasbourg.' We looked up the address in the phone-book; I noted it on a scrap of paper and set off to the rue du Dôme the next morning.

'Good morning!' I said, doffing my hat to a large, handsome woman who was serving behind the counter.

'Good morning,' she replied affably.

A good beginning, I thought.

'I have come,' I said, and added with emphasis, 'especially from London, to talk to M. Hubert Bijon about *foie gras*.'

And with this I produced with a flourish the warm-hearted letter.

The lady did not take the letter or even attempt to look at it, but without any trace of irritation and with calm authoritarian conviction, said. 'At this moment Monsieur Bijon will be in conference with his senior staff.'

'Maybe,' I said, noting that she had not even looked up to see the clock's time, 'but I am sure Monsieur Bijon will want to see me. Perhaps you can tell him I am here.'

Even more calmly, the lady said, 'After that, Monsieur Bijon makes a tour of the factory.'

'Look,' I said, now quite annoyed, 'if you would just look at this letter you would see that Monsieur Bijon will *want* to see me. Dammit! I have come hundreds of miles just to call on him.'

'Can't you go out to Schiltigheim?' said the woman calmly.

Of course, her utter imperturbability made me more and more furious.

'No, I can't go out to Schiltigheim or any other damned and blasted one-horse heim,' I thundered.

'Monsieur Bijon is a very busy man,' said the woman.

I exploded. 'Well, what in the name of stuffed geese do you think I am? One of the——idle rich?' I tried to look venom, but the woman gave me a sweet smile.

If at that moment a young girl had not come in to make a purchase I think I would have picked up one of those placid china geese and hurled it through the window.

'Six ounces, please,' said the girl. She had a maid's uniform under-neath her coat, so I jumped to the conclusion that she had been sent to get a little *foie gras* for a luncheon, and that Feyel sold it by the slice from a special large block. Well, I thought, watching this being done would at least be something to record after this disastrous meeting. I'll bet that damned woman will give the pretty little maid short measure;

FOIE GRAS AND FEYEL

I was surprised that she hadn't said six ounces was too little.

The woman pulled out a drawer and then, to my surprise, got hold of one of those brass scoops formerly used for serving loose sugar and general cereals in grocers' shops before all was prepacked. She dug into whatever was in the drawer, put a piece of paper on one side of the scales, and out of the scoop cascaded a stream of glittering, light-golden sand. This was deftly wrapped, the maid handed over a very small coin and went out.

'What on earth was that for?' I said. I was too surprised to stand on my dignity any more, and asked the question most deferentially.

'That was special savoury salt which the *foies gras* are cooked in,' said the woman. 'Would you care to see it?' And in anticipation she poured a little on a plate. I wetted my finger and tasted; it was curiously spicy, rather like a gravy-browning cube, only desiccated. It was rather nice.

'It's delicious,' I said, feeling more relaxed now.

'Would you like a little packet to take away? I am sure Monsieur Hubert—you see, I call him by his Christian name, because I have been with the firm for thirty years—won't mind if I give you some.'

'Very kind, I'm sure, but what is this doing in a *foie-gras* shop?' I said.

'Yes, that does surprise people. But, you see, a lot of people cook their own *foie gras* at this time of the year, and they come to us for the savoury salt to do this with. Ours is the best in town: there's ground nutmeg and caraway seed and cinnamon and several other spices all blended in with the salt.'

'But do many people cook their own?' This was news to me. 'I mean apart from the local farmers who have the geese?'

'The farmers never cook their own,' said the lady. 'But yes, quite a number of people do make their own, especially now that such good livers are coming over from Israel.'

'Israel?'

'Yes, they say these are better than our own. After all, it doesn't matter where they come from if they have been fattened properly.'

We were chatting away like Darby and Joan now, and suddenly we both remembered that seconds before all was going so wrong.

'You know,' said the woman, 'I don't think you are such an impossible person as I first thought you.'

'And I think you are very nice,' I said, and added, 'Now!'

My new pal's name was, I soon found, Mme Simone Lotz ('The

surname is most difficult to pronounce, call me Madame Simone') and we were getting on so famously now that I wondered whether if I put my sixty-four-thousand dollar question I would get an answer. This was, 'Where can I go to a farm at which they actually stuff the geese?'

At times I wondered if, in order to protect this Strasbourg industry, all the inhabitants of the town and around had come to an unspoken pact *not* to let visitors see the artificial stuffing. Nothing so crude as 'No, I won't tell you', but the pattern was always the same.

'Hey, Jean!' calls out the man in the café to whom you have put the question, 'Do you know of a farm where they stuff geese still?'

'Well, yes,' says Jean, 'doesn't that old chap outside [unpronounceable Alsatian village] do a few still?'

'How do you get there? Hey, Pierre, how do you get to ——?'

'It's not easy to find. You go [fantastic directions].'

'What's the name of the owner?' you say.

'The name is Smith, but that won't help you very much when you get to —— because there are five Smith brothers and only one does the geese.'

'Never mind. Well, thanks, I think I'll be getting along now. Goodbye.'

You make towards the café door.

'Oh, by the way . . .' says one.

'Yes?'

'It's not much good your setting off for there *now* because by the time you get there it will be pitch dark and all the geese are shut up at dusk till the next morning.'

So I had very little hope when I asked Mme Simone if she could help. Again, a pleasant surprise.

'You go to [unpronounceable village] and call on Père Schultz. He will show you.' I noted it down. 'And when you go there give him my regards.'

I said I would.

'And now perhaps you would like me to phone Monsieur Hubert?'

'But I thought you said he was busy?' I said.

'But I think he will be able to see you.'

'Do you know, I've heard so much from you that I think I'll wait to see him until I come over again. But I suppose you wouldn't have any leaflets on *foie gras*?'

'Ah! That's a coincidence,' said Madame. 'Quite an important work is coming out shortly by a most distinguished gentleman whom I am sure you would like. He is a good friend of Feyel and comes in here a lot. When could you meet him?'

'Hi!' I said. 'I've got to get back to London.'

'Well, if you will give me your address I'll post a copy on to you.' And sure enough, she did!

From a little booklet, 'The Wonderful Story of the Foie Gras of Strasbourg and its Makers', compiled by Marius Veyre, I learned quite a bit about the subject.

Both the Greeks and the Romans used the livers of geese to embellish their savoury dishes, but the first written description of the actual stuffing of the geese is by the Consul Metellus Pius Scipio, father-in-law of Pompey, who in 52 B.C. described how he 'fed figs to geese in semi-darkness'. After that the idea caught on greatly and there are several references to professional goose-fatteners.

In France the making of pâtés and terrines of liver and pork, as well as game, in different shapes and forms, went on all the Middle Ages, but it was not until the reigns of Louis XV and XVI that they really came into their own. Then there were three goose-liver-pâté regions vying with each other for supremacy.

First in chronological order were the *terrines de Nérac,* created in January 1769 by a chef called Taverne in his inn at Nérac, in the south-west. Quickly following on these, the pastrycook Courtois at Périgueux made a pâté which found customers, even then, all over the world.

Finally, around 1780, Jean-Pierre Clause made his first *foie-gras* pâté-in-a-crust at Strasbourg. Actually, although Clause was the creator of this remarkable dish, he might never have conceived it had it not been for the Marquis de Contades, Maréchal de France, who in 1762 was nominated as Governor of Alsace by Louis XV.

On taking over his post Contades at first installed himself in the Military Governor's Palace, which was in the ominously named rue de la Nuée-Bleue, or Street of the Blue Thundercloud, and is now appropriately occupied by the City Police. At this period it is fair to hazard a guess that the Maréchal de Contades was a man who liked good food but had got himself saddled with a bad chef. I say this because, at the end of 1765, Jean-Jacques Rousseau was received by the Governor and recalled that he was 'honoured by the kindness and good wishes of everyone from M. le Maréchal de Contades down to the most menial of the poor'. But he also adds in another letter that he would have stayed on a bit longer 'if the frequent dinners of M. de Contades had not been too fatiguing'.

The Maréchal stuck the Governor's Palace for three years, and then a château came up for sale which seemed to him just the thing. Near Strasbourg there are several islands formed by the Rhine, and one of these, where the soil is extra lush, was found to be particularly suitable for the rearing of geese, and so became called (and still is today) the Île Jars, the Island of Ganders.

Here, only twenty minutes on horseback from the centre of Strasbourg and in the château formerly occupied by the octogenarian Comtesse de Lutzelbourg, the Maréchal de Contades settled down to get away from the hurly-burly of city life, but also to entertain his friends.

How good the first chefs were at the château is not known, but towards the end of 1778 there arrived a young man with quite a reputation. The son of Sébastien Clause, a cask-maker, and Françoise Tancer, Jean-Pierre Clause was born at Dieuze, in Lorraine (now in the *département* of Moselle), on 24 October 1757. He started as a kitchenhand at an inn in Évreux (which has caused some biographers to say, erroneously, that he was a Norman) and then went to Paris with his uncle Dumoulin. But he was doubtless attracted to Strasbourg because he had a brother there, who had started up on his own as a pastrycook. Thither he went, and there he remained until the brother died in September 1778, which was how Jean-Pierre came to join the Maréchal in that same year.

Clause soon became head chef in the Governor's household, but exactly how good he was—or rather, how good the Maréchal thought him—we are not told. Perhaps we may guess that he was good but occasionally lapsed into giving rather humdrum food, because one fateful day de Contades said to him, 'Tomorrow I am entertaining certain people of quality and I do not wish to give them the usual rabbit and noodles and the eternal Alsatian dumplings. I want proper French cooking.'

Jean-Pierre spent a sleepless night, but by the morning he had really thought of something. He made a thick pie-crust in a completely round form, which he stuffed with whole *foies gras*, then added a *farce*, finely chopped veal and lard. He then put a lid on, made of a crust of the same consistency as the main dish, and cooked it in a slow oven; the lard slowly melting and the livers cooking gently to perfection but remaining whole.

This was the dish of which, in his great *Physiologie du Goût*, Brillat-Savarin wrote:

> This Gibraltar of a *foie gras*, the moment it appeared, immediately stopped all conversation in full spate by the over-brimming happiness it caused in all hearts.... Then followed among the guests an overwhelming desire to have more of this wonderful dish, after that came the ecstasy of gourmandizing, ending up with the beatitude of repletion.

That was what Brillat-Savarin wrote, but the Maréchal, being a man of action, called for Clause and congratulated him warmly in front of the guests.

Then followed an extraordinary occurrence, one which shows that even in those leisurely days people always had their eye to the main chance. The very next morning the chef was commanded to make another pâté, and as soon as it was prepared the Maréchal sent one of his gentlemen-at-arms hot-foot to Versailles to present it to Louis XVI. And legend has it that the monarch granted de Contades a gift of land in Picardy and bestowed twenty pistoles upon the chef.

Did the creation of the famous pie go to Jean-Pierre's head? We may surmise that it did, for he did not stay long with de Contades after this incident. In February 1784 he married the widow of a Strasbourg pastrycook, three weeks later he took out the necessary papers to make him a Master-Pâtissier, and from this moment the hot *foie-gras* pie or *pâté en croûte*, which hitherto had only been seen on the Maréchal's table and was known as '*à la Contades*', was given to civilization on a far wider scale.

For forty years more Clause continued to make his speciality, dying in his home in Strasbourg in 1827, at the age of seventy. As for the Maréchal the Marquis de Contades, he was relieved of his post in 1788.

At this point it is necessary to remark that the *pâté-de-foie-gras* dish created by Clause was not as yet exactly as it is today. Down in the deep south-west of France another creative brain in the kingdom of the kitchen was at work.

Nicolas-François Doyen was born in Paris on 18 January 1760, and after an uneventful youth in the capital found himself, around 1785, in Bordeaux, where he soon got a position as chef to M. Leberthon, the First Magistrate of Parliament for the town and the surrounding region.

Came the Revolution, and with it the suppression of parliaments, which meant that Leberthon was obliged to draw in his belt, and so Doyen found himself out of a job. Then providence took a happy hand: Doyen decided, without rhyme or reason, to try to make a living in Strasbourg. He hastened to make the acquaintance of Clause, and of his famous pâté. Having worked so close to the region for several years Doyen had, of course, tried out in his dishes many a time that precious tubercle, the truffle of Périgord. Now he proposed putting the 'black diamond' into Clause's confection, which soon changed its name from *Pâté à la Contades* to become what it still officially is, the *Pâté de foie gras de Strasbourg aux truffes de Périgord'*.

And if the first creation was good, what shall we say of the second? It created a furore! Soon Clause came to realize that he now had far more orders than he could cope with, and, seeing that there was clearly room for another supplier, François Doyen himself set up a rival business. Where he started is not known, but he was certainly successful from the start, for in 1792 he moved to larger premises in the smart rue du Dôme, at number 22. And on a sign outside was the punning trademark of the firm, a placid goose looking at an escutcheon, on which were the words '*Moult Foi*'.

Clause, as I have said, personally supervised the making of his dish for forty years after he started in business; Doyen went one better and did the same for nearly sixty, dying in his eighty-seventh year in 1846; on the assumption that he enjoyed eating what he made, a very good advertisement for fattened goose-livers.

Before the turn of the eighteenth century, and for some six years, these two creators had the field to themselves; but then again, I suppose, the demand exceeded the supply, and in 1803 Philippe-Édouard Artzner started up in a shop in the rue du Miroir and a few years later had built up a useful connection in Paris. At first the pâtés went by the diligence or public stagecoach, but this method of transport was found to be too slow (or too tempting?) and so later they were dispatched by couriers.

Eight years later Jean-Antoine Muller opened up in the rue des Juifs, and this was the firm to get the first Royal Warrant, granted in 1861 by Emperor Napoleon III. The words *The Foie Gras of Napoleon* appear on the firm's jars to this day.

So far, then, only four firms had opened up to supply *pâtés en croûte* in over twenty-five years, and this seems to have been enough to maintain an adequate supply for the demands of the period, for there is no record of another supplier's starting up for a whole sixteen years more.

What I think must have happened is that around 1827 it dawned on a number of small pâtissiers in Strasbourg that the crust paste creation of Clause and Doyen was neither patented nor so difficult to do as had been imagined. From now on hardly a year passed without someone opening: in 1846 there were five newcomers, and at least six in 1860.

It is important that the reader should understand that the *foie gras* we have been discussing was not marketed in the same form as ninety per cent plus of the *foie gras* sold today, which is either in an earthenware terrine or in a tinned block, as distinct from the old pie-crust. Experiments in cooking the livers in earthenware were started in 1850 by Édouard Artzner, who covered them with a layer of butter or lard and after cooking them obtained a conservation period of two to three weeks. This was an innovation of which the older generation would have disapproved, and so what is interesting to note is that the first pottery terrines were moulded to look like a *pâté en croûte*.

By about 1875 this new form of presentation had come into its own, and pottery-manufacturers were vying with each other in producing jars with the most exquisite designs on the outside. They started off, quite naturally, with the inevitable placid goose being tended by a girl with the typical Alsace head-dress in a field. This was followed by pictures of Strasbourg Cathedral, coupled with the arms or shields of the surrounding towns, but soon more ambitious subjects were done, and there were series on the Vosges forests, Obernai, Sainte-Odile, le Markstein, Sélestat and Colmar.

But meanwhile something else was happening which was going to cut down the demand with a vengeance.

François Appert cannot have been all that well known in his time, since details of his life are somewhat contradictory, but he was the inventor of a process which for the first time enabled various foods to be preserved in tins and glass jars. Some biographers say that he was a cook at the court of King Christian IV, later becoming a confectioner in Paris, and that it was from the premises that he took on in that city that he perfected his invention. Others say that he was a chemist born in 1750 in Massy (Seine-et-Oise), working all his life in that town and dying in 1841. The basis of Appert's 'invention' was that all fermentation, and in consequence all decomposition, could only take place when in contact with the air—Pasteur's great theme later on. The other part of his brainchild was to use an *autoclave* (pressure-cooker, which had certainly been used before to boil up other things) for food products.

When François died a son or relation called Chevallier-Appert started to improve on his predecessor's work and to combine this with perfecting a contraption known as a manometer, now called a steam pressure-gauge. Like the autoclave, the manometer was not new, but it was totally inefficient for Chevallier-Appert's work. Till then these gauges could only tell the temperature of whatever was inside the cooker to within some three or four degrees either way; if food was to have all the bacteria killed and also to retain the original flavour the heat measurement would have to be accurate to a half-degree—which was achieved. Chevallier-Appert was pleased with his experiments; he also saw their commercial usefulness, so much so that in 1852 he took out a patent. This was the year in which the vast present-day canning industry can be said to have started; it also greatly helped the export of Strasbourg *foie gras*.

By 1900 I would say that the crust pâté had passed its peak demand, the earthenware terrine was in the ascendant and the tinned terrine well established.

In 1860 was started the firm of Joseph Brendel; a plain Martin set up in 1875, but in spite of the absence of a Christian name he had absorbed the former firm by 1880. Let us look at his list.

First come round crusted pâtés of truffled *foie gras*, which were for six to forty people, the price ranging from seven to fifty francs. Then come earthenware terrines of *foie gras* or game, both with truffles, at the same prices as the pâtés. These are 'in tall form', but next is offered the same in the *forme écuelle* (bowl or porringer), at slightly less. Most expensive of all is the crusted pâté of game with *foie* and truffles, which cost eight francs for five people. Finally, of the serious pâtés, comes one in tins, 'for consumption in summer or hot countries, which will keep *several years*'. These italics are mine; present-day makers and literature seem to hint that a year is about enough.

Messrs Martin ('By Appointment to His Royal Highness the Grand-Duke of Baden') also had a sideline, 'Speciality of sending to the provinces and abroad complete dinners and buffets, for balls and routs.' With this sideline it was clearly advisable to ring the changes on the presentation of *foie gras*, and so Martin offered sausages with truffled *foie gras* at eight francs the kilo, *timbales de foie gras* with a Madeira jelly, truffled turkeys, chickens, pheasants and partridges.

Such was the Strasbourg world of stuffed goose-livers at the turn of the century; the oblong *bloc* had obviously not yet arrived.

Whether they are Emden, Toulouse, Grey-back, Pendle, Roman or Chinese, all geese are of the sub-family Anserium; family Anatidae.*

The goose used to be far more abundant, popular and more of a delicacy than it is today (would this be because it thrives so well on grass and does not need as much corn for fattening as chickens and ducks?), so much so that in Paris the itinerant rôtisseurs served such a quantity of these birds that they became known as *oyers*. They all sold their goods in the same quarter of Paris and eventually one road became called the Street of Geese—the rue aux Oyes. As the years passed people slowly forgot this etymology and so the name became the Street of Bears—rue aux Ours—which it is to this day.

According to several references in English and French, the Strasbourg goose is said to be a variety of the Toulouse goose, but in not one of these works is there any hint or suggestion as to the form in which the two differ. I strongly doubt that there is any difference whatever, and suspect that the *foie-gras* goose was called after Strasbourg for publicity purposes.

The common goose of France is known as the ash-grey or farm goose (*oie cendrée* or *oie de ferme*), and is much smaller than the Toulouse variety, which is built close to the ground and has a loose fold of skin on the belly which provides an excellent space for fattening, a ready-made reservoir for goose-grease. One of the most popular fattening foods is noodles, which produce livers very light in colour, almost a cream, shading to pink.

Incidentally, it is not a hundred per cent certain that the Romans employed forcible feeding. They waited till the bird was dead and then immediately extracted the liver, which was placed, while still warm, in milk. In this way it soaked up a great deal of the liquid and became rich and heavy and most succulent.

* But not a Winchester goose, which was an eighteenth-century name for a prostitute. In the times of popery the Bishops of Winchester licensed in the City of London, along Bankside, eighteen houses to keep prostitutes—hence the name.

15

MORE ABOUT FOIE GRAS

THE season for fattening and killing the Strasbourg geese, and then cooking and conserving *foie gras*, is a short one: though most references say that it lasts from October to the end of March, it would be nearer the truth to say that it runs from mid-November to the end of February.

In view of this, it was most kind of M. Hubert Bijon to pick Alice and me up at our Sofitel Hotel on the last Saturday of the year.

Whether this newly built palatial hotel was put up in Strasbourg because it is the Council of Europe's headquarters I do not know, but for its comfort, the great spaciousness of its entrance foyer, and its charm, this establishment is hard to beat. Its extreme modernity is in a way curiously stimulating, and though to a middle-aged person like me with a very warped sense of humour the gadgets were greatly amusing, there was not one of them which did not in some small way either save time or add to the guests' comfort. At the hall-porter's desk, for example, instead of either waiting till someone took your key from you or leaving it on the top of the desk to clutter the place up, you dropped it down a chute to be sorted out when a quiet moment came. The ordering of one's meal in the bedroom was utterly simple too, even if one did not know a word of the language, for the excellent menu was all done pictorially. As for the lifts, I have never before come across anything so silent and supremely swift. And even the permanent, subdued piped music in the foyer seemed just right.

Hubert Bijon and his pretty young wife arrived punctually at twelve forty-five and although I was not expecting someone uncouth, I had anticipated meeting a man whose *embonpoint* would have advertised the fact that its owner was fond of good goose living.

M. Bijon was half the age I had imagined, very well dressed and so spare I at once formed the impression that such an of-the-earth-earthy thing as a Toulouse goose was the last thing he would be interested in.

Well, I said to myself, good-bye to learning anything connected

MORE ABOUT FOIE GRAS

with *foie gras*. I suppose we shall start lunch with cold consommé. How wrong can you be?

I had already greedily looked up the Strasbourg restaurants in the *Guide Michelin*, and the 'Maison des Tanneurs *dite* Gerwerstub' had enough knives and forks against it to show it was in the near-luxury class, but also it had a 'rustic interior in an old Alsatian house with a pleasant view over the Ill'. It was also in the famous rue du Bain-aux-Plantes, and oddly enough I had been there not ten minutes before the Bijons arrived at the Sofitel. This street in the old quarter of Strasbourg is considered to be, and is, one of the most attractive tourist sights in the region; you can hardly fail to find it, because it is signposted from nearly every street corner of the town. It runs its narrow, curving way along the side of the Ill, and nearly every house is an old, oak-timbered work of art.

Just by the Maison des Tanneurs, one of the loveliest houses of all, the road broadens and there is a gap in the buildings so that one gets a view of the river—a wonderful sight, for little can have changed since the Middle Ages. As I was standing here and wondering what it must have been like in the past I noticed that the thing on which my hand was resting, and which I had thought was a parking-meter, was actually a clever little talking machine, which invited you to put a franc in the slot and hear in French, German, English or Spanish what happened along the banks of the Ill in bygone days. I duly inserted a coin and turned the knob to *English*, mainly hoping to get a giggle from a ghastly translation in a worse accent.

But no, the girl had a most melodious voice, and I listened, fascinated, to the whole story. The main trade carried on along this stretch of the river in the sixteenth century was tanning, and that was why the first-floor windows used to have no frames, since they were always open so that the skins could dry. On the right of where I was standing, said the girl, was the famous Maison des Tanneurs, now an excellent restaurant (good puff!), but if I would look opposite on the other side of the road I would see the wine bar called [unpronounceable]. This name, unfortunately, could not be translated into any language, but what happened was that all the residue from the tanning was trodden down—always by convicts, be it noted—and turned into hard cakes, which were then sold to the poor as fuel. But now, talking about convicts, would I turn my head the other way and look down the river to the left, where I would see a bridge. It formerly had cages underneath in which thieves were put to be ducked in the river; as the water was red-brown from the washing of the skins and had a terrible stench it was a pretty nasty punishment. Still, it was better than being left under just too long and coming up dead, as often happened.

'We are going to the old part of Strasbourg,' said M. Bijon now, as we motored along, 'so you can see it.'

'Then we are going to the Maison des Tanneurs,' said Madame, and she proceeded to give it a good build-up.

Two minutes later, when we drew up at the restaurant, Alice and I were drooling with anticipated hunger.

'Damn!' said the Bijons together.

Some Frenchmen say that the only good legacy the Germans left from their four years of occupation in the Second World War was their scheme for making all restaurants shut for one full day of the week. It is called the *jour de repos* and, to my amazement, all the café-proprietors and restaurateurs I spoke to about it seemed quite pleased with the idea. I am not quite certain how each establishment was allocated its day: but no one seemed to object.

'Aren't you furious at being obliged to shut on Fridays?' I persisted to one quite contented owner. (Friday is pay-day.)

'It doesn't seem to harm the business,' he replied.

'Supposing you had Sunday?' I said.

'I shouldn't worry.'

Of course, customers cannot remember on which day each restaurant is shut, and that is what had happened here.

Five minutes later we were back at the Sofitel; it was rated higher even than the Tanneurs, so I was not too unhappy to miss the ancient rustic interior.

The ease with which Monsieur got us on to *the* subject was charming. Waving aside the vast menu the maître d'hôtel brought us, he said, 'The first course is easy—*foie gras*.'

'Since you have started the subject,' I said, 'tell me, don't you get sick and tired of it at times?'

'Never!' said our host. 'The more I eat, the better do I feel.'

'How did you come into the business?' I said.

'Ah! That's an odd story, and has quite a connection with my fondness for *foie gras*. My father was the sole owner of the business, as was his grandfather. Well, one day he asked me if I would like to go into the business. Now, my father and I had made a pact when I was quite young that we would always speak our minds with the utmost candour, with the result that we got on exceptionally well.

'I had a very good job with prospects when my father made me this offer, so I said to my father I wasn't quite sure.

' "What?" said my father, surprised.

' "I'm not sure, Father," I said, "how much I like *foie gras*."

'Now he was really astonished, and said that he didn't see that that had got much to do with coming into the business.

' "On the contrary, so far as I am concerned, it has everything to do with it. I'll tell you what I'll do," I said, "I will eat your and other firms' *foie gras* for six months hard, and if I find I really enjoy it I shall be proud to join the family firm." '

'And it still never palls?' I said.

'Not a bit. I'm always finding excuses to give *foie-gras* parties at our private house—nothing whatever to do with business.'

Just then the wine-waiter came up with a couple of bottles of Tokay d'Alsace, and another waiter brought some lovely fresh-curled pats of butter.

'For Heaven's sake, take that away!' said Hubert Bijon.

There is a feeling among dedicated *foie-gras* connoisseurs that the delicacy should not be eaten with butter as it takes the palate off the liver. I personally do not agree with this: my face fell, and I even hinted to our host that I thought this was not true, hoping he would agree.

'They are perfectly right,' said Bijon. 'Good butter is so delicious that it does take just that something away from the dish.'

But I still do not agree.

As the meal progressed (and we next had a lovely local Rhine fish in a frothing Champagne sauce), I began to feel I was at last learning something about the subject.

The least-known thing was that there are two sorts of straightforward *foie gras* as we know it, and by this I do not mean the *croûte* and the plain terrine. No: there is a very seasonal *foie gras*, cooked and tinned in the usual way but without the preserving salty spice; it is very delicate (but nothing like so nice, I feel) and its life is only some four weeks, even in a refrigerator.

Perhaps the most interesting thing that our host talked to us about was the ideal size that a liver should have attained before the goose is killed. The point here is that so many books on this subject seem to like to vie with each other in recording just how big a liver can get, and the figure is often put at over two pounds, or ten per cent of the total weight of the bird.

'I suppose a pound is about right,' I interrupted, as Bijon started explaining.

'Incorrect!' said he incisively. 'It should be *une livre et un quart*. *Une livre* is just not enough for all the goodness of the liver to have filled out, and it would remain stringy. If on the other hand the liver grows above a pound and a quarter, then it cannot absorb the fat, and this melts away from it in the cooking, just producing a greasy mess of goose fat.'

This gave me a clue as to how a local Strasbourg dish (and my theory is greatly strengthened by the fact that it is highly seasonal—November to March) has come to be thought of as an exquisite speciality, when in fact it is nothing of the kind. This dish is called *Foie gras frais aux pommes*, and it had been pressed on Alice and me several times. Neither of us liked it, since it consisted of little bits of sour apple fried up with runny goose-fat, and I suspect that it has grown up because factories have not known what to do with the overgrown livers I have described.

With the sweet I let everyone have a little peace from my questioning, but with the coffee I returned to the attack. In reply M. Bijon fished in his pocket and brought out a little leaflet, devised by himself, which gave a great number of answers.

The delicate flavour of
FOIE GRAS
demands that a certain amount of specialized
care be exercised in the service

It is essential to serve it very cold. Those in tins should be refrigerated (but out of the tin) for several hours before serving. Those in earthenware terrines should be placed in the refrigerator after the top metallic cover has been removed.

Foie gras is always served in Strasbourg at the beginning of a meal.*

It is a crime to accompany it with a salad since the acidity kills the unctuosity.

The only decoration should be a clear aspic, preferably of Madeira, or if not of Port.

Even prepared *en brioche*, or *à la financière*, or *en escalope*, *foie gras* should be accompanied by a white wine: Alsatian (preferably Riesling);

---

* A dig at those who would have it at the end. How right he is!

MORE ABOUT FOIE GRAS

Cramant nature;* a great white Burgundy;† or even, if preferred, a Bordeaux of a great year.

All tinned *foie gras*, once opened, should be consumed quickly.

Conservation Times

Fresh Foie Gras
- Terrines .. .. 4 weeks in refrigerator
- Blocks .. .. 20 days in refrigerator

Conserved Foie Gras
- In tins .. .. 2 years
- Hermetically sealed terrines .. .. 1 year

The three hot dishes mentioned in the pamphlet are considered the most important ways of serving this delicacy by most French cookery-books, so much so that some comments on them and perhaps a few recipes would not be out of place.

Foie gras en brioche (hot) is one of the pinnacles of great cuisine, and any reader who proposes to serve it is in for a treat de luxe.

First you must make your *brioche* paste. Take 6 oz. of butter, 1 lb. of flour, 3 large eggs, salt, a veritable pinch of sugar, ½ oz. of extra dry yeast, and a little tepid milk. Make the leaven with a third of the flour, the yeast and the milk, and set it to ferment while the paste is being prepared. Prepare the paste, and keep it fermenting for 8 hours.

Now you must deal with your *foie gras*. First stud the liver with truffles, and then wrap it in slices of bacon and poach it in savoury salt for half an hour.

Now for the cooking. Here comes a tricky problem, for you will need a thing called a timbale mould, which *must* be of a size in proportion to that of the liver. It is a complete waste of an expensive liver to fail to surround it with exactly the right amount of *brioche* mixture, and each time you buy a liver it will almost certainly be of a different size to the last.

Line your timbale mould with a thick layer of *brioche* paste, then put the *foie gras* upright into the mould, which it should almost fill.

---

* A still white wine from one of the best districts of the Champagne vineyards —rarely seen in England.

† The logical extension of this is that M. Bijon does not think an *average* good white Burgundy good enough, which I think is carrying regional chauvinism too far.

Now fill up the mould with the same paste, and surround the top with strong buttered paper, which prevents the paste from running over. Now let it rest for a quarter of an hour, at a temperature of 80° F., to allow the paste to work.

Put a long thin skewer through the mixture from top to bottom; bake in a fairly hot oven until the skewer withdraws quite clean.

The reason for the superlative gourmandise of this recipe is that the fat from the outside of the liver, such of it as there is, melts away into the brioche paste.

Foie gras à la financière is a whole, cooked, truffled *foie gras* served with a rather vulgar garnish, which consists of a brew of cocks' combs, tiny, fluffy dumplings (or *quenelles*), cut mushrooms, olives and sliced truffles.

Foie gras en escalope is an example of how words change in meaning from country to country. I suppose that most people reading the word *escalope* on a menu in a London restaurant would take it to mean a flattened-out piece of veal (or chicken) cooked in any one of a dozen different ways. Indeed, when I started checking up on escalopes in my more classical recipe-books, I looked up veal, firmly expecting that what the Feyel brochure had in mind was indeed fried veal with the *foie gras* placed, spread or dotted on the top in a variety of ways. But no: the sense meant here is the correct one. An escalope is 'any piece of meat or fish cut thin, or slightly flattened out, which is cooked in butter or any other fat'.

There are some dozen classical ways of serving *foie gras* in this manner.

Montrouge involves placing a fried slice on a buttered *croûton* and garnishing with a purée of mushrooms.

Aux raisins is the same as above, but the garnish is cooked peeled and seeded white grapes, which have been sprinkled with a dessert wine called Frontignan.

À la Romaine is the same fried slices of *foie gras* on hot buttered toast, with a Romaine sauce. This was created by the great (but rather heavy-handed to our modern way of thinking) Carème, and modern French cookery-books call it *sauce ancienne*.*

---

* Cut up finely the heart of a stick of celery and put it in a casserole with a good pinch of coriander, a pinch of powdered sugar, a clove of garlic, a little basil, and some bay-laurel and two glasses of Champagne. Simmer till the celery is cooked, and then add two tablespoonfuls of a ragoût of consommé and the same of *sauce espagnole* (a very rich heavy brown sauce which takes about three

Bellevue is a sort of savoury truffle blancmange, with whites of egg as a garnish.

À la Ravignan is an open, round, hot flan of *brioche* paste cut in segments, on which are placed first chicken forcemeat and then *foie gras*, then more chicken forcemeat and more brioche paste on the top. It is then glazed and baked in a hot oven for fifteen minutes. This is not madly expensive, sustaining yet light, and original yet exquisite— I recommend it unreservedly.

À la Talleyrand I do not recommend. Before I give brief details of this recipe, which I wouldn't waste a *foie gras* on trying out, I must explain that it was probably created between 1850 and 1900,[*] which is considered (and I generally wholeheartedly agree) as the Golden Age of cuisine in Britain. But they were not always right, and Escoffier tells us that he recommends with hot *foie gras* an accompanying garnish of macaroni, or spaghetti—what a ghastly thought! *Foie gras à la Talleyrand*, then, is an open, hot cheese-and-macaroni tart with truffled *foie gras* on the top.

À la Périgueux is a remarkably good dish, created, I suspect, by Escoffier. Cut some slices, about 3 oz. in weight, from a raw *foie gras*, season with salt and pepper, dip in beaten egg and roll in finely chopped truffle. Sauté in clarified butter. Before serving, pour over a Madeira sauce flavoured with truffle essence.

When we got outside the Sofitel another, smaller car had materialized, and M. Bijon suggested that we divide up and drive in cortège through Strasbourg to Schiltigheim. This was much nearer than I had expected, and we were there in only a few minutes.

The firm had only recently moved out there, all the conserving having previously been done behind the shop in the rue du Dôme. These new premises were small, well laid out and as bright and clean as a new pin. Alice and I were whisked up to the first floor, where we left our coats in M. Bijon's most spacious, plush Managing Director's office; then down a corridor, and we were in the factory.

Having had my share of visiting food factories I was not expecting to

days to make and has in it every vegetable under the sun, and a generous portion of thyme which comes out terribly strongly in all cooking). Reduce this liquid, and when this has been done add another glass of Champagne and then reduce it again. Then pass the sauce through a cloth sieve under pressure, and add a little butter and lemon-juice.

[*] Talleyrand wouldn't necessarily have had to be alive to have a recipe called after him.

see much going on, but here there was even less activity than usual. There were a number of staff, all in spotlessly clean overalls, a row of gleaming stainless-steel boilers and two or three very small baker's ovens.

Somehow, seeing this factory brought to my mind a conversation I had had with my friend Edgar Bender, of Bender and Cassell, now of turtle- and kangaroo-soup fame. Before the war the firm had been the only British conservers of real *foie gras* (as distinct from the purée, which is seldom good and can be execrable), and Mr Bender recounted how he and his father had been at pains to bring over Strasbourg chefs who really knew the secrets of the trade. This had made my ears prick up; I felt that, at last, I would have something revealed which would unravel the mystique of cooking these over-fattened livers which people—disarmingly, I imagined—had made out to be rather a simple job. So I pressed Mr Bender to spill the beans. His answer surprised me. 'Very little skill is needed in the cooking,' he said, 'but it is essential that the chef should know his livers when they arrive in their raw state. You see, very few terrines of *foie gras*, especially large ones, come from one single liver, so the secret lies in sorting the livers out so that one batch is all of the same colour. Deft fingers are the most important thing of all, for the livers must be so packed that you cannot see the join, and also that when they are cooked the surplus fat does not run into the centre.'

Naturally, all firms who conserve *foies gras* have other tinned and potted sidelines of less expensive things, and looking at the rather barren stainless-steel carving-tables it dawned upon me that this in itself was an excellent unspoken testimony to the success of Feyel's as purveyors of the real thing, for if the place had been littered up with dead geese and giblets it would have meant that they had been obliged to concentrate on more humdrum things.

Just then a man passed us wheeling an aluminium trolley. It was perhaps four feet six to five feet tall, and around two feet square, exactly like those used to push around self-service restaurants for taking away the dirty dishes. It was loaded with tins of *foie gras*.

'Those are the new season's livers,' said M. Bijon. 'The ones that have to be eaten fairly quickly. That is an order for the French railways.'

'They must be worth a tidy penny,' I said. 'What, a couple of hundred pounds?'

M. Bijon took a tin from the trolley and handed it to Alice as a gift.

'One thousand, five hundred pounds.'

'! ! !'

16

ROUGET DE LISLE

Are readers of the *Times Literary Supplement* all kindly people who have trained themselves to give a little of that most valuable thing, time, to others, or have I just been lucky? Often I have written for help in solving knotty problems, and always I have had the most helpful replies. So when I wanted to know a bit more about the man who, in Strasbourg, composed the 'Marseillaise', I pooped off a little letter to the *T.L.S.*, and of all the pleasant letters I had in response the most remarkable was from a man who has since become a friend—Norman Peterkin. He not only wrote to me, but trustingly posted to my home a huge parcel of books on Strasbourg, as well as several lives of the man who, under the most stirring circumstances, composed in one short night the French National Anthem.

On the 10 May 1760 a young, newly married woman left the tiny village of Montaigu to do some shopping on market day at Lons-le-Saunier, in the Franche-Comté (now in the *département* of Jura).

She was very much with child, but we can assume that she felt she could comfortably get back home after she had made her purchases. Things, however, do not always go as planned; her labour pains suddenly came on, and she was obliged to call at the house of a friend at 24, rue du Commerce. One hour later, Claude Joseph Rouget saw the light of day.

Here Rouget stayed until his sixteenth birthday, when he set off to Paris, adding a grandfather's name of Lisle and also the particle of nobility, which was always useful if you were going to take up a military career.

Why his parents sent a somewhat timorous boy, who had already shown a penchant for music, to learn the rudiments of arms is not known, but Rouget spent six years at Saint-Cyr, and in 1782 he was made a second-lieutenant in the Corps of Engineers.

He was clearly not very good at his job; here is his commanding officer's first report on him:

He is only meticulous in his work because there is no other choice, and it seems that he works far less from choice than from necessity. He does his work slowly and clumsily, and, while it is clear he possesses a certain over-all intelligence, he does not transport this into his work. His morals seem good, his general conduct is that of a man more occupied with pleasure than with his duties. He has finesse, and a gay spirit. But he is not all that stable and seems almost incapable of serious reflection. His character is soft, pliable and honest, but with a strong tendency towards rakishness.

Poor Claude Joseph! Still, he survived; but only just. It would appear that this young officer not only did not care for his military career but was also thoroughly lazy.

His next post was at Grenoble. He was sent here, in 1782, because Bonaparte was reputed to be trying to pick a quarrel with the French monarchy, and it had been thought wise to create a sort of eighteenth-century Maginot Line in the region. Shortly he was detailed to Mont-Dauphin, a little town near the Italian border, which, surprisingly, for all its remoteness was a gay little place. So much so that at the end of three years, spent much more in serenading young ladies by lantern-light, attending balls and writing languorous love-sonnets than in attending to the defence fortifications, his commanding officer, de la Rozières, a kind-hearted man, wrote to the Maréchal de Ségur, then Minister of War: 'Without wishing to reproach him with anything definite, I feel I should ask your lordship that while he should not be sent too far away, he should not be under my command in the following year, but be granted a pension.' In fact the poor man was genuinely sorry to see de Lisle go: no one liked gay young people with pleasant manners better than he did, but it just didn't mix with the military discipline he needed at that crucial time. He therefore tried to get rid of this young spark without causing him to be punished too severely. And that was what happened; Rouget received a gratuity, ostensibly for having drawn up the fortification plans for the defence of Mont-Dauphin. He was also transferred to the Château de Joux in his native Franche-Comté, as desolate and barren a spot as can be imagined.

Rouget seemed to manage to 'have fun' wherever he went; this talent was matched, however, by an unfortunate propensity for running up debts. Equally unfortunately he found himself up against a much tougher commanding officer. Aumale, as soon as the creditor called at the mess, complained loudly and bitterly to the young lieutenant, and demanded that he should contact his parents to see if they could settle his debts. Eventually he too was obliged to write to the Minister for War: 'The merits of Lieutenant Rouget de Lisle are very pawky. He is given to loose living, and his captain requests with justification and with insistence that he be removed to another brigade.' That settled things! Rouget was ordered to report to the la Rochelle garrison; a definite come-down. But somehow he managed to wangle out of this and to be granted a holiday. He immediately went to Paris, where he spent the whole of 1790 and part of 1791.

With M. Bailly, his uncle, being the Mayor of Paris, Rouget was at last able to realize his ambition, namely to get 'in' with the gay society of the capital. What he really wanted to do was to make enough money writing lyrics for operettas to be able to give up the army, and as soon as he had got settled down in the city he took along three pieces he had written at Joux to the directors of the Opéra de la Comédie Italienne. Two were turned down, but the third, *Créqui et Clémentine* (later *Bayard en Bresce*), was actually put on—it ran for two nights, and de Lisle's name did not even appear on the hoardings or receive mention by the *courriéristes*, as theatrical critics of the time were called.

But his leave was up, and de Lisle was ordered to report at once to Strasbourg.

Ici
s'élevait l'hôtel
où retentit pour la première fois
la Marseillaise
chantée par Rouget de l'Isle
chez le maire Dietrich
le 26 avril 1792

It is not a very large one, and the stone is an ugly colour, but this modest plaque at 4, place Broglie, now the premises of the Banque de France, certainly recalls some stirring days. As will be seen, its message ('Here stood the house where was heard for the first time the Marseillaise, sung by Rouget de l'Isle, at the home of Mayor Dietrich, on 26 April 1792') is inaccurate in one important particular.

When Rouget arrived in Strasbourg excitement was at fever-pitch. Some days before, the Legislative Assembly had declared war against Austria and Prussia, who had banded together to restore the absolute monarchy. And so, threatened with the same fate as Poland, France, instead of submitting, had answered by a general call to arms. This was on 20 April 1792.

But before we come to the fateful day of the creation of the 'Marseillaise', let us go back a little.

Although his one piece at the Opéra-Comique had been a flop, Rouget had been accepted as a musical collaborator with the Parisian Grétry, one of the most distinguished French musicians of his time, and because of this fact alone had gained a certain amount of fame. But he was also making a minor name for himself as a novelist and—more important—as a poet.

He must have got to Strasbourg some time between May and August 1791, and immediately secured an introduction to a man who—with his whole family—in truth deserves as much credit for the 'Marseillaise' as de Lisle does.

Baron Frédéric de Dietrich, known to history principally as the first constitutional Mayor of Strasbourg, was one of the most charming of figures. A cultivated gentleman and high-minded citizen, he had welcomed the French Revolution, but from a point of view which is overlooked or forgotten these days. Along with the Duc de Liancourt (a great friend of Arthur Young) and many others, he believed in the possible eventual establishment of a constitutional monarchy. And to Dietrich's cost he had trusted the last words of Louis XVI: '*Puisse mon sang cimenter votre bonheur.*' We are jumping well past the time of our story now, but this outlook caused the Baron's once well deserved popularity quickly to wane among the more violent faction at Strasbourg, and ultimately led to his tragic end on the scaffold.

But in 1791 and 1792 the Dietrich salon in place Broglie was the centre of all that was public-spirited and refined in Strasbourg. The Baron possessed a magnificent tenor voice and played the violin, his wife played charmingly on the harpsichord, and there were also two nieces who were accomplished musicians. The Baron also had two sons, Frédéric and Albert, both in the army. The elder was the head of a battalion of volunteers called '*Les Enfants de la Patrie*'.

An important day in these turbulent times was the fête of the promulgation of the constitution, celebrated on 25 September. For the parade of 1791 the Mayor of Strasbourg had asked de Lisle if he would write something. The lieutenant therefore retouched and brought up to date his 'Hymn to Liberty', which he had written at the beginning of the Revolution. On the day, it was sung in the place des Armes (now place Broglie), accompanied by a full orchestra and chorus, in front of all the dignitaries of the town and the crack battalions. Mayor Dietrich was very proud of his young friend as the hymn was a great success.

After this, as the weeks passed, de Lisle seems to have gone more and more to musical evenings and dinners in the place Broglie. Then came a blow: he was ordered to go to Neuf-Brisach and to report there on 1 May 1792. He was now, incidentally, a captain (nominated 25 February), but still not a very good soldier ('he could become a good officer when common sense has made him fully mature'), and his promotion seems to have been due almost entirely to the fact that 'posts had to be filled when others went off to the Front'.

Some biographers of Rouget say that when it was known that he was to be posted the Dietrichs planned to give him a farewell dinner; others, that it was just a dinner-party at which he was present. It does not much matter, but if it was because the young officer was going away one cannot but be fascinated at the way the speed of transport has changed in those hundred-and-eighty-odd years; why, with a fast car I wouldn't mind going from Strasbourg to Neuf-Brisach for lunch, returning, and going back for dinner.

War was declared in Paris on 20 April, and the news reached Strasbourg and became publicly known on the night of 24 April.

What happened in Strasbourg on the morning of 25 April is well documented. In fact, there is only one small piece of conjecture necessary: did the infantry captain definitely read, and on *that* morning, an inflammatory recruiting poster which was on all the walls of Strasbourg?

> To Arms, Citizens! The standard of war has been unfurled. The signal has been sounded. To Arms! We must fight, conquer or die. To Arms, Citizens! If we persist in wanting to be free, then all the other powers in Europe will see their sinister plots fail. Let them tremble, these crowned despots! The blaze of Liberty will shine radiantly for all men; hurry towards Victory, scatter the armies of the despots. Let us March! Let us be free down to our last breath, and see to it that your vows are always for the well-being of your Country and for the happiness of all the human race!

One author of a very factual book, written some sixty years ago, on de Lisle, has allowed himself a little conjecture concerning this eventful morning, but as the newly appointed captain had in fact got a small apartment in the rue de la Mésange in the centre of the town it is most likely, in view of the striking similarity between the poster's wording and that of the French National Anthem, that the following, or something like it, really did happen:

In those days one was very far from being able to disseminate news as efficiently as today, and it was necessary to get very close to walls on which [official] posters were displayed in order to read any proclamations, which were then printed in type which would now seem minute. Rouget de Lisle used his elbows to good effect and by a coincidence found himself standing beside the very Ignace Picyel, Master of Music to Strasbourg Cathedral, who had collaborated with him in his 'Hymn to Liberty'. They exchanged greetings and then were making some optimistic comments to the bystanders, when suddenly there was heard a tremendous roll of drums which sent everyone hurrying to the place d'Armes. Here a military parade was beginning to take place. Soon the music got louder, rising to a terrific crescendo, which started the now huge crowd of bystanders singing 'Ça ira!', the popular marching song of the time.

Suddenly the music stopped and all the soldiers stood to attention. This made the crowd silent and also curious; they looked around and suddenly saw Mayor Frédéric Dietrich, riding into the centre of the square with a paper in his hand. In a loud voice he now officially announced the declaration of war.

Rouget de Lisle, who had watched this emotional manifestation, now walked back to look at the poster and re-read those inflammatory words: 'To Arms, Citizens!' He also thought of his friend in the battalion of the Enfants de la Patrie.

He looked up at the huge spire of Strasbourg Cathedral rising into the Alsatian sky. A rhythm came into his head, and at that moment he conceived the first words of the immortal hymn he was going to compose:

Allons, enfants de la Patrie!
Le jour de Gloire est arrivé!

That evening de Lisle made his way to the Dietrichs' salon and found a very military gathering assembled. There was General Desaix, who had renounced his title of nobility and was to be the hero of Marengo. Also present was General Victor de Broglie, later to give his name to the very square they were in.

There are several versions of the early events of the evening. One says that several *chopes* (glasses) of beer were downed before dinner started, while another, by Miss Matilda Betham-Edwards, says that 'Champagne circulated freely'. There were, it seems, only three ladies present, Mme Dietrich and the two nieces, so it is not surprising that the conversation turned almost entirely on matters military. It was the practice in those days for the ladies to remain at the table with the men to the last, and so it is quite likely that Mme Dietrich, tired of hearing so much martial talk, suggested a change of subject.

This brought the conversation round to the question of patriotic songs, and what Dietrich said next has been remembered word for word.*

> What I think is such a pity is that our soldiers have not got their very own song which they can sing when they advance on the enemy. All they know is that 'Ça ira!', which is nothing more than a dreary quadrille or country folk-dance tune and incapable of arousing fervour. Do you know, my friends, of an idea I have had?
>
> Well, it is to open a competition for a battle hymn which we will call 'Le Chant de guerre de l'armée du Rhin', and the first thing I shall do tomorrow is to get busy with it.

Everyone thought this excellent, and loudly applauded their host's idea. But the Mayor became somewhat pensive, and turning to Rouget:

> But you, Monsieur de Lisle [said the Baron with charming persuasiveness], you who are the cherished Darling of the Muses, you who speak the language of those on Mount Olympus and who play Orpheus' harp, why don't you turn your lyre to these thoughts? Find us a stirring tune for our soldier-people which will rouse them when danger is imminent. Do this and you will receive the thanks of the Nation.

At first Rouget demurred, but there is no doubt that it was a very convivial evening and doubtless his comrades pressed him—perhaps a little extra out of politeness to their host—to do what was suggested.

'All right,' he said at last. 'I'll do my best.'

Loud applause greeted this announcement; more bottles of Champagne—and Alsace wines, say some biographers—were opened and

---

* Probably by Rouget de Lisle himself when reminiscing about the evening in later life.

the grand clock of the cathedral was striking one as Rouget walked home to his lodging in the rue de la Mésange. As he walked back both the words and music came into his head. Back at his lodgings he feverishly jotted down the words, then got out his violin and played to himself the air. Dawn was breaking when he finished and he flopped, quite exhausted, onto his bed and slept.

When he woke he still felt he had got something worth while but, not absolutely certain, he took his rough notes to a great friend, Lieutenant Marclet, who said it was first rate and suggested he took it straight to Baron de Dietrich. The Mayor was in his garden at the time; he took a look at the papers and said, 'From what I can make of it, you have written either something perfect or something very bad. Let us go inside to the music-room.'

Dietrich called his wife and his two nieces to him, and one of the girls sat herself down at the harpsichord, while the composer gave her one or two instructions on how to play the music. Dietrich listened with great attention. Then he turned to his wife and said, 'Listen, my dear, write this very moment to all our friends who were with us last night and ask them to come and have dinner with us this evening. Tell them I have something of some importance to impart to them, but don't say anything else.'

So there was Rouget again, only twenty-four hours later, at what is now 4, place Broglie, and there were all the same guests, again drinking Champagne but this time continuously asking their host what it was all about.

The Baron did a Brer Rabbit on them. When the meal was over Dietrich asked his wife to seat herself at the harpsichord and he stood beside her. Then with his magnificent tenor voice he sang for the first time those words which were soon to go all over Europe and then the world, and become the hymn of liberty:

> *Allons, enfants de la Patrie!*
> *Le jour de Gloire est arrivé!*
> *Contre nous de la tyrannie . . .*

The guests were deathly silent, spellbound.

> *Aux armes, citoyens!*
> *Formez vos bataillons!*
> *Marchons,*
> *Marchons . . .*

Then pandemonium broke loose: it is recalled that several tough soldier guests had tears in their eyes as they stood up and put their arms around their next-door neighbours. 'Le Chant de guerre de l'armée du Rhin' was sung there and then again and again, and everyone joined in.

Claude Joseph Rouget de Lisle was congratulated in such a sincere and warm way that, while obviously terribly pleased, he was visibly moved.

On the very next Sunday the new hymn had its first public hearing. This was at the time fixed for playing of martial music by the band of the National Guard of Strasbourg (always an exceptionally military garrison-town, but at this period even more so). They were instructed to play the new tune, and were just about to strike up when an announcement was made that an eight-hundred-strong battalion of volunteers of the Saône-et-Loire was waiting to make its formal entry march into the town before proceeding later to the frontier. It was these soldiers who heard the hymn, or rather marched to it, for the first time. The rhythm was startlingly and strangely suitable for marching; here it has been recalled that the men straightened themselves up, held their muskets straighter and quickened their pace. A few seconds later, when they had been called to the halt, an old sweat made the comment that history has never forgotten: 'What ever is this devil of an air? Here is a strapping tune which knows how to command us. *Il y a des moustaches!*'

Though there is the aforementioned plaque to de Lisle, the tragedy is that nothing was done to perpetuate the memory of Baron Dietrich and his wife. For let us be clear on one point: these two had a great hand in the whole affair. Rouget, though he almost certainly wrote the tune, had no idea of orchestration. As soon as the tune got around Strasbourg all the friends of the Mayor and Rouget de Lisle were bombarded with requests for copies of the composition, and Mme Dietrich, who seems to have had considerable experience in musical techniques, had set to and fully orchestrated the work. We know this because of the famous letter she wrote to her brother, Ochs, who was the Chancellor of Basle.

Dear brother, This is to write and tell you that for the last few days I have done nothing save copy and transcribe music, an occupation which I like and which takes my mind off things; especially at this juncture, when no one talks of anything but politics and suchlike.

As you must know, we are always inviting a great number of people to the house, and in order to change the eternal subject my husband suggested that a song to suit the occasion be composed.

A Captain of the Engineers, a most pleasant poet called Rouget de Lisle, speedily did the music of a real war song. My husband, who has a good tenor voice, sang part of the song, which is quite haunting and somewhat original. It is in the style of Gluck at his best, but more lively and sharply defined. I, for my part, have used my knowledge of orchestration to some use and arranged the keys for the harpsichord and for other instruments. The piece was played at our home to the great satisfaction of our guests.

This letter caused the artist David to paint a picture based on its contents. Like the plaque at 4, place Broglie, it contains one error of fact: de Lisle is shown doing the declaiming, whereas on this occasion it was the Baron who sang.

Poor Dietrich! And what a fantastic ironical twist of fate. Because of his zeal and patriotism he was eventually sent to the guillotine, and it is almost certain that the very song he had had such a large hand in launching was played at his death.

There was another terrible tragedy for de Lisle personally in connection with his song. He was very fond of his uncle Bailly, the Mayor of Paris, who had been so kind to him when he had been in the city. Bailly too went to the guillotine, and writing several years after the worst days of the Revolution, a journalist was to say, 'Ah, de Lisle! You so loved your uncle! Well, those cruel beasts, while you were imprisoned, sang *your* song as a sign of happiness as they dragged him to the scaffold.'

Yes, indeed, de Lisle was imprisoned. In August, with the King chased from the Tuileries, the entire army was invited to sign an Act of Fidelity to the new régime: 'Will you agree simply and solely to submit to the decrees issued by the National Assembly: Yes or No?' Rouget de Lisle replied 'No' with all his heart. Why? Why? He was not of the nobility, and he had no attachments to the Ancien Régime. The answer generally accepted is that he was a sentimental and undecided person. De Lisle left the army, went to Paris; the rigours of the revolution got worse and he was for a short while arrested as a general suspect.

As for the song itself, it is little exaggeration to say that so devastating was its effect that it was not unlike one side having tanks and the other being without them.

There are many factual stories to substantiate this. One incident is recalled by that prolific writer Jules Michelet, in his *Histoire de la Révolution Française*. It happened when the Palais des Tuileries was given up to pillage on 10 August 1792:

> One of the assailants, M. Singier, who has since become well known and respected as a theatrical director, has recounted how on entering the Queen's sitting-room he saw the crowds breaking the furniture and throwing it out of the window. He espied a magnificent harpsichord on which were some magnificent paintings. The crowd were about to subject this to the same fate; M. Singier did not lose time; he seated himself down to play the 'Marseillaise', and to sing it. Suddenly, all these men, grimed and bloodstained, started to join in the chorus and then to dance quietly around the clavecin.

Much has been read into this incident; it has been suggested that the reason this infuriated mob was quietened by this hymn was that they realized for the first time that here was not just another music-hall song but the future National Anthem of France.

This occurrence was freakish in that all the other memoirs of the 'Marseillaise' are accounts of how it drove the soldiers to victory. That fiery military adventurer Charles Dumouriez, later Minister of War for the Girondins, who eventually gave himself an army to fight the Austrians, issued an order of the day: *Close your ranks, lower your bayonets, sing the 'Marseillaise' and you will conquer!* But the most telling tribute of all is from a Prussian officer who, having soldiered in the winter campaign of 1792, wrote in his memoirs: 'The French, who had come up close to us several hours ago, confronted their enemy in repeatedly singing that terrible song of the Marseilles battalions. To describe the effect of this hymn sung by thousands of voices is humanly impossible.'

It will be noted that in these memoirs the hymn is still not called the 'Marseillaise'. The way in which it got this name is interesting.

A large number of copies of the tune and words had been made in Strasbourg, whence they had been sent all over France. One went to Marseilles, where it had an even greater success than elsewhere. Now, it happened that the Legislative Assembly had ordered the formation of a camp of twenty thousand men to be stationed at Paris. Battalions of volunteers had been raised in all parts of France, and soon started to converge on Paris. One such was a contingent from Marseilles who entered Paris singing Rouget de Lisle's song. This was the first time it was heard in the capital; it was quickly adopted by the Parisians, who christened it the 'Marseillaise'.

And the final irony is that Claude Joseph Rouget de Lisle, then thirty-two years of age, was actually in Paris at this time and had no idea whatsoever that his composition had got there. This was one of the many times he was in disgrace with the authorities, and so he had to lie very doggo. Going out one evening, though, he was surprised to hear some youths playing at soldiers and singing his song.

He could not forbear to approach them.

'What are you singing?' he asked.

'The "Marseillaise",' they replied.

'The "Marseillaise"? But this tune comes from Strasbourg.'

'No, sir,' they replied, 'the Marseilles battalion brought it to Paris, where it was sung for the first time.'

17

THE PRESENCE OF STRASBOURG

DOMINATED by its pink sandstone Gothic cathedral, which, in spite of apparently missing a spire, is of great if severe beauty, Strasbourg is one of the pleasantest towns in which to stay in all France. And, let's face it, this may well be because it is half German.

This time Alice and I put up at a hotel which goes by the curious name of the Maison Rouge, an enormous, very old-fashioned luxury hotel which overlooks Strasbourg's main square, the place Kléber.*
I love ancient de luxe hotels, and the older they are the more I love them. If they have kept up their standards of service as has the Maison Rouge, they are ideal.

Alice and I were shown into two single rooms overlooking the square, in which a soccer team could easily have bivouacked. All the fittings were in keeping, too, and the wash-basin in my room was of such ample proportions that you could have bathed a St Bernard in it. That evening we were to dine as guests of the Maison Kammerzell, an establishment which deserves a special description. It lies under the shadow of the enormous cathedral; the ground floor was built as early as the middle of the fifteenth century, while the upper floors date from the end of the sixteenth. The place has been restored with consummate taste, and between the old criss-cross beams of the whole outside of the building are the gayest collection of frescoes you can imagine.

Our 'invitation' was not of the usual type: it was over three months old, and I was by no means certain it was still on, for the only proof that I was invited was an illegible signature scrawled on a menu, which I had obtained under rather strained circumstances.

I had dined there some while before, and while I had eaten excellently I had found the Riesling—probably because I had been imbibing it at growers' cellars for the past six hours—very poor. And I said so in no

---

* One of the great generals of the revolutionary era, Kléber was born in the town in 1753 and assassinated in Cairo in 1800. He it was who said to the English Admiral Keith, when asked to surrender, 'Soldiers only reply to such insolencies by victory; prepare, sir, to fight!'

uncertain terms. In fact, I am ashamed to say I was quite rude.

The waiter, visibly taken aback, went away and came back with a tiny little man whom I took to be the manager. I repeated my complaint. The little man in turn went away and came back with one of the largest men I have ever seen. Oh, my giddy aunt! I thought. I hope the pavement isn't too bumpy. The man sat down at my table, and immediately a cup of black coffee was placed in front of him.

For seconds, which seemed like hours, silence reigned.

That's what I should be drinking, I thought. Perhaps that is a hint. Oh, well, I suppose I deserve it, even his spinning it out. Anyway, I've never been chucked out of a restaurant before, so I suppose it is experience. I wonder if I will fall on my proverbial ear.

'I hear you don't think much of our Riesling,' said the giant. His tone was neither heavy with sarcasm nor menacing. Was I being given a chance to recant? I weighed up the alternatives: a bruised face against saying that a wine I honestly disliked was good. No! I was darned if I would tell a lie on this sacred subject. Still, there was a glimmer of hope.

'You see,' I said, 'I am a student of wine and very fond of it, and I have been tasting fine Rieslings all day . . .' I paused and looked at the giant. There was certainly no murder in his eyes. He continued to sip his coffee; a waiter hovered at his side with a coffee-pot, waiting to pour out another cup. '. . . and your Riesling just wasn't true to type, and I'm afraid I said so rather forcefully.'

'Did you try our Traminer?'

'No.'

'Bring the gentleman a glass of Traminer,' said the giant.

It arrived in a twinkling and I sipped it critically.

'Hardly any Traminer nose,' I said; 'quite clean otherwise.'

'Well, I'm very grateful,' said the giant. 'You see, I suffer from a fairly severe liver complaint and am totally forbidden any form of alcohol. Can I open you a bottle of Champagne?'

'No, thank you,' I said, feeling I'd had enough for one day. 'But I tell you what I'll do. I'd like my daughter Alice to see your place, and you can invite us to dinner when I come back in December.'

'All right,' said the giant.

'Ah, but you might forget,' I said, and had the inspiration to seize hold of one of the excellent menus (day of rest, Monday; annual holiday, 15 January to 15 February) and ask him to sign it as an earnest.

So now here I was, and I must confess to feeling a little uncertain of my welcome. But no; they remembered perfectly, dinner was on the house, I congratulated myself, and then the main course came—it was our old enemy, *Foie gras frais aux pommes*. There was no escape. It seemed a little unfair on Alice.

When we left the restaurant it was gently snowing outside, but this by no means deterred the crowds who were beginning to throng the streets, all making for the place Kléber. For tonight was New Year's Eve, the day on which, shortly before midnight, I came into the world. We walked around the great cathedral, which was floodlit, but one could hardly say the scene was peaceful: for the past two hours the noise of jumping-jacks and fire-crackers had been deafening. And now, as it got near to twelve, it got very much worse, and so we decided, especially as the snow was falling thickly, that we would get back to the hotel and watch the festivities from our balconies.

Now, the Maison Rouge proclaims its distinguished existence by a huge and appropriately brilliant red neon sign on its enormous façade which gives onto the place Kléber. This sign was placed between our two bedrooms and above them, and so it was that, accompanied by the terrific din of hundreds and hundreds of thunderflashes, we saw the New Year ushered in with an unforgettable sight—bright red snow descending from the skies.

The following day we planned to make a culture one, but Alice had firmly hinted that she wanted a break to get herself ready for a reception Geoffrey de Freitas had asked us to. We had met in London only a few weeks previously, when I had asked him to lunch with me after I had seen that we had had letters side by side in the *Sunday Telegraph*, his refuting an allegation in connection with his presidency of the Assembly of the Council of Europe, and mine stating that I thought that 'the recipes of the Ministry of Food during the war were not only brilliant invention, but saved food which had to come from abroad, and were above all polished, professional and gastronomic'. (I went on to say that we were now living in such an era of prosperity that the present-day British housewife had lost all her wartime techniques because she imagined that heaving chunks of butter over badly cooked vegetables was as good as taking proper trouble.)

'As you aren't going to look at museums,' I said, 'you can do one chore for me. Go into a delicatessen shop and see how many different types of sausage you can rout out. We'll meet outside the cathedral to see the clock at twenty-five past twelve.'

'I thought it did its stuff at midday,' said Alice.

'Yes,' I replied, 'but it runs half an hour slow.'

Strasbourg has seen more strife than any other town in Western Europe. In Julius Caesar's time it was called Argentoratum, but it grew and grew, mainly because it stood at a crossroads for all the peoples of the Rhineland, and so it was christened *Strateburgum*, the Town of the Roads. Only once did this warlike city gain a reputation for peace: in 842, when two sons of Louis le Débonnaire, Louis and Charles, signed a peace pact known to future generations as the Oath of Strasbourg. It was a very minor treaty and would soon have been forgotten save for one thing: it was the first official document written in both the Romanesque and the Teutonic languages.

Walking towards the museums, I went across the place Gutenberg, a charming little square. Gutenberg was born in Mainz in 1400, but fled for political reasons to establish himself in Strasbourg sometime around 1433. In 1436, with three associates, he formed what I suppose would now be called a limited-liability company to try out certain 'secret processes', of which Gutenberg was acknowledged to be the inventor. But Gutenberg seems to have been a bit of a firebrand for he soon brought an action against them, where he talked vaguely of presses and lead. In 1444 he returned to Mainz, where he perfected his great invention.

After this Strasbourg remained, probably without caring too much about it, without any great men for three hundred and fifty years, until in 1770 Goethe, as a young student, came on the scene. He stayed in a family *pension* run by two elderly spinsters, but the place was none the less open house for a number of bright young things of the town, and Goethe, himself a beer-drinker, was staggered by their vast wine-imbibing capacities. Goethe found the cathedral useful to him too, and for an extraordinary reason. He suffered terribly from vertigo but he also had a will of iron and so, regularly twice a week, he would, holding like mad to the balustrade, climb to the top of the lofty spire and force himself to look down.

That cathedral! How it dominates the city—probably more, with the exception of Chartres, than any other cathedral in France.

Its beauty has struck many great people, but perhaps the most enthusiastic description comes from Victor Hugo, who visited the region in 1830 in connection with his great book *Le Rhin*:

THE PRESENCE OF STRASBOURG

Suddenly the road made a turn and at the same time the fog lifted and I saw the Munster.* The enormous cathedral with a spire the tallest ever built by man save the pyramids, was set against a background of sombre mountains and looked magnificent, especially as the sun bathed here there and everywhere the undulating valleys. A work of God made for man, and the work of man made for God, the mountains and the cathedral were equal in a struggle for grandeur.

Never have I seen anything more imposing....

Yesterday I visited the cathedral. The Munster is in truth a marvel. The principal doors of the church are very beautiful especially the Romanesque one. On the façade there are three magnificent figures of men on horseback; the rose window is noble and well sculptured and all the façade of the cathedral is a poem sagely composed. But the true triumph of this cathedral is the spire, with its crown and its cross it is a veritable tiara in stone. It is a prodigy of giganticness and delicacy. I have seen Chartres, I have seen Antwerp; all that was needed to see the greatest was Strasbourg.

Victor Hugo, a forthright and rude man, spends a lot of time in the cathedral, so much so that he is several times accosted by sightseers and others:

At the most profound moment of my reverie I was interrupted by an Englishman who started asking questions concerning the Affair of the Pearl Necklace and about Madame de la Motte and expecting to see in the cathedral the tomb of the Cardinal.† Anywhere else I should have burst out laughing, but on reflection I should have been wrong. All of us have our corners of tremendous ignorance.

To return to my cathedral. In an alcove on the right is a chapel

---

* An attractive name for the cathedral—we have *Minster* for a church of considerable size.

† Handsome, profligate and immoral, Louis de Rohan comes to believe that if he can only give a fabulous pearl necklace to Queen Marie-Thérèse he will get into her good books. He buys it on credit but his mistress, Mme Jeanne de la Motte, takes the real necklace and then the creditors start demanding their money. Scandal all round. De la Motte is publicly whipped and de Rohan, exiled, eventually dies at Ettenheim in 1803—was that the reason Victor Hugo thought the Englishman's question so stupid?

obscured by a scaffolding so I was unable to see it. Beside this chapel is a fifteenth-century balustrade fixed to the wall. A sculpted and painted figure can be seen leaning against this balustrade, and it seems to be admiring a pillar which is surrounded by statues and is indeed a marvellous sight. Tradition has it that this figure represents the first architect of the Munster, Erwyn de Steinbach.

Statues talk to me and tell me a lot; furthermore I have always got an insatiable desire to ask them questions, and when I find one I like I stay in front of it for ages. So when I came face to face with the great Erwyn I stood there, profoundly pensive, a good hour until some damn fool came to disturb me. It was the church porter (guide) who, for thirty centimes, offered to tell me all about the cathedral. Can you imagine?! Some ghastly guide speaking half-Alsatian and half-German offering me his *Explications*: 'Sere 'ave yew seened ze chawpel?'* You can be assured that I sent this jabberer away with a flea in his ear.

Having calmed himself, no doubt, with this outburst, Victor Hugo feels restored enough to climb up the tower, which he describes equally vividly:

You know of my predilection for perpendicular travel. I would have been unwise to fail to leave out the tallest spire in the world. The Munster of Strasbourg is nearly five hundred feet tall, and is of the type which is reached by a very open-to-the-light-of-day stairway and it is wonderful to be able to walk about this colossal mass of stone at all points penetrated by air and light, a lantern and a pyramid which vibrates and trembles with every gust of wind. I met on ascending a visitor who was coming down; he was as pale as death, trembling like a leaf and half being carried by his guide. There is however no danger whatsoever.

The danger probably starts where I stopped, that is when the true spire of the cathedral starts. Four completely open spiral staircases lean against the stone-work, and they get smaller and smaller as you mount, so much so that the uppermost ones are barely larger than a foot-print. There is no hand-rail or if there is, there is so little of it as to be hardly worth talking about. This entry is shut by an iron

---

* This is as near as I can get to Victor Hugo's, 'Monsir, fous afre pas fu le champelle?'

THE PRESENCE OF STRASBOURG

grille and it is only opened by special permission of the Mayor of Strasbourg and even then you are only allowed up if accompanied by two workmen who tie a cord round you and attach it to iron rings and continue this operation until you get to the top. A week ago three women, German women, a mother and two daughters, did in fact do this ascent. Further up still, that is up to the lantern, there are not even steps, only iron rungs.

Victor Hugo twice says that this spire is the highest in the world, but he is wrong, for the *Michelin Green Guide* tells us that the height from the ground is a hundred and forty-two metres, nine metres less than the cast-iron spire of Rouen 'which is the tallest in France', and for accuracy my money is on them.

The spiral staircase is still just as much closed to the public as it was a hundred and forty years ago, and I doubt if the Mayor would now have the time to give special permission.

There is, incidentally, a curious and mysterious legend that there is a huge pond under Strasbourg Cathedral. 'When there is deadly silence in the streets outside passers-by can hear the faint noise of the oars of a boat rowing in this subterranean lake.' The legend may possibly have started from the fact that there might have been several underground wells where victims were washed and then, with the arrival of Christianity, where the faithful were baptized.

We met punctually to see the astronomical clock do its stuff, but I'd spoiled Alice's morning completely. As it was the first day after the holidays all the shopping mums were out in ravenous force. I think most of the shops were desperately short-staffed, and those staff that had turned up had got such thick heads they were in a foul temper and hardly in a mood to give a young girl gratuitous advice without even the prospect of a sale. After she had tried at a half-dozen shops someone had written out for her a list of a dozen different sorts of sausages, but the hand-writing was so bad that I could only decipher eight: Lyons, Beer, Liver, Ham, Frankfurt, Tongue, Galantine and Pistachio.

The clock, which is situated in the south-east corner, is a terrific tourist draw (tickets seventy-five centimes from a little ticket-office in a courtyard outside) and a surprisingly large crowd had flocked to see it, even on this bitterly cold winter's day.

When Victor Hugo paid his visit it was being repaired, 'it was covered with a shirt of match-boarding', but he describes it as a 'charming little edifice of the seventeenth century'. I should have called it an enormous edifice, so I feel it is fairly certain that it was not being restored when Victor Hugo saw it, but was being replaced by the much larger one which in fact was ready in 1838.

The seven days of the week are represented by chariots driven by the divinities of Roman mythology, which appear over an opening above the dial: Diana is for Monday, then come Mars, Mercury, Jupiter, Venus, Saturn and Apollo.

Every quarter of an hour two strokes are sounded by various automata studded around the huge face of the clock. The first is sounded by one of the two angels which frame the dial called 'Modern Times', at the centre of the Gallery of Lions. The second is sounded by one of the 'Four Ages of Man', who file past Death in the upper part of the clock (Childhood strikes the first quarter, Youth the second, Manhood the third and Old Age the fourth). The hours are sounded by Death. At the last stroke of the hour the second angel in the Gallery of Lions turns his hour-glass round.

All the above goes on every hour, but at midday—or rather, at half-past—out come the twelve apostles to pass in front of Christ, who gives them his blessing, while a cock perched on a turret to the left of the clock vigorously flaps its wings and crows three times in commemoration of St Peter's repeated denial.

After seeing the clock, Alice and I went round to the main façade of the cathedral, which is truly a marvel. The wealth of detail is immense, but before taking it all in one should stand back and take in the front as a whole. First, the huge main door with two smaller ones on either side, then the splendid rose window, and then the giant, but elegant, spire. Above the door is the tympanum, considered to be one of the oldest and most richly decorated of all cathedrals in France. Here in the most meticulous detail is depicted the whole story of the Passion: Christ's entry into Jerusalem, the Last Supper, the kiss of Judas, St Peter cutting off the soldier's ear, Jesus taken before Pontius Pilate, Christ crowned with thorns, and so on.

Opposite the south side of the cathedral is the famous Château des Rohan, which contains a number of museums; and next to the Château the Musée de l'Oeuvre Notre-Dame. There were two things in the latter museum that I had read about so much that I was childishly excited about seeing them. One was the celebrated Head of Christ (originally from the Church of St Peter and St Paul at Wissembourg) which dates from the eleventh century and is the oldest stained-glass figure known; the other was an adorable miniature medieval herb-garden.

After this orgy of culture Alice and I set off for Saverne and lunch.

18

SAVERNE

This ten-thousand-strong town to the north-west of Strasbourg has several claims to fame; including one unpleasant incident which almost caused the First World War to break out a twelvemonth earlier than it did.

A really nasty piece of work, a Prussian officer as disdainful as they come, called von Forstner, was in the habit of offering payment to those German soldiers who were prepared to maltreat Alsatian recruits. Naturally, to say that he became unpopular in the town is a gross understatement; he was so hated that when he went out he was obliged to have an escort of eight fully armed soldiers. Then some boys made fun of him; this caused their parents to be arrested by the occupying German army. This, in turn, resulted in a complaint from the Alsatian magistrates of Saverne, and to the disgust of all France they themselves were arrested. At this point many decent Germans felt that von Forstner had gone far enough; the incident was hotly debated in the Reichstag, with the result that the regiment received orders to withdraw from Saverne. But as it marched out a cripple from a near-by village made an insulting remark to von Forstner, who drew his sabre and gave the man a nasty wound. The whole affair now became international, especially when a military court-martial acquitted the Prussian officer; for many months the situation between France and Germany was tense indeed.

But, *au fond*, Saverne is the home of those remarkable Cardinals de Rohan who to all intents and purposes ruled Alsace, the town of Strasbourg and over a hundred other towns and villages around it from 1704 right up to the Revolution. None of them were especially talented; they were certainly not virtuous and not the slightest whit religious. They were just powerful lords, very proud of their birth, their ostentation and their prodigality. But they had two other things which greatly endeared them to both the populace and the nobility, namely charm and fantastically good looks.

The first of the de Rohans to make the headlines was Armand-

Gaston de Rohan-Soubise who in 1704 and at the age of thirty became the first Bishop of Strasbourg. But when he was only fifteen Madame de Sévigné was writing of him as 'this fine-looking priest, so handsome and (yet) too handsome'.

And that crotchety, very elderly diarist the Duc de Saint-Simon said more or less the same thing in his well-known comment on the Cardinal:

> He was a fairly big man, a little too fat, and with the looks of a Greek god and with, apart from this remarkable beauty, something else: a face in which shone all the graces in an imposing and unaffected way.
>
> Furthermore, he had a splendid command of language which he used in such a free and easy way that without giving any signs of affectation or pride, he retained all those advantages of being a prince and cardinal without causing any embarrassment to himself or to others.

And Saint-Simon (who hated the guts of the whole Rohan tribe) was not exaggerating for we have another record from the Marquis de Valfrons, who was also keeping a diary, and was quite a young officer at the time:

> The handsomeness of his open smiling face inspired great confidence. He had the true bearing of a man destined to lead others. The ensemble of these traits caused all people to adore him and a smile from him (which cost nothing) was remembered with lasting gratitude.

Handsome, a true patron of the arts, a man of exquisite taste and a good administrator, Armand Gaston de Rohan's interest in the church was less than nil. Saint-Simon writes that: 'He put the ecclesiastical affairs of Alsace into the hands of a servant and did nothing to further the interests of the church other than lending his palace and his table to the priests of the party.'

A later historian commenting on Saint-Simon's remarks says, however, that there are many worse ways of serving a cause, even a theological one.

The château at Saverne which Armand-Gaston inherited and embellished was by all accounts one of the marvels of the eighteenth century. I say 'by all accounts', because it was destroyed completely in 1779 and 'embellished' because it was actually started by his predecessor, Prince François-Egon de Furstenberg. He was a German but was in the pay of Louis XIV, was totally loyal to him and sought only to please and flatter him down to copying his clothing, his uniforms and particularly his style of architecture. To this end he demolished at Saverne the medieval castle stronghold of Guillaume de Diest and started to build, in 1670, a veritable little Versailles, employing for the job the brilliant Italian architect Tomacio Comacio, who in turn took on two gifted men, Robert le Lorrain, who remained almost unknown, and Coysevox, who became famous.

Four years after he became the first Cardinal of Strasbourg, Armand-Gaston, probably spurred on by a fire which demolished the entire right wing, started rebuilding, enlarging and embellishing the place, and in so doing created a marvel.

The place was, of course, vast, but its huge size was given a very harmonious air by being placed at the end of an immense esplanade which appeared to be guarded by two huge stone sphinxes and two lions holding up the arms of the Cardinal. Lined along the lawns were twenty-four sculpted statues in the pink Vosges sandstone, there was a bronze statue of Louis XIV and, to show that Saverne was the centre of the world, of all things, a huge stone obelisk had been erected, giving the distances in Germanic miles (Prague 75, Jerusalem 495, Peru 1,350) of all the most important places in the world.

Although only one single print of the outside and nothing within remains of the old château, one can get a pretty good idea of the expanse of the place from the memoirs of the Marquis de Valfons, an officer with the garrison of Strasbourg who was a frequent visitor.

> The huge edifice causes those who see it for the first time to gasp with surprise. There are no less than seven hundred beds in the place and a hundred and fifty horses in the stables where a large number of *barouches* are always ready waiting for any guest who wishes to use one. I have attended one or two magnificent shoots where over six hundred peasants have been strung out at a distance of several miles shouting and beating the woods and copses with sticks. These shoots would go on to one o'clock when both the men and women would assemble in a marquee which had been erected at some enchanting spot by the river, where an exquisite meal would be served, spiced with much gaiety. And as it was necessary that everyone should be

happy benches and tables were laid out on the grass for the peasants. Then when the lunch break was over, and it was a little cooler, everyone went to take up new stands and the shoot re-started. Each person chose a suitable cover or hiding-place and so that the women should not be afraid each one was put in the company of the gentleman she disliked least. Everyone was sternly warned not to leave their post until a certain signal was given; this was to avoid being shot by accident. Then when the day was over all the beaters were paid off, and all they asked was that the shoot should take place again. This went for the women too.

The fact that the men were paid I find revealing. One hears so much of the peasants being down-trodden in France at this period that one would have thought it quite normal for them to have been fully expected to do a day's beating for nothing, and yet here they were, being well fed and paid into the bargain.

But there was another amenity which the ladies liked much more than a good day's shooting, and that was a gondola ride along the newly built canal.

In 1718 Armand-Gaston de Rohan made a deal with the abbess of Saint-Jean-des-Choux, whereby she received from the cardinal the village of Eckartswiller and ceded him a property at Zomhof which he badly wanted to extend his estate. As soon as the deal was through, the Cardinal started to dig a lovely winding canal which meandered out several miles to the village of Steinbourg. But no ordinary canal was this one, for at irregular intervals it had been widened into lakes and pools where the guests of the cardinal could forgather and pelt each other with flowers or indulge in mock battles.

With all this sumptuousness went a good deal of loose living. Says the Marquis de Valfons: 'Always there were in attendance twenty to thirty young women, the most amiable of the province, and these would be augmented by those from the court in Paris.'

As the years went by the Cardinal became more profligate, and one of his most remarkable indiscretions was to permit a rumour to run around that Louis XIV had been in love with his mother, Madame de Soubise, and that he was an offspring of this affair.

When things really went too far, the old Abbot of Ravennes, a counsellor of state, would remonstrate: 'I shudder at your indiscretions in public,' he once said. The Cardinal shrugged his shoulders. 'The whole place is covered with scented powder, and the furniture is being terribly knocked about,' continued the Abbot. 'Liberty and free and easy going should be the order of the day,' replied Armand, 'otherwise this place will be a backwater.'

Armand-Gaston de Rohan died in 1749 and was succeeded by his great-nephew, François-Armand de Rohan-Soubise-Ventador, who made only the very briefest appearance on the scene, for he visited Saverne to make his solemn entrance and then to be buried there in 1756. The next cardinal, Louis Constantin de Rohan-Guemenée-Montbazon, was equally colourless—he was in his early sixties when he succeeded to the bishopric, but he was the only one of the four who felt that someone in his position should be reasonably pious and should occupy himself with the affairs of the Church.

But do not run away with the idea that this de Rohan was living in a much more modest way: far from it, for he was permitted, in 1770, to receive Marie-Antoinette at his palace when she was on her way to marry the Dauphin, the future Louis XVI. The festivities that day of 8 May were magnificent, but there was one rather poignant episode —poignant, that is, if one looks at the event with hindsight. As Marie-Antoinette was leaving a very old woman on the estate was presented to her, and this centenarian wished the future queen the good fortune to live as long as she had. 'Yes, I wish that too, if it can be for the benefit of France,' replied Marie-Antoinette. And to think that in only a few years the peasants would be chanting, 'Little Queen, little Queen of twenty years, soon you will be swinging!'

What with this much-publicized visit, the gondolas on the lakes, the huge orangery, the comic obelisk, I get the impression that the château at Saverne was a sort of Longleat and Woburn rolled into one, the only difference being that at the latter places you don't get the added spectacle of watching their Lordships of Bath and Bedford sitting down to their midday meal. For this is exactly what happened at Saverne, and we have an interesting account of a visit by Goethe, who was then taking his degree at Strasbourg University:

> With my two good friends, Englebach and Weyland, from Lower Alsace I took myself on horse-back to Saverne and as it was such a pleasant day this gracious little town smiled down upon us most charmingly. We admired the aspect of the episcopal château; the size and luxury of the new stables gave a good clue to the affluence of its owners; the magnificence of the stairway* surprised us;

---

* I wonder if it was a spiral one like that at Blois?

we walked respectfully around the bedrooms and salons, but the bearing of the Cardinal himself was in strong contrast; he is a little man decaying with age. We saw him take dinner. The view over the garden is superb, and a canal about two miles long, running as straight as a bow-line to the centre of the building* gives one an excellent idea of the capabilities and taste of ancient craftsmen. We promenaded along the canal's banks, then around various parts of the domain and cogitated with pleasure the magnificence of the ecclesiastical outpost of a powerful monarchy.'

The last of the de Rohan cardinals, who became nicknamed 'Cardinal Necklace' on account of his stupidity over a diamond necklace intended for the Queen, was Louis-René-Édouard. He arrived at Saverne to make his 'solemn entry' in the very first days of September 1779. He can literally hardly have had time to inspect anything like all of the seven hundred bedrooms of his palace when, at three o'clock in the morning of 8 September, a terrible fire gutted the place and the new Cardinal himself only just escaped with his life.

I do not think there is much doubt that this Louis de Rohan was twice as good-looking as Armand-Gaston, was twice as profligate, but had half his intelligence.

With all his money—or, more accurately, with the vast taxes he was able to raise among his peasants—the new château was quickly built and is the austere and forbidding place we see today.

Between the rebuilding and the Revolution it saw a great deal of pomp and some remarkable goings-on, including occupation of the orangery by Cagliostro, who had persuaded the credulous Cardinal that he could manufacture gold for him.

But the rumblings of the Revolution were beginning to be heard, and the long-suffering peasants were getting fed up with paying for Louis de Rohan's silly extravagances. They may well have heard rumours of, or have guessed at, the colossal cost of a fabulous Persian kiosk which was built in 1783 on an island in the canal. It was a true belvedere, because from it there was a wonderful panoramic view over the Vosges. The Cardinal had the entire roof covered in gleaming copper and here it was that his guests came to repose themselves after paddling themselves in gondolas up and down the canal.

But the Cardinal's popularity had by no means sunk to zero, as

---

* It meandered after this.

witness the affair of the diamond necklace. When the scandal broke, de Rohan stood trial and so did the instigator of the plot, Mme de la Motte-Valois. The latter was found guilty and her punishment was to be branded and whipped through the streets. The Cardinal was found not guilty—he was, said the gossips, found 'innocent' in two senses of the word—but was ordered to exile himself for a period in Auxerre. When he returned to Saverne his peasants were there to greet him and we have several contemporary accounts of what happened. A fanfare of trumpets sounded, cannons galore were let off, and five miles outside the town the traces of his carriage were cut and scores of peasants pulled it to the château.

But his perks were too much to stomach for ever: he received as dues a tenth of the barley, of grapes and all fruits and, since 1743, this had been augmented by a tithe on potatoes. More valuable still, it was only the Cardinal who was allowed to sell his wine a fortnight before Pentecost and, even more financially useful, he alone was allowed to sell the new wine fourteen days before the annual autumn wine fair.

As the years passed, though, the grip weakened. In 1789 a company of guards refused to officiate at the château, and this occurrence may well have led the Cardinal to think the end was near, especially as at the same time the inhabitants of Wirterswiller found courage to ask for their forest rights back. Louis Gaston left, never to return.

That was the end of Saverne in its glory. In 1794, when the Revolution was at its cruellest height, the kiosk was demolished as being a sign of 'despotism and excessive luxury', and not much later eight hundred peasants fell on the place, destroyed the orangery and broke into the pheasantry, taking away all the game for their own larders.

Under the first Empire the Légion d'Honneur acquired the château to house a number of its troops, and then in 1852 Louis-Napoleon, President of the Republic, wishing to ingratiate himself with the populace, had the place restored and turned into a gigantic retreat for widows whose husbands had been killed in the service of their country, and the place was divided into seventy-eight apartments—several reserved for Napoleon personally in case he wished to pay a visit to Alsace—and became known as the 'Imperial Asylum of Saverne'. In 1871 the conquering Germans turned it into a barracks to house their own troops there; in 1918 the French turned them out but still kept it as a barracks. But it is now well worth a visit, especially when it is given a *son et lumière* treatment in the summer.

Alice and I were pretty peckish by the time we reached Saverne, so I left her in the car to keep an eye on our belongings while I started ferreting around for a restaurant.

The first place smelt so badly of Lysol that I was forced to beat a quick retreat to avoid being sick; in the next the juke-box was playing so loudly that it started to hurt my ear-drums. Next door was a small restaurant, with a menu affixed to the window offering a choice of half a dozen snails or hors d'œuvres, followed by cutlets of baby kid with noodles, then cheese—all for six francs. I pushed open the door; the place was charming.

'Ah!' I said. 'What an appetizing menu! Can we have a table for two?'

'I'm afraid we cannot serve you,' said the waitress.

'Are we too late?' I said.

'We cannot serve you,' said the woman, whom I took by her looks to be the daughter of the most handsome lady owner behind the bar.

'Have you run out of something on the table d'hôte menu?' I persisted.

'Monsieur, we cannot serve you,' said the older woman, speaking for the first time.

'Why on earth not?' I said. 'Is it some dislike of foreigners?'

'We do not take smokers in this restaurant,' she replied.

'But, damn it all,' I said, looking at the remains of the miniature cigar I was smoking, 'I won't be smoking at the meal.'

'No matter,' said the woman. 'If we even suspect that someone smokes we cannot take him.'

At the next two places the *patron* and his wife were sitting down to their own lunch and made it quite clear that they had no intention of getting up again until they had finished their copious meal. I was beginning to get desperate and so slipped into a little side-road that gave off the main street. On my left was a canal (a more modern one than that built by the de Rohans), on the right a row of houses, and one had a sign: *Hôtel Restaurant de la Marne*.

My heart sank as I pushed open the door, for the place was deserted, save for a middle-aged couple just about to embark on a gargantuan meal. I felt I hadn't a hope of getting lunch here, but at least they could serve me with a *pastis* before I walked back to the car to give Alice the bad news.

The man showed no sign of annoyance when I asked for my apéritif, and the woman said, 'Would you like a little ice with it?'

'Well,' I said, as they had both jumped up, 'I don't want to spoil your lunch.'

They really didn't seem in any hurry to get back to their food, the most interesting and appetizing part of which were some flat fried potato cakes I had never seen before, so I thought I would have a final try.

'No trouble at all,' they both said, and that was how Alice and I were shortly sitting down to one of the most copious blow-outs ever. The first course was *Charcuterie alsacienne Lucullus*, and is worth describing. On a huge oval wooden platter, perhaps two feet long, were arranged in tempting profusion—certainly enough for a full meal for six—a terrine of hare, a tasty liver pâté, three different sorts of sliced sausages, sliced tomatoes sprinkled with chopped onions and parsley, chopped beetroot, potato and onion mayonnaise, egg mayonnaise, plain sliced cucumber, sweet-sour cucumber, diced cheese and snippets of fried bread, shredded lettuce, radishes and, that great favourite of mine, *céléri-rave*.

We started eating, we tucked in, we ate well, and when we could do no more we looked at the wooden platter. It seemed scarcely dented.

After a longish pause, mountainous steaks followed with potato chips, so correctly dry you could have broken them in half and heard them snap.

'Oh, where are the potato cakes you were eating?' I said, not disappointed but curious.

'They are rather a peasant's way of doing them,' said *la patronne*. 'That was why we took so long; I was frying you some fresh chips.'

Two minutes later a mountain of sizzling round potato cakes were placed before us. They looked just like the little flat, three-inch round cold pancakes they give you in Glasgow tea-shops.

We were sitting at a great, typically French, marble café table which had been overlaid with paper tablecloths, and we were so placed that we looked out (through the enormous plate-glass window which covered the whole of the front) over the canal and on to the little houses beyond. The rain had lifted sufficiently for one to be able to see clearly how clean the little lace curtains were, and while I was enjoying my steak I vaguely wondered if, in the high season when the restaurant would have been packed, little old ladies in lace caps were in the habit of peering unseen through the windows to satisfy their curiosity as to what the tourists were eating.

When I looked up again from my food plate I noticed that the room had darkened considerably, and then I saw, to my astonishment, that the houses opposite had altogether disappeared and that a great iron curtain had descended, blocking out their view. Remembering that *pastis*, which is absinthe, can cause hallucinations, I jumped up and went over to the entrance to find, to my relief, that a monster barge had arrived in the lock part of the canal. I went back to our table and told Alice I was going outside, and would she say I did not want anything more to eat even if it was included in the set price.

The old boy in charge of the lock—it was most curious seeing one in the very middle of a busy town—was a real charmer, with a very bad club-foot and minus an arm; how he managed the heavy machinery which opened the sluices, I cannot imagine.

The small cigar I gave him made him pleasantly communicative, and when he had told me a bit about his job I said maliciously, 'I suppose you make quite a nice bit on the side with the tips you get from the bargees.'

He took a slow puff and gave me a look which he fondly hoped was one of incomprehension.

'Come off it!' I said. 'With your disability no one could ever lodge a complaint if you worked a bit slowly on opening the sluices.'

'Oh, I can be a bit of a bastard on occasions,' said the man. 'When these young foreigners come through and ask me to empty in double quick time it's amazing how my gammy leg will slow me down.'

'Well, then,' I said, 'so——'

'Ah! But,' he interrupted, 'if it was known that I took tips I would not be able to do that, and I prefer to forfeit the cash in exchange for the right to be awkward when I choose.'

'These barges fit pretty snugly,' I next said.

'I'll say they do,' he replied. 'Look here.'

We went closer to the side of the great barge and stood at the very edge of the lock. He then pointed to the other side.

'You can see from here that the barge is touching that side,' he said. 'Now try and put your hand down there.'

I bent down. By Jove! I could get my fingers and the palm of my hand between the lock side and the barge, but there wasn't enough room to clench my fist.

I went back to our seats, where the patron's wife was standing, arms akimbo.

'Time for us to be going,' I said to Alice.

She gave me a curious look which I couldn't interpret, but she seemed very amused.

'Monsieur,' said the woman, 'wherever have you been? Your daughter here said you had both finished, but I *never* let anyone leave Saverne until they have eaten my apple fritters.'

The next day we polished off our Strasbourg culture. Alice went and looked over the Orangerie, a very pretty park laid out by le Nôtre in 1692, while I went to look at the headquarters of the Council of Europe, which looked like a hangar for a squat dirigible which someone had tried to camouflage as a barracks, or vice versa. Then on to the Church of Saint-Thomas which houses the mausoleum of Maréchal de Saxe. It is a most curious affair: this huge piece of marble statuary shows France in tears, holding the Marshal by the hand and at the same time brushing back Death, who is holding open the warrior's tomb. In the background Hercules is stricken with emotion, Love, weeping, snuffs out his torch, while the Lion (Holland), the Eagle (Austria) and the Leopard (England) cower in a corner in deference to the all-conquering might of the national flag. Whether the sculpture is more hideous than the ghastly church, which is kept locked, is hard to say.

With all this dashing around I had, perforce, taken several taxis, and with one which seemed most modest I mock-seriously questioned the cost.

In reply the man produced a little pad which turned out to be a sort of municipal form on which were printed the main places where taxis were likely to go to and from in the town. There was a blank dotted line for the taxi-driver's name and another for the price, and a third for the time of day. Slowly the man filled it in.

'But I was only joking,' I said.

'I must insist that you take it,' said the man.

The last thing we saw in Strasbourg I had seen before, but I must say that it rather grew on me. It had the unusual distinction of having been recently 'discovered', although it had in fact been there for centuries. This was a covered fortified bridge built over the river in the old part of the town, by that master military architect Vauban, and the municipality were clearly rather proud of it as they had plastered every hotel and hoarding with exquisitely designed posters urging the tourist to visit the *terrace panoramique*, and stressing how very recently it had been brought to light.

The first time I paid my new franc to visit it I thought they had rather over-egged the place, but when we went back I realized that the view of old Strasbourg from the bridge was a very charming sight.

19

WISSEMBOURG, AND A NEW ROUTE DU VIN

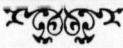

WITH both the commercial and cultural sides of the trip now finished, our last day could be one of relaxation. So we set off north from Strasbourg to see Wissembourg, and the 'region of typical little picturesque villages' we had heard so much about.

The place we wanted to see most was Hunspach which had 'conserved its typical Alsatian character intact', and which 'had conserved intact its mullioned windows and tessellated roofs, going back to the Baroque era'. Here perhaps I would take a glass or so of Riesling, or more if no breathalysing gendarmes were about—anyway Alice was a good driver and she could take a fine photo of the gay rooftops topped by the storks' nests while I was imbibing.

The heavy snow had stopped in Strasbourg the night before, and in the town there was little evidence of it left, but as we motored north it was a very different story, and when we got to Hunspach we found the little hamlet completely snowed up; not a mullioned window, not a roof to be seen.

Disappointed, we motored on up to Wissembourg, where we found the snow gone. On the outskirts of the town we came to a large roundabout so bristling with signs that I thought myself quite clever to have seen the one directing us to the town centre without having to go round twice. As we left it, Alice said, 'Did you see the arrow to the Route du Vin back there?'

'That's quite impossible,' I replied. 'The route finished miles and miles away, at Marlenheim.'

'But there really was one, Daddy,' Alice retorted.

'Well, if there *was* one,' I said, still quite disbelieving and for quiet's sake, 'let's go and have lunch. We will see about it on the way back.'

The frontier town of Wissembourg, with nearly six thousand inhabitants, is so much part of history that it needed 'doing' in depth in spite of my promise to Alice that we should relax.

It cannot be stressed too often that the history of the whole of Alsace and Lorraine is tied up with wars—probably more so than that of any other corner of Europe. And Wissembourg has been hit worst of all, although you hardly credit this as you walk round the charming, sleepy old canal part of the town—the Quartier Bruch.

There have been four major battles around Wissembourg, in 1704, 1744, 1793 and 1870, as well, of course, as those of the Second World War.

I owe my knowledge of these dates to an engraving of a medal struck to commemorate the unveiling of a huge war memorial at Geisberg, outside Wissembourg, the scene of the first French reverse on 4 August 1870. This huge edifice is incorrectly known as the *monument des morts*, and if it had been so called instead of by its correct name, the *monument français*, there would never have been the fantastic amount of trouble which its sponsors had in getting it erected—a story of behind-the-scenes frustration I found in a tattered forty-year-old magazine I unearthed in a little secondhand book-shop in Colmar.

We are apt to think of *le tourisme* as a quite recent phenomenon, but in fact it was getting well under way in the last decades of the nineteenth century. In those days the equivalent of a charter flight to Málaga was a steamer trip down the Rhine, including visits to surrounding towns and villages. Wissembourg was one of these places, and it suddenly occurred to four extra-loyal *French* Alsatians that 'until now there has been absolutely nothing to remind or tell tourists that the blood of thousands of our brave soldiers has reddened the soil of Wissembourg and then in 1870 the heights of Geisberg'.

They then went on to suggest a monument and asked for subscriptions, adding, '*N'importe quelle obole sera la bienvenue*' ('Even the widow's mite will be gratefully accepted'). An *obole* was a tiny French silver coin (later made of *billon*, or debased metal) used in the tenth to fifteenth centuries, and later came to mean a trifling sum. It was this word that caught the imagination of the Alsatian public.

The committee of four had originally asked for a sum total of thirty thousand marks, but soon they had collected five times that amount and it therefore seemed time to consider closing the subscription. This was agreed upon, and then one of the four, who had an important position on the French daily paper then printed in Alsace, the *Journal d'Alsace*, proposed, solely as a gesture of thanks to the subscribers, the printing in the paper of all the names of those who had made donations. No further cash was asked for, but the publicity flew around the world. Frenchmen who had left their native Alsace were thrilled to find there was an outlet for their nostalgia, and subscriptions poured in from Africa, the United States, Brazil, Indo-China and France.

The sum of money now collected was so great that the original committee of four felt that they could no longer cope alone and officialdom had to be called in. And that was when the troubles started.

The reader may have been surprised to see the name of France among the countries from whence subscriptions came. But at this time (1907–9) Alsace and Lorraine were what nearly every history book of the region calls 'under the German yoke'.

So now permission had to be granted to erect the monument. This was given by the local *Kreisdirektor*, and great was the happiness of the French Alsatians' Monument Committee when they stumped one morning over the heights of Geisberg 'so that we could buy the land and find a site *which would dominate the landscape more than did the existing German monument*'.

Yes, there was already a German one!

When it came to the exact wording there was more trouble: the French Alsatians wanted to draw attention to the terrible casualties sustained by the French soldiery on the battlefield in 1870 and the permission to erect the monument was given if only the words *Aux soldats français morts pour la Patrie* were chiselled on the plinth.

This was accepted, but a few weeks later officialdom changed its minds and asked the Committee to substitute *leur* for *la*, on the grounds that '*on ne voulait pas que la génerosité alsacienne de 1909 se réclamât de la patrie française.*' In other words 'It was not desirable that because the Alsatians had been generous, they should be able to put in a claim that Alsace belonged to *la patrie*'.

The Committee refused, and the Government gave way.

As to the form of the monument, it was felt that the best way to go about things was to open a competition, which eventually was won by the sculptor Albert Schultz.

But he was not given a free hand—far from it; the monument was now national news, and having got so far the Committee did not wish the whole project cancelled by a suspicious Government. 'The general tone,' they told Schultz, 'should be one of calmness and dignity, and the monument must be large. It must have nothing aggressive or theatrical about it. The idea of glory must be tempered by that of Death.'

Schultz produced a model, and to everyone's surprise put a gallic cockerel on the top of the monument. This, thought the Government, would be bound to court trouble, as the Alsatian Germans would imagine that the Alsatian French were crowing over them. The decision was too important for them to take, and they decided the question should be taken up by the powers-that-be in Berlin; they, in turn, dared not make a decision without asking Kaiser Wilhelm II. He, wanting to cut a father-figure in Alsace and Lorraine, surprisingly enough said yes.

Then Albert Schultz pulled another fast one.

At this point I should explain that there was a strong back-to-France nationalist movement in Alsace, and that the German Government was not being too unreasonably harsh about it. And I feel that the Monument Committee and Schultz, sensing this, were trying to get everything they could get. Anyway, the sculptor had the bright idea—which was *not* shown on the original model—of putting four extraordinary motifs on the four corners of the huge plinth, commemorating four great periods in France's military past. These were four circular bas-relief plaques: the Sun of Louis XIV; the Fleur-de-Lys; the Lictors' fasces with the Phrygian cap; and the Eagle of Napoleon. This was prosaic enough; but an extraordinary added touch was that above each plaque was sculptured a military hat appropriate to the period. But this time they had gone too far; the *Kreisdirektor* ordered the removal of the plaques, and only three days before the inauguration a party of workmen obliterated the motifs on the plaques (not the four hats, as these had been passed on the model) with chisels.

This, though, did not deter a crowd of fifty thousand Alsatians attending the unveiling.

Wissembourg, sometimes called the 'Alsatian Bruges', can cling to two memories not connected with war.

The present hospital of the town, a charming old building with a lovely courtyard, was two-hundred-odd years ago the scene of one of the more emotional moments in history.

The dethroned King Stanislas of Poland had been exiled from his country after a quarrel with his nobles, and the King of France had lent his 'brother', his family and a small number of faithful servants a modest house in Wissembourg. Louis had supplied furniture with the house but that was all, and Stanislas and his entourage were so short of funds that often they literally did not know where the next meal was coming from. His chief worry was on account of his daughter, Marie Leczinska. Though witty and clever, she was far from a beauty, but if he could only marry her off some of the family worries would be over.

One suggestion for a consort was Louis XV's current Prime Minister, the duc de Bourbon, and hopes ran very high when an artist arrived from Paris to paint Marie's portrait.

The Duke, however, had a mistress with a great deal of power over him, Mme de Prie, and she, not wishing to be ousted, suggested instead that Marie should marry the fifteen-year-old Louis. This turned out to be a brilliant suggestion, because at that moment, for balance-of-power reasons, an English or Spanish princess was out of the question, and what was needed was a royal personage whose family held no dangers.

So the family waited at Wissembourg for the news that Marie might possibly become the Duchess of Bourbon, and when galloping messengers arrived, headed by the duc d'Antin, hopes ran high.

He was received by Stanislas who, after a few minutes, went into his daughter's bedroom and fell on his knees before her.

'God be praised, you are to become Queen of France!'

Wissembourg's other happy memory is that its old part was used—and so perfect was it that hardly any studio sets were needed—in filming that great novel of Erckmann and Chatrian, *l'Ami Fritz*, some years ago.

We had lunch in a little café-restaurant which was remarkable for a sort of finicky, exaggerated kind of cleanliness which gave one the impression that, although there were plenty of people there, it was hardly lived in. The floor was almost too shiny, the ashtrays too free of ash and the tables so scrubbed that the veins of the harder part of the wood stood out like ridges. And the food somehow, though excellently cooked, seemed to match it; the helpings were minute and almost too neatly dished up.

As we were taking our coffee in thimble-sized cups (a thing I normally warmly approve of, for I loathe breakfast-size cups of coffee after a lunch or dinner) I said to Alice, 'I bet I could describe the chef-proprietor of this restaurant.' A second's pause to impress. 'A little man, as thin as a rail, perhaps with rimless spectacles, and so neatly clad in his white chef's clothing that if so much as a speck of soup fell on his trousers he would rush up to change; probably teetotal.'

I ordered a Williams, that liqueur I like so much, and idly watched a table for one being laid up for a very late lunch. A bottle of red and one of white were deposited in *papier-mâché* coasters accompanied by outsized glasses; a third glass, much smaller though still large by normal standards, was placed in front of the others and filled by the waitress with what I took to be a local spirit.

As I was paying the bill a man walked out of the kitchen. He was so far from the immaculate figure of my description that I thought he could be neither the owner nor the chef, but this possibility was quickly dispelled when he ambled up to the cash-register, riffled through the notes and quickly, and very surreptitiously, slipped several into his jacket pocket. He was immensely fat, unshaven, and wore the filthiest outfit I have ever seen, the dirtiest patches being on his buttocks where he was in the habit of wiping his grimy hands. As we left we saw him draining his apéritif in one gulp.

On our way home we again passed the multi-sign roundabout and there, sure enough, was a *Route du Vin* sign off to the right. I was still not very surprised because I assumed that, although the Wine Road began at least forty miles to the south-west of us, this was a valiant attempt to allure German tourists along it.

As we had oodles of time to get back to Strasbourg we turned off, and a few miles later we saw two signs: *Route du Vin—Grands Crus de Rott*, and then again, *Caves Co-opérative vinicole de Cleebourg*.

This was now becoming a mystery! My wine map clearly showed, and several guide- and text-books had confirmed, that Marlenheim was the very final *Route du Vin* town.

We were surrounded by vines now, all in tip-top condition, and a few minutes more brought us to the impressive, neat Co-operative of Cleebourg. As I got out of the car I wondered if it could possibly be that we were not on the *Alsatian* Route du Vin at all, but in some little wine area hitherto unknown to me. This, I felt sure, could hardly be the case, because I was certain that when I had visited the decrepit, dreary, inefficient little region of Côtes de Toul, outside Metz, some weeks before, I had trod the grapes—as I put it to myself proudly—on the last V.D.Q.S. region of France still left, after thirty years of seeking, unvisited.

A pleasant workman greeted me, and the speed with which he comprehended that I would like to meet the manager, together with a number of other little portents, such as a stand where special commemorative glasses were sold, made me feel certain that the place was much visited by tourists.

As we were walking through the cellars and along innumerable rows of great oak casks Alice pointed out a series of chalk squiggles on the nearest and asked what they were.

I have already explained how the new wine ferments so violently that the bubbling causes quite a noise in the cellars. It is useful to be able to tell at a glance how this fermentation is going.

Accordingly, when the wine is 'working', a wavy horizontal line is chalked on the cask. When it is 'working fast' the wavy line is replaced by a violent zig-zag, like the sales graph of a firm doing fantastic business one month and almost on the rocks the next. When it is quietening down comes a gently rippling line; and, when it is finally finished, a straight line.

The room we were presently shown into was a combination of office and tasting-room, and the manager, who courteously introduced himself as Michel Wust, bade us be seated at a long, narrow old oak table with trestles at both sides.

I briefly explained my Alsatian mission, and produced one or two impressive letters of introduction, which caused M. Wust to press a button by his desk. I heard three separate buzzes outside, and in a twinkling a man appeared with a collection of glasses and bottles on a tray, which he proceeded to array before us. The wines, and my notes on them, were: Riesling, 1966 (full, dry, with a pronounced Palatinate Hock taste about it); Tokay, 1966 (full, surely unusually dry for this type of wine); Gewürztraminer, 1966 (excellent nose, very spiced); and Gewürztraminer, 1964 (surprisingly, a less pronounced nose).

As we sipped Monsieur told us the whole story.

The little enclave we were in was indeed part of the *official* Alsace wine region, with full *appellation* rights, and had been so, Michel Wust said, for seven hundred years. But it so happened that it was also dead between the Maginot and Siegfried Lines, and so when the last war broke out the wines had to be totally abandoned, as this very narrow area was now between the two front lines.

After the war the growers of the four hamlets which form this enclave, Rott, Oberhoffen-les-Wissembourg, Steinseltz and Cleebourg, put in a claim to the government for loss of *récolte* and got eight million *anciens francs*. Many took their share of the money and sold off their best vineyard slopes to better growers who started up again.

'So do you realize what this means?' said M. Wust, with considerable pride in his voice.

'Not exactly,' I replied.

'It was a fantastically lucky coincidence,' said our host excitedly. 'The old vines were utterly useless, and the growers, just at the right moment, had sufficient capital to replant with only the very best species.' He paused. 'The result is that we are the *only* part of the Alsatian *vignoble* which hasn't got a single Chasselas or Knipperlé vine on it.'

I took a sip of the Riesling. It really was extra good. Then I reached for my briefcase and pulled out my Route du Vin leaflet maps. There were six of them, all very slightly different, all printed by different organizations and all unanimously showing Thann in the south and Marlenheim in the north as the starting- and ending-places on the Route du Vin.

There are times when a dumb-crambo act is a thousand times better than the spoken word. With a pencil I theatrically pointed to Marlenheim on the first map, then I lifted it up with a flourish and pointed at Marlenheim on the second, and so on for all six, and each time I smiled, as if to say, 'How do you account for *that*?'

M. Wust had shown a certain amount of animation when I had produced the first map, but by the time I had displayed all six and done my little theatrical act he was hopping about on his seat like mad. He was too polite to interrupt me, but the second I had finished he jumped up and produced from his desk yet another Route du Vin map leaflet, which I could see was far better printed and more modern in design than mine. With terrific aplomb he opened it and spread it all over mine, and pointed, also with a pencil, to the northernmost end of the Route. And there, with a suitable break to show that there were no vines in between, were his four villages prominently displayed.

'Well, if you have had *appellation* rights and been part of the Alsatian vineyards for seven hundred years,' I said, 'why on earth haven't you been shown before on the earlier maps?'

M. Wust explained, and it indeed made sense.

'In the first place, it is not so many years since we came back into full production, so under these circumstances it would have been foolish to have shown us as part of the official Wine Road with no wine to offer. Then, when we were ready, the local authorities were too busy to put up those little cement plaques to guide the motorist. But now at last they have got around to it.'

'Quite recently?' I said, a little excitedly.

'Oh, very. The maps were printed in advance.'

'Then we are perhaps the first English people to visit you?'

'I haven't had any before,' said M. Wust.
I sipped my wine again.
'May I please buy a mixed dozen bottles?' I said.
'Assuredly,' said Michel Wust.
While the parcel was being done up I looked at my little tasting-glass and saw that it was engraved with a three-leaf clover, with a C, a V and a C on each of the leaves, and *Cleebourg* underneath.
'Please take it,' said my host.
And exactly a year later I drank from it my last Cleebourg Alsatian wine as I finished this book.

APPENDIX A
Place-names differing in French and German

Below will be found two lists of Alsatian and Lorrainer place-names which have been changed since the annexation in 1871. In some instances the alterations have been slight, but in some others the difference is great. The French terminals *ville* and *willer* (from the Latin *villa* and *villare*) have become *weiler* in German. *Bourg* also has, not unnaturally, been changed to *burg*. It is not claimed that the following lists are complete; nevertheless they may prove useful for the identification of some of the localities mentioned. In the first list the French and in the second the German names are given in the first column alphabetically.

French	*German*
Alsace	Elsass
Aubure	Altweier
Ban de la Roche	Steinthal
Belmagny	Bernetzweiler
Bischwiller	Bitschweiler
Bitche	Bitsch
Bonhomme, Le	Diedolshausen
Boulay	Bolchen
Bouxwiller	Buchsweiler
Broque, La	Vorbruck
Cernay	Sennheim
Château-Salins	Salzburg
Châtenois	Kestenholz
Chavannes-sur-l'étang	Schaffnat-am-Weiher
Courtavon	Ottendorf
Dabo	Dagsburg
Éteimbes	Welschensteinbach
Faulquemont	Falkenberg
Fenestrange	Finstingen
Ferrette	Pfirt
Fouday	Urbach
Guebwiller	Gebweiler
Haguenau	Hagenau
Huningue	Hüningen

French	German
Levoncourt	Luffendorf
Lièpvre *or* Lièvre	Leberau
Longueville	Longeville
Lorquin	Lorehingen
Lorraine	Lothringen
Main-du-Prince, La	Herzogshand
Marmoutier	Maursmünster
Massevaux	Masmünster
Montreux	Münsterol
Mulhouse	Mülhausen
Neubois	Gereuth
Neuf-Brisach	Neu-Breisach
Obernai	Oberehnheim
Orbey	Urbeis
Petite-Pierre, La	Lützelstein
Phalsbourg	Pfalzburg
Porcelette	Porselt
Poultroie, La	Schmerlach
Ribeaupierre	Rappoltstein
Ribeauvillé	Rappoltsweiler*
Riquewihr	Reichenweier
Romagny	Willern
Rouffach	Rufach *or* Ruffach
Saint-Hippolyte	Sankt Pilt
Saint-Louis	Sankt Ludwig
Sainte-Croix-aux-Mines	Sankt Kreuz im Leberthal
Sainte-Marie-aux-Mines	Markirch
Sainte-Odile	Odilienberg
Sarralbe	Saaralben
Sarreguemines	Saargemünd
Sarre, le	Saargebiet
Saverne	Zabern
Schlestadt	Schlettstadt
Soultz-les-Bains	Sulzbad
Soultz-sous-Forêts	Sulz unterm Walde
Thionville	Diedenhofen
Trois-Fontaines	Dreibrunnen
Val-de-Ville	Weilerthal
Valdieu	Gottesthal
Vancelle, La	Wanzel
Ville	Weiler

* Rapperschweir in the local dialect.

APPENDIX A

French	German
Vosges, les	Wasigen *or* Wasgenwald
Wasselonne	Wasselnheim
Wesserling	Husseren
Wihr-au-Val	Weier im Thal
Wissembourg	Weissenburg
Xouaxange	Schweizingen

German	French
Altweier	Aubure
Bernetzweiler	Belmagny
Bitsch	Bitche
Bitschweiler	Bischwiller
Bolchen	Boulay
Buchsweiler	Bouxwiller
Dagsburg	Dabo
Diedenhofen	Thionville
Diedolshausen	Le Bonhomme
Dreibrunnen	Trois-Fontaines
Elsass	Alsace
Falkenberg	Faulquemont
Finstingen	Fenestrange
Gebweiler	Guebwiller
Gereuth	Neubois
Gottesthal	Valdieu
Hagenau	Haguenau
Herzogshand	La Main-du-Prince
Hüningen	Huningue
Husseren	Wesserling
Kestenholz	Châtenois
Leberau	Lièpvre *or* Lièvre
Lorchingen	Lorquin
Lothringen	Lorraine
Luffendorf	Levencourt
Lützelstein	La Petite-Pierre
Markirch	Sainte-Marie-aux-Mines
Masmünster	Massevaux
Maursmünster	Marmoutier
Mülhausen	Mulhouse
Münsterol	Montreux
Neu-Breisach	Neuf-Brisach
Oberenheim	Obernai
Odilienberg	Sainte-Odile

Wines & People of Alsace

German	French
Ottendorf	Courtavon
Pfalzburg	Phalsbourg
Pfirt	Ferrette
Porselt	Porcelette
Rappoltstein	Ribeaupierre
Rappoltsweiler	Ribeauvillé
Reichenweier	Riquewihr
Rufach *or* Ruffach	Rouffach
Saargebiet	Sarre, le
Saargemünd	Sarreguemines
Salzburg	Château-Salins
Sankt Kreuz im Leberthal	Sainte-Croix-aux-Mines
Sankt Ludwig	Saint-Louis
Sankt Pilt	Saint-Hippolyte
Schaffnat-am-Weiher	Chavannes-sur-l'étang
Schlettstadt	Schlestadt
Schmerlach	La Poultroie
Schweizingen	Xouaxange
Sennheim	Cernay
Steinthal	Ban de la Roche
Sulzbad	Soultz-les-Bains
Sulz unterm Walde	Soultz-sous-Forêts
Urbach	Fouday
Urbeis	Orbey
Vorbruck	La Broque
Wanzel	La Vancelle
Wasigen *or* Wasgenwald	Vosges, les
Wasselnheim	Wasselonne
Weier im Thal	Wihr-au-Val
Weilerthal	Val-de-Ville
Weissenburg	Wissembourg
Welschensteinbach	Eteimbes
Willern	Romagny
Zabern	Saverne

APPENDIX B
Justification that Rouget de Lisle was definitely the author of the "Marseillaise", by Valerie Walkerdine

THERE has been considerable inquiry since the death of Rouget de Lisle as to whether or not he actually wrote the 'Marseillaise'. After his death, several people, notably Germans, made claims that unknown German musicians wrote the music. These are discussed in Julien Tiersot's biography, *Rouget de Lisle*. These claims were, however, not supported by any tangible evidence, and can to a certain extent be dismissed as attempts by Germany to steal France's glory, its 'Marseillaise'. The Germans were, on the other hand, so impressed by the 'Marseillaise', that two of their composers, Schumann and Wagner, used it as themes in their music.

There were, too, during the Revolution, after Rouget de Lisle's death, several French claims that Rouget had not written the music. These claims were connected with people who would have liked the 'Marseillaise', their battle-cry, to have been composed by a supporter of the Revolution, not by a man who was never particularly in agreement with, and sometimes violently opposed to, their revolutionary machinations. There are those too who would have liked the 'Marseillaise' to have been composed by a great man, befitting a great song, for a great nation. Rouget de Lisle was not known for any other work and so they wondered how he could have composed such a soul-stirring song as the 'Marseillaise'. One must consider the situation—a young, aspiring poet of very emotional temperament just returned home after a very patriotic party having drunk a considerable amount of Champagne. At the party, he had been asked to compose a song worthy of Frenchmen going into battle, and had been filled with patriotic fervour. When he got home, he was in such an emotional state that he was capable of this one great act of composition.

These are, however, merely my own thoughts. To my mind conclusive proof of the authorship of the 'Marseillaise' is contained in an article written by an inhabitant of Lons-le-Saunier, Rouget de Lisle's birthplace. He has amassed considerable evidence about Rouget de Lisle, his character and works. He wrote an article in the local newspaper, in reply to one in the same newspaper written by the great-great-granddaughter of the musician Playel; it was he who wrote the music for Rouget de Lisle's 'Hymne à la Liberté', and she claims that it was

Playel who wrote the music for the 'Marseillaise'. She does, however, cite no evidence, basing her argument on a tradition passed down in her family. M. Génévaux, the defender of Rouget de Lisle, claims that this was a mistake, which probably results from a confusion with the 'Hymne à la Liberté', written just before the 'Marseillaise'.

In the manuscript of his *Fifty French Songs*, Rouget de Lisle put a heading above the 'Marseillaise', stating that he wrote the words and music on the night of 25 April 1792 at Strasbourg. Above the 'Hymne à la Liberté', he states that this is the only song in the book to which he did not write the music.

Manuscripts, including the *Fifty French Songs* (*Cinquante chants français*), are to be found in the municipal library at Lons-le-Saunier. The writer of the article quoted above, Monsieur Génévaux, is Vice-President of the Société d'Émulation du Jura. The relevant articles appear in the newspaper *La Croix jurassienne*, 29 August 1963, and 17 October 1963. Further information for those interested in Rouget de Lisle and the 'Marseillaise' may be found in Julien Tiersot's books *Rouget de Lisle* and *La Marseillaise*, published by Delagrave and obtainable from the French Institute Library in London.

In absence of any proof to the contrary, there seem no reasonable grounds for doubting Rouget de Lisle's authorship of the 'Marseillaise'.

VALERIE WALKERDINE
May 1968

BIBLIOGRAPHY

ACKER, PAUL, *Le Beau Jardin* (Paris, 1912)
ADAM, DR FRANTZ, *Voyons . . . de quoi s'agit-il? La question d'Alsace exposée aux anciens combattants* (Paris, 1932)
BARRÈS, MAURICE, *Le Génie du Rhin—les bastions de l'est* (Paris, 1921)
BATTIFOL, LOUIS, *Les Anciennes Républiques alsaciennes* (Paris, 1918)
—— *Colette Baudoche—histoire d'une jeune fille de Metz* (Paris, 1923)
BAUTY, ED, *En Alsace reconquise—impression du front 1915: dix documents photographiques* (Paris, 1915)
BAZIN, RENÉ, *Les Oberlé—roman* (Paris, 1916)
—— *Les Nouveaux Oberlé* (Paris, 1919)
BEVER, A. VAN, *L'Alsace vue par les écrivains et les artistes—recueil de textes* (Paris 1920)
BORDEAUX, HENRI, *Sur le Rhin* (Paris)
CHAGNY, ANDRÉ, *Basse-Alsace–Strasbourg* (Lyons, 1932)
—— *Haute-Alsace* (Lyons, 1932)
CHAMPION, CLAUDE, *Sainte Odile* (Paris, 1930)
COMITÉ ALSACIEN D'ÉTUDES ET D'INFORMATION, *L'Alsace depuis son retour à la France* (vols 1 and 2) (Strasbourg, 1932–3)
DELAHACHE, GEORGES, *Alsace-Lorraine* (Paris, 1904)
—— *Strasbourg* (Paris, 1931)
DIETERLIN, JACQUES, *Le Roman de la cathédrale* (Paris, 1926)
DOLLINGER, F., *L'Alsace* (Paris, 1929)
DORAY, A., *Colmar et ses environs* (Paris, 1933)
EDWARDS, GEORGE W., *Alsace-Lorraine* (Philadelphia, 1918)
ENGLEHARD, MAURICE, *Souvenirs d'Alsace* (Paris, 1890)
ERCKMANN, E., and CHATRIAN, A., *L'Ami Fritz* (London, 1933)
—— *Histoire d'un paysan* (London, 1933)
—— *Les Rantzeau* (London, 1940)
FERRACQUE, PIERRE, *L'Alsace minée ou l'autonmie alsacienne* (Paris, 1929)
FLORENT-MATTER, *L'Alsace-Lorraine de nos jours* (Paris, 1909)
FRAIPONT, GUSTAVE, *Les Vosges* (Paris)
FRITSCH, LOUIS (ed.), *Les Vosges et l'Alsace* (Strasbourg)
FROELICH, JULES, *L'Esprit alsacien* (Paris, 1919)
GARROS, LOUIS, *Rouget de Lisle et la Marseillaise* (Paris, 1931)

GOLBÉRY, PHILIPPE DE, *Mémoire sur quelques anciennes fortifications des Vosges* (Strasbourg, 1823)
GOSSE, JEANNE, *Alsatian Vignettes* (London, 1946)
GRAD, CHARLES, *L'Alsace—le pays et ses habitants* (Paris, 1921)
HALLAYS, ANDRÉ, *À travers l'Alsace* (Paris, 1926)
—— *Sites et monuments* (Paris, 1929)
'HANSI', *L'Alsace* (Grenoble, 1933)
HERBIG, M., *Die Dreissenstein Schlösser* (Strasbourg, 1903)
—— *Die Ottrotter Schlösser* (Strasbourg, 1903)
—— *Schloss Landsberg* (Strasbourg, 1933)
HINZELIN, ÉMILE, *En Alsace-Lorraine* (Paris, 1904)
—— *Légendes et contes d'Alsace* (Paris, 1933)
KLEIN, E., and COLLARIUS, E., *Sainte-Marie-aux-Mines et ses environs* (Strasbourg, 1904)
LELONG, M. H., *Pélérinages d'Alsace* (Strasbourg, 1933)
LICHTENBERGER, ANDRÉ, *Juste Lobel, alsacien* (Paris, 1911)
LINTIER, PAUL, *Avec un batterie de 75—le tube 1233—souvenirs d'un chef de pièce 1914-16* (Paris, 1917)
LOUFTI-DUPERTAL, F., *Le Château de Freundstein—légende et histoire* (Paris, 1920)
MADELIN, LOUIS and HANSI, *Les Vosges* (Grenoble, 1933)
MARTONNE, EMMANUEL DE, *Les Grandes Régions de la France—les marches de l'est: Lorraine-Vosges-Alsace-Jura* (Paris, 1927)
NEWMAN, BERNARD, *Cycling in Northern France* (London)
ODILE, CLAUDE, *Alsace* (Paris, 1934)
PFISTER, CHRISTIAN, *Le Comté de Horbourg et la seigneurie de Riquewihr sous la souveraineté française* (Paris, 1889)
—— *Lectures alsaciennes—géographie, histoire, biographies* (Paris, 1920)
—— *Pages alsaciennes* (Ltd edn, 1,000 copies), (Strasbourg, 1927)
PITNAM, RUTH, *Alsace and Lorraine—from Caesar to Kaiser* (New York, 1915)
PITON, E., *Promenades en Alsace—monographes historiques, archéologiques et statistiques* (Strasbourg, 1856)
POINCARÉ, RAYMOND, *Le Visage de la France* (Paris, 1925)
REDSLOB, ROBERT, *Entre la France et l'Allemagne—souvenir d'un alsacien* (Paris, 1920)
REUSS, R., *Histoire d'Alsace* (Paris, 1934)
ROSNOBLETS-SCHUTZENBERGER, HÉLÈNE, *Gens d'Alsace* (Paris, 1920)
ROUF, MARCEL and GURNONSKY, *La France gastronomique* (Paris, 1921)
SCHUTZENBERGER, H., *À l'ombre de Sainte Odile* (Paris, 1931)
SPETZ, GEORGES, *Légendes d'Alsace* (Paris, 1912)
SPINDLER, CHARLES, *Ceux d'Alsace—types et costumes* (Paris, 1928)
STAUB-GRANDMOUGIN, G., *Sainte Odile d'Alsace* (Strasbourg, 1934)
TOWNROE, B. S., *A Wayfarer in Alsace* (London, 1926)
UMBRICHT, ABBÉ, *Le Mont Sainte-Odile et ses promenades* (Rixheim, 1932)
VARIOT, JEAN, *Légendes et traditions orales d'Alsace* (Paris, 1910)

BIBLIOGRAPHY

VARIOT, JEAN, *Contes populaires et traditions orales d'Alsace* (Paris, 1936)
VIZETELLY, E. A., *The True Story of Alsace-Lorraine* (London, 1918)
WAGNER, E., *Les Ruines des Vosges* (vols 1–3), (Paris, 1927)
WELSCHINGER, HENRI, *Le Retour de l'Alsace-Lorraine à la France* (Paris, 1917)
—— *Sainte Odile—patronne de l'Alsace* (Paris, 1925)
WERNER, L. G., *L'Alsace et les Vosges* (Mulhouse)
WETTERLÉ, ABBÉ E., *L'Alsace et la guerre* (Paris, 1919)
—— *Au service de l'ennemi* (Paris, 1917)
WOLFF, HENRY W., *The Country of the Vosges* (London, 1891)
WRANGEL, COUNT F-U., *La Vie rustique en Alsace—territoire de Belfort* (Paris, 1919)
ZANTA, LÉONTINE, *Sainte Odile* (Paris, 1921)
L'Alsace et la grande révolution 1789 (Colmar)
Notre-Dame de Dusenbach 1221–1894: le pélérinage, son origine et son histoire (Mulhouse, 1894)
Le Château de Haut-Koenigsbourg—Guide (Mulhouse, 1936)
Blue Guide to North-Eastern France (London, 1930)
Guide Fridolin de Strasbourg
Guides Bleues: Vosges—Alsace—Lorraine (Paris, 1928)

Periodicals

L'Alsace française (1934–7)
La Vie en Alsace (1934–9)
Voix d'Alsace (1946–7)

INDEX

Abordant blanc (grape): 56
Agencies, for wines: 2, 78 & *n*., 79
Agricultural games, origins of: 8
Albrecht, Louis: 78–9
Almanach des Gourmands (Régnière): 119
Alsace: history, 1 & *n*., 31–3, 39–40, 46–8, 77, 94, 104, 114, 154–5, 172–6, 178, 185–8; geography, 28–9 *and see* Route du Vin; language difficulties, 32–3, 42–3, 44; food, 6–7, 44–5, 52–3, 54, 81, 94–5, 97–8, 116–19, 124, 128–30, 131–50, 179, 180–1, 182, 188–9; wines, *see under* Wines, Alsatian
Altkirch: 46
L'Ami Fritz (Erckmann & Chatrian): 119, 188
Ammerschwihr: 96, 97–8, 106
Andlau: 115
Anthony, St: 91
Antonians, Order of: 91
Appert, François: 140–1
Armagnacs: 77
Armes de France (rest.), Ammerschwihr: 97–8
Arnold, Allan: 6–7, 111
Artzner, Philippe-Édouard: 138, 139

Barker, Edward Harrison: *quoted*, 105
Barr: 115–16
Bartholdi, Auguste: 90
Baumard, Jean: 27
Baumé Scale: 35*n*.
Beer, Alsatian: 94, 124–8; rules for brewers, 126–8

Belfort, Lion of: 90
Belgium: 11–12
Bender, Edgar: 150
Bernardswiller: 119
Bijon, Hubert: 131–4, 142–7, 149–50
Birds, ravages of in vineyards: 71, 74–5
Blanchemer, Lac de: 29
Bollinger (Champagne): 6, 18
Boniface VIII, Pope: 91
Bouquetraube (grape): 56
Boutmouss, recipe: 129–30
Boutwood, Daphne: *quoted*, 102
Brand vineyard, Turckheim: 94, 97
Brillat-Savarin: *quoted*, 137
Broadbent, J. M.: 34

Café Royal, London: 5
Cagliostro: 177
Cahors, wines of: 3 & *n*.
Campbell, Moira: 18
Carp: 130
Le Carrosse (rest.), London: 4
Cassis: 122–3
Caves coopératives, wines of: 21–2, 26–7, 76
Champagne: 15–19, 99–100
Chaptal, Jean-Antoine: 86
Chaptalisation: 86
Charles I of France (Charlemagne): 31, 77*n*.
Charles II of France (le Chauve): 31
Charles III of Germany (le Gros): 115
Chasselas: grape, 48, 50, 51, 56; wine, 51, 62

203

Château des Rohan (Strasbourg): 170
Château des Rohan (Saverne): 173-5, 176-7, 178
Châteauneuf-du-Pape: 3
Châtenois: 113
Chatrian, A.: 119, 188
Cheese: 4-6
Cheese and Cheese Cookery (Layton): 4-7
Chevallier-Appert: 140
Cipolla, Louis: 5
Claridges, London: 21
Clark, Guy Gordon: 2
Clause, Jean-Pierre: 135, 136-7, 138, 139
Cleuvenot, M.: 20, 24
Cleuvenot, Mme: 20, 27
Clevener (grape) *see* Pinot blanc
Clonal technique: 69
Cognac: 2, 3, 99
Colmar: 28, 35-6, 42, 47, 51, 54, 58, 68, 80-1; place de la Gare, 83; Voltaire in, 87; wine fair, 87-9; architecture of, 89-90
'Colmar Pocket': 77, 97
Comité Interprofessionnel du Vin d'Alsace: 54-5, 68, 69, 83
Commerce, medieval: 60-1, 106-9
Common Market: 51
Confrérie St-Étienne: 54, 61-2, 67-8; seal of quality, 63-4; rules for, 64-7
Contades, Maréchal de: 135-7
Côtes de Toul: 189
Courtois: 135
Couvreur, Jean: 7, 13, 18-19
Croix d'Or (hotel), Orbey: 36-8

Daily Express: 88
Daily Telegraph: 100
David, Louis: 160
Decapolis, the: 32
Dietrich, Baron Frédéric de: 154-5, 160; and composition of the 'Marseillaise', 156-8
Dietrich, Mme de: 157, 158; quoted, 159-60
Dijon: 123
Diocletian, Emperor: 107
Dorchester Hotel, London: 4, 5-7
Dosage, in Champagne: 18 & *n*.
Dove, George: 111
Dover: 11
Doyen, Nicolas-François; 137-9
Drouet, Théo: 4
Dumouriez, Charles: 161

East Malling Research Station, Kent: 70
Ebhart, Bodo: 114
Edelzwicker: 26, 51, 57, 81
Eguisheim: 82
Ehretwantz: 119
Eierküchas, recipe: 130
Épinal: 20-5, 38
Erckmann, E.: 119, 188
Evesham Flan: 5; recipe, 5*n*.

Faller, Théo: 99
Faller, Mme: 103-4
Fermentation: 34, 190; Champagne, 15
Feyel: 131-5, 144-5, 149-50
Field: quoted, 100-1
First World War: Reims, 16-17; Orbey, 36
Le Florence (rest.), Reims: 19
Foie gras: 98, 129; Feyel's shop, 131-5; cooking of, 133; history of, 135-9, 140; feeding of geese for, 141, 142; serving of, 144-5, 146-9; size of, 146; recipes for, 148-9; conserving of, 139-40, 150
Foie gras frais aux pommes: 146, 165
Forstner, von: 172
Franco-Prussian War: 32, 47, 185

INDEX

Frankfurt, Treaty of (1871): 32, 48
de Freitas, Geoffrey: 165
Frogs: 81
Furstenberg, Prince François-Egon de: 174

Gamay (grape): 56, 107
Geese: 141
Geisberg, monument at: 185–7
Gerard, John: 13
Gérardmer: 28
Gewürztraminer: 22, 35, 53, 73; *and see* Traminer
Giordano, René: 5
Gladstone, W. E.: 99
Goethe, J. W. von: 166; *quoted*, 176–7
Goldriesling (grape): 48, 50
Gourmets: 109–11
Grande Taverne (rest.), Épinal: 20–4
Grétry, André: 154
Grünewald, Mathias, *see* Nithardt, Mathis
Gueberschwihr: 82
Guebwiller: 76–7
Guilds, origins of: 60–1
Guillaume Tell (rest.), Mulhouse: 41, 44–5
Gutenberg, Johann: 166

Hallays, André: *quoted*, 89–90, 114–15
Harding, Gilbert: *quoted*, 101
Harpers Wine and Spirit Gazette: 4
Hattstatt: 82
Haut-Koenigsbourg: 113–15
Heiligenstein: 119
Heim, M.: 79, 80–2
Histoire de la Révolution Française (Michelet): 161
Hohneck, the: 29
Hops: 128; diseases of, 69–70
Hugel, Jean: 6, 7, 63, 74–5, 111–12; family of, 74–5, 112

Huglin, P.: 69; *quoted*, 69, 70, 71
Hugo, Victor: 166; *quoted*, 167, 167–8, 168–9, 169–70
Hunspach, 184
Husseren-les-Châteaux: 82
Hyams, Edward: *quoted*, 55–6
'Hymne à la liberté' (de Lisle): 154–5

Île Jars: 136–7
Ill, River: 47, 143
Illustrated: *quoted*, 101
Images of Épinal: 24–5
Ingersheim: 27
Ireland: 4
Issenheim: 9; altarpiece of, 92–3

Jerez de la Frontera: 30, 72
Journée Vinicole: 2–3

Kaefferkopf vineyard (Ammerschwihr): 51, 97
Kaufeler, Eugene: 4, 5–7
Kaysersberg: 98–9, 106
Kientzheim: 62, 104, 106
Kintzheim: 113
Kir: 123
Kléber: 163*n*.
Klevner *see* Pinot blanc
Knipperlé (grape): 48, 50, 56, 63
Kougloupf, recipe: 129
Kuehn, François: 98

Lac Blanc: 29
Lac Vert: 29
Language problems: 12–13, 41–3, 81, 134
Lattre de Tassigny, General: 77
Layton, Alice: 28, 86–7, 105, 184, 188, 190
Layton, Peggy: 4
Lebègue, Ltd: 99, 103; annual tastings, 100–2

Lebègue, Jean: 99–100
Lee, Marjorie: 5, 6
Liberty, Statue of: 90
Lille: 12–13, 30
Longemer, Lac de: 28
Lothaire I, Emperor: 31
Lotz, Mme Simone: 132–5
Louis I of France (le Débonnaire): 31, 104, 166
Louis XIV of France: 175
Louis XV of France: 135
Louis XVI of France: 137, 164
Louis II of Germany (le Germanique): 31–2
Lutzelbourg, Comtesse de: 136

Maginot Line: 48
Maison Kammerzell (rest.), Strasbourg: 163–5
Maison Pfister, Colmar: 90
Maison Rouge (hotel), Strasbourg: 163, 165
Maison des Tanneurs (rest.), Strasbourg: 143–4
Maison des Têtes, Colmar: 90
Marie Antoinette, Queen of France: 176, 177
Marlenheim: 123
'Marseillaise', the: 151, 153, 155–62
Martell: 2
Martin, Messrs: 140
Maurois, André: 1n.
May Fair Hotel, London, 5
Meistermann (rest.), Colmar: 80–1
Menus, preparation of: 22–3
Metellus Pius Scipio, Consul: 135
Metz: 32
Meurseult: 28
Michelet, Jules: *quoted*, 161
Michelin Guide—France: 1, 90, 98, 105, 143, 144, 169
Michelin Guide—Vosges: 40, 115
Molsheim: 121–2

Moselle: source of, 39–40; wines of, 71–2
Monopole-Métropole Hotel, Strasbourg: 131
Mulhouse, 40–5, 87; Town Hall, 40; *Weinstuben*, 41, 43–4
Muller, J-A.: 138
Muller-Thurgau (grape): 48–50
Mumm: 6, 17–19
Murbach: 77n.; Prince-Abbots of, 77
Muscat: grape, 50, 52, 56, 61, 62; wine, 52
Musée de l'Oeuvre Notre-Dame, Strasbourg: 170–1
Music: use of in vineyards, 8

Napoleon I, Emperor: 24–5
Napoleon III, Emperor: 138, 178
Newman, Bernard: *quoted*, 40, 98
Neymeyer-Petitdemange, A.: 27–8, 29–31
Nijmegen, Treaty of (1678): 32
Nithardt, Mathis: 91–3
North Thames Gas Board: 4

Obernai: 119–20
Oberlin Institute, Colmar: 68–9, 70–1
Oechslé Scale: 35n.
Old Man's Beard, *see* Traveller's Joy
Orbey: 36–8; Val d', 36
Orschwihr: 77–9
Orschwiller: 113
Ortlieb, J-N.: 62–3
Ottrott: 120
Oxford English Dictionary: 46–7

Paris: Rouget de Lisle at, 153
Patois: 32, 42–3
Paulée, la: 28
Peacock Inn: 69
Pérignon, Dom: 15
Perfume: and wine-tasting, 101–2
Peterkin, Norman: 113, 151

206

INDEX

Pfaffenheim: 82
Pfifferday: 113
Physiologie du Goût (Brillat-Savarin): 137
Piers Plowman (Langland): 47
Pinot blanc (grape): 50, 51, 56, 73, 119
Pinot gris, *see* Tokay d'Alsace
Pinot noir (grape): 50*n*., 56
Piquette: 107 & *n*.
Port: harvesting of, 8
Poujade, Senator: 122-3
Pourriture noble: 56
Pratt, Anne: *quoted*, 13-14
Prince, Guy: 99, 100, 101
Prince, Hervey: 99

Quenelles: 6

Régnière, Grimod de la: *quoted*, 119
Reims: 6, 12, 15-19
Relais des Ducs de Lorraine: 20, 24-5
Remiremont: 39
Retournemer, Lac de: 28-9
Revolution, French: 153-62 *passim*, 177-8
Le Rhin (Hugo): *quoted*, 166-70 *passim*
Rhine, River: 32
Ribeaupierre, Counts of: 106, 107
Ribeauvillé: 104, 113
Richarde, Princess: 115
Riesling: grape, 50, 53, 56, 57, 62, 69; wine, 21-2, 31, 35, 52-3, 73, 78
Riquewihr: 6, 104, 105-6, 112; annals of, 106-11
Rohan, Cardinal Louis de: 169 *n*., 177-8
Rohan-Soubise, A. G. de: 173-6
Rohan-Soubise-Ventador, F-A. de: 176
Rohan-Guemenée-Montbazon, L. C. de: 176-7
Ronus, George: 6-7
Rouen, Cathedral of: 169

Rouffach: 82
Rouget de Lisle, Claude Joseph: early life, 151; military career, 151-3; musical career, 153-5; and 'Marseillaise', 156-60, 162, 197-8
Rousseau, Jean-Jacques: 135-6
Route du Vin, Alsace: 76-7, 79, 82, 94, 96, 97, 98, 104, 105, 113-14, 119, 120, 121, 123, 184, 189; of Wissembourg, 189-92

St-Hippolyte: 113
St-Quentin: 13
St-Simon, Duc de: *quoted*, 173
Sauce ancienne (recipe): 148-9 *n*.
Sauerkraut: 94-6
Sausage, varieties of: 169
Saut des Cuves: 28
Sauternes: 53
Saverne: 172-82
Schiltigheim: 131-2, 149-50
Schweitzer, Albert: 98
Schwendi, Lazare de: 52, 98-9, 104
Second World War: 48, 77, 97, 190
Sélestat: 47
Shakespeare: 9
Sharp, Geoffrey: 4
Sichel, Alan: 87-9
Siegel, Léon: 131-2
Sigolsheim: 104
Simon, André: 17
Sisters Alsace-Lorraine, The (Newman): 40 & *n*., 98
Snails: 116-17; trade in, 117; preparation of, 118-19
Sofitel Hotel, Strasbourg: 142, 144-6, 147
Soil, influence of on wine: 30 *n*.
Sonnenglanz vineyard, Beblenheim: 51
Soultz: 76
Soultzmatt: 79
Stanislas, King of Poland: 187-8

Storks: 121–1
Strasbourg: 32, 42, 47, 87, 108, 182–3; brewing in, 124–8, 131–2, 135, 136, 138–40, 142–4; cathedral, 119, 121, 163, 166–9, 170; clock, 169–70; history, 166; museums, 170–1; Rouget de Lisle and, 151, 153–60, 163
Strasbourg Hotel, Mulhouse: 40, 45
Sunday Times: quoted, 102
Sylvaner: grape, 50, 56, 69; wine, 23, 26, 51–2, 73

Tanet, le (Tanneckfels): 29
Taverne: 135
Terminus-Bristol (hotel), Colmar: 35–6, 83
Thann: 76
Thirty Years' War: 47, 108
Thoman, M.: 36–8
Times, The: quoted, 100
Times Literary Supplement: 151
Tokay: 52, 98, 99 n.
Tokay d'Alsace (Pinot gris): 50, 52, 56, 62 & n., 73, 99 n.
Traminer: grape, 50, 56, 57, 61, 69, 74; wine, 43; confusion with Gewürztraminer, 52–7
Traveller's Joy: 13–14
Trockenbeerenauslese: 56–7
Trout: 129
Turckheim: 94
Turenne, Marshal: 94

Unterlinden, Musée d', Colmar: 90–3
Urban II, Pope: 91

Valfons, Marquis de: quoted, 173, 174–5, 175
Vignerons: 9–10, 27–8, 29–31, 33–6; history of, in Alsace, 48–9; organization, 78, 79–80, 81
Le Vin (Hyams): 55 & n., 56

Vineyards: sizes, 26, 27; total area, 49; location of, 58–60, 82; 'named', 51, 94, 97; soils, 30 & n.
Viniculture: 68 *et seq,* 86; history of, 46, 47, 48–9; music used in, 8; racking off lees, 10 & n.; unguents in, 57, 86
Vintage: 8–10, 68
Viticulture: 70–1; weather in, 71–3
Viticultural Research Station, Colmar: 68–9, 70–1
Vologne, River: 28–9
Voltaire: 87
Vosges Mts: 32

Waffelpasteta (recipe): 129
Wangen: 123
Wayfaring in France (Barker): 105
Weather: 71–3
Weinbach, Château: 102–4
Weinbach, Monastery: 62
Weinstuben: 41, 43–4
Westphalia, Treaty of (1648): 32
Wettolsheim: 82
Whiting: 21, 22
Wilhelm II, of Germany: 114, 115, 187
Williams (liqueur): 24
Wilm, M.: 116, 118
Wine: harmed by oxygen, 33; harvest, 8, 9–10; serving of, 33–4; storage of, 34; tasting, 30–1, 87–9, 100–2; weather and, 71–3; women and, 101–2; young, 34–5
Wine, Alsace: 1, 21–2, 46–86 *passim,* 164, 189–92; export of, 26–7, 46–7, 78 & n., 79; grape-varieties, 50, 51–7, 62–3, 107–8, 191; growers, 33, 48–9, 78, 79–80, 81; history, 46–9, 60–3, 106–11; nomenclature, 50–1, 58–9, 68; production figures, 26; red, 50n., 120; tax, 86, 103, 106–7, 123; trade administration

Wine Alsace—*cont.*
   63–9, 76, 79–80, 81, 83, 86; types of, 51–3, 98–9, 190; viticulture, 70–1
Wine, German: 71–2, 73, 120
Wine, Swiss: 120
Wine Fairs: 30
Wine Frauds, Inspector to: 83–6
Wine Trade, British: 2, 49–50
Wines and Vineyards of Alsace: quoted, 54

Wintzenheim: 33, 94
Wissembourg: 46, 170, 184–5, 187–9
Worshipful Company of Vintners: 31
Wust, M.: 190–2

Year at the Peacock, A (Layton): 69*n*.

Zind-Humbrecht, M.: 31, 33, 34–6
Zwicker: 26, 51

INDEX

Wine, Alsace, 126
61–2, 76, 79–81, 84, 85, 86, 89, 90,
96, 92–3, 96, 98, 99, 100, 101, 105,
107
Wine, (German) 71–2, 73, 120
Wine, Cape, 120
Wine, Jura, 120
Wine, Loire & Bordeaux, 81–9
Wine, S.A. Bottled, 39–50
Wine, and Liqueurs of above, 79, 91, 80

Würzenberg, 73, 91
Weinsberg, 91, 130, 134, 137, 129
Wine, Inghill Company of Vintners
71
Wine No. 1, 199–2

Stein de Bernd... (Lavrin), 1905.
Wine-Instituten M., 19, 25, 58, 93
Zwichen, 70, 91